HMS *Fowey* Lost and Found

New Perspectives on Maritime History and Nautical Archaeology

UNIVERSITY PRESS OF FLORIDA

Florida A&M University, Tallahassee
Florida Atlantic University, Boca Raton
Florida Gulf Coast University, Ft. Myers
Florida International University, Miami
Florida State University, Tallahassee
New College of Florida, Sarasota
University of Central Florida, Orlando
University of Florida, Gainesville
University of North Florida, Jacksonville
University of South Florida, Tampa
University of West Florida, Pensacola

HMS *Fowey*
Lost and Found

Being the Discovery, Excavation,
and Identification of a British Man-of-War
Lost off the Cape of Florida in 1748

RUSSELL K. SKOWRONEK AND GEORGE R. FISCHER

Foreword by James C. Bradford and Gene Allen Smith

University Press of Florida
Gainesville/Tallahassee/Tampa/Boca Raton
Pensacola/Orlando/Miami/Jacksonville/Ft. Myers/Sarasota

Copyright 2009 by Russell K. Skowronek and George R. Fischer
Printed in the United States of America. This book is printed on Glatfelter
Natures Book, a paper certified under the standards of the Forestry
Stewardship Council (FSC). It is a recycled stock that contains 30 percent
post-consumer waste and is acid-free.

14 13 12 11 10 09   6 5 4 3 2 1

Library of Congress Cataloging-in-Publication Data
Skowronek, Russell K.
H.M.S. Fowey lost and found : being the discovery, excavation, and
identification of a British man-of-war lost off the Cape of Florida in 1748 / by
Russell K. Skowronek and George R. Fischer; foreword by James C. Bradford
and Gene Allen Smith.
p. cm.—(New perspectives on maritime history and nautical archaeology)
Includes bibliographical references and index.
ISBN 978-0-8130-3320-4 (alk. paper)
1. Fowey (Man of war) 2. Underwater archaeology—Florida—Biscayne Bay.
3. Shipwrecks—Florida—Biscayne Bay. 4. Excavations (Archaeology)—
Florida—Biscayne Bay. 5. Biscayne Bay (Fla.)—Antiquities. 6. Underwater
archaeology—Law and legislation—United States. 7. Historic preservation—
Law and legislation—United States. I. Fischer, George R. II. Title.
F317.D2S56 2009
910.9163'48—dc22   2008033885

The University Press of Florida is the scholarly publishing agency for the State
University System of Florida, comprising Florida A&M University, Florida
Atlantic University, Florida Gulf Coast University, Florida International
University, Florida State University, New College of Florida, University of
Central Florida, University of Florida, University of North Florida, University
of South Florida, and University of West Florida.

University Press of Florida
15 Northwest 15th Street
Gainesville, FL 32611-2079
http://www.upf.com

For David Brewer, who pushed us to tell the *Fowey*'s story.

In memory of David Lyon (1942–2000) of the National Maritime Museum and Dr. J. Leitch Wright (1929–1986), professor of history, Florida State University, whose support of our research never wavered. And Gerald Joseph Klein (1938–1982) of Perrine, Florida, whose dreams of finding a shipwreck led us on this odyssey.

Contents

Figures

Foreword

Water is unquestionably the most important natural feature on earth. By volume, the world's oceans compose 99 percent of the planet's living space; the surface of the Pacific Ocean alone is larger than the total land surface. Water is as vital to life as air. Indeed, to test whether the moon or other planets can sustain life, the National Aeronautics and Space Administration (NASA) looks for signs of water. The story of human development is inextricably linked to the oceans, seas, lakes, and rivers that dominate the earth's surface. In fact, 50 percent of the world's people live within sixteen miles of a coast. The University Press of Florida's series New Perspectives on Maritime History and Nautical Archaeology is devoted to exploring the significance of the earth's water while providing lively and important books that cover the spectrum of maritime history and nautical archaeology broadly defined. The series includes works that focus on the role of canals, rivers, lakes, and oceans in history; on the economic, military, and political use of those waters; and on the people, communities, and industries that support maritime endeavors. Limited by neither geography nor time, volumes in the series contribute to the overall understanding of maritime history and can be read with profit by both general readers and specialists.

HMS *Fowey*, a fifth-rate ship constructed in Hull, England, and launched in September 1744, had a brief yet notable career during the War of the Austrian Succession, known as King George's War in North America. Carrying forty-four guns and named for the town of Fowey in Cornwall, its first three years witnessed the capture of two French ships and the sinking of a twenty-six-gun French ship protected by shore batteries along Normandy. *Fowey* convoyed British troops to the recently captured Fort Louisbourg on Cape Breton Island and thereafter began patrolling the waters off Virginia during summer months and off Jamaica during winter months. When twenty-four-year-old Francis William Drake, a descendant of the famed English sea-dog Francis Drake, took command in late January 1748, *Fowey* deployed to the Caribbean to hunt Spanish and French ships.

In early June 1748 *Fowey* captured a twenty-gun Spanish ship in the Bay of Campeche, carrying to Havana a cargo of cocoa, indigo, and some

60,000 pieces-of-eight. Drake manned his prize, and along with two merchant ships the convoy departed for his summer station along the coast of Virginia. While it was passing through the Strait of Florida in late June, misfortune struck. *Fowey* ran aground on a reef on the morning of June 27, 1748; the prize ship also ran aground. During the following day, Drake and his crew did all within their power to refloat the ship. They cut loose anchors and threw overboard yards, heavy guns, and even drinking water to lighten the ship's draft, all to no avail. Prisoners and sailors transferred to the nearby merchant ships shortly before *Fowey* slipped below the water on the morning of June 28, 1748. Some five months later, in early December 1748, a court-martial convened in Portsmouth, England, acquitted Drake and his officer for the loss of the ship. While Drake's name and reputation did not suffer from the episode—shortly after the court-martial he gained command of a sixth-rate warship, which was not appropriate for his rank— the fifth-rate *Fowey* had been lost. The next ship to bear the *Fowey* name was a sixth-rate warship with twenty-four guns, whereas all of the previous vessels with the same name had been fifth-rate ships. So *Fowey* had been lost in more than one way.

In October 1978, when Gerald Klein discovered a shipwreck off Elliot Key in Legare Anchorage, he believed that he had found a Spanish treasure ship and that his dreams had come true. During the following months, convinced that the shipwreck represented part of the famed Spanish *flota* (fleet) of 1733, Klein began collecting artifacts from the site, with many of them ending up in his wife's restaurant. In October 1979 Klein filed a "Complaint in Admiralty" in the U.S. District Court, for the Southern District of Florida, Miami Division in Admiralty, to gain legal salvage rights over the site. Thus began a legal struggle lasting more than two decades to define federal laws concerning shipwrecks and salvage. As the proceedings advanced, the authors of this book found themselves on the front lines of the case. They ultimately participated in a historic episode that now stands as a landmark in historic shipwreck litigation and preservation. Moreover, these nautical archaeologists gave an identity to the sunken vessel, determining conclusively (based on evidence recovered from the site) that the wreck was not a Spanish ship or part of the *flota* but rather a British warship from the 1740s. From the mountains of archaeological, historic, and circumstantial evidence, they concluded that the shipwreck site of Biscayne National Park must be considered the final resting place of HMS *Fowey*. In doing so, they found and identified the British ship and, more importantly, helped to lay the groundwork for future protection of shipwrecks from illicit salvage.

James C. Bradford and Gene Allen Smith
Series Editors

Preface

Life is short. If you are lucky in that life you will cross paths with some wonderful people and perhaps do some wonderful things. If you are truly lucky you will do a fascinating thing and have a great colleague and friend who is equally fascinated with doing that thing. This is a story about two such lucky people (one the teacher, the other the student), who came together originally for a single ten-week course and instead embarked on an "adventure of a lifetime" more than a quarter of a century ago. As we look back on those heady times in the early 1980s we can now see how special they were. The right people and the right circumstances jelled in the halls of the Bellamy Building on the Florida State University campus, creating a whole that was greater than the sum of its parts. That may seem to be a hackneyed phrase, but those of you who have been fortunate enough to experience a similar circumstance can attest that it is a magical occurrence. Oh, to have such energy and passion again! If only the stars would again align . . .

What developed might best be seen as a love affair, and this book represents the tangible evidence of that passion. This might seem to some to be hardly the stuff of archaeology, but we would challenge you to think about those once-in-a-lifetime projects that so intrigue you that you do more and more: not because "you have to" but because you want to. That is the story we are telling here. This is a story about an archaeological site that we saw, and still see, as "our" child, which needs to be seen and heard *and* protected. This analogy may seem overblown; but, just as we teach our children, you can't always spot the molester. We do everything to make our children safe and then we let them go. If anything or anybody threatens to harm them, we become the mother bear all over again, no matter how old the child is.

In October 1979 our paths crossed for the first time when the Legare Anchorage Shipwreck first came onto the National Park Service's radar. Within eight weeks we had completed the first focused research on the wreck (Skowronek 1979). Nine years later, following field and lab research in the United States, Canada, and the United Kingdom, an initial stab at stabilizing the site, and the publication of a report (Skowronek 1984a), articles (Skowronek 1985; Skowronek et al. 1987), and conference proceedings (Donnellan 1988; Fischer 1988; Johnson 1988; Skowronek 1988; Vernon 1988; Wild 1988), we thought it was time to put the site to bed. We wanted to protect it from further illicit salvage and erosion through monitoring and, better yet, burial (Fischer and Johnson 1981; Skowronek 1984a: 55–56). Those recommendations were never acted upon. We never even considered that the site might suffer more from benign neglect.

Today we know that we were naïve; but we genuinely believed that our opinions counted, when we received news on August 7, 1986, that the report we had written was of "superior quality." The letter, dated July 21, 1986, said in part:

> Chief Anthropologist Scovill and Chief Historian Bearss have read the draft and they commend Archeologists Russell K. Skowronek and George R. Fischer for providing the [National Park] Service with a report that more than meets standards, as well as the canons of their professions. The interdisciplinary approach followed, and methodology employed, enhance the value of this undertaking. (Jerry L. Rogers July 21, 1986, H30[418])

Not too shabby.

Yet the wheels had already begun to turn imperceptibly. Within days of the conclusion of the 1983 project three "Case Incident Records" were reported in Legare Anchorage or nearby at Elkhorn Reef regarding the disturbance of shipwreck remains (Bidwell, July 14, 1983, #830240; Childs, September 1, 1983, #830317; Curry, October 20, 1983 #830352). Shortly thereafter, personnel from Biscayne National Park removed one of the remaining iron guns from the wreck to "protect" it from looters.

We moved on with the more traditional events of our lives. Everyone knows these things—weddings, children, health issues, funerals, and jobs. In the late 1980s the National Park Service began developing interpretive exhibits on the Legare Anchorage site, to be placed on Adams Key, one of the barrier islands in the park. It was pointed out at the time that it might be unwise to place artifacts out there, because of the danger of storm surges. Those admonitions were ignored.

In 1992 Hurricane Andrew pounded Homestead, Florida, and Biscayne National Park. The storm surge destroyed the exhibits on Adams Key and washed much of the sand off the wreck.

The condition of the wreck was assessed during the summer of 1993 under the auspices of the Submerged Cultural Resources Unit of the National

Park Service. In 1995 members of a "think tank" got together to decide how best to preserve and thus protect the wreck.

For *Fowey* scholars, the most sobering part of the past twenty years began in October 1996 with the publication of an article in *Naval History* (Adams 1996) that claimed the Legare Anchorage wreck was uncovered by the storm. None of the earlier works were mentioned or cited, though it seems certain that they were consulted, based on the article's content. We wrote to the journal to clarify what had been done in 1983 (Fischer 1997; Skowronek 1997), but by then it was water under the bridge. Not long thereafter (Delgado 1997: 445) a discussion of the Legare Anchorage wreck appeared in the pages of the *British Museum Encyclopedia of Underwater and Maritime Archaeology*. This time only the work conducted in 1980 and 1993 was discussed. Daniel Lenihan (2002: 103) referred to the work in the 1980s as "preliminary" until a "major excavation" could be mounted. As recently as February 2004 the Submerged Resources Center (formerly the Submerged Cultural Resources Unit) "Projects" webpage ignored the work of the 1980s and focused only on the 1993 project. It makes sense that they should spotlight their work, but it also made us want to tell the rest of the story before it was too late. Some might feel that the work of the 1980s was meaningless. We don't.

We feel it is important to show how research is conducted and to tell the whole story. Rarely in research is there a straight line from problem formulation to conclusions. Anyone who tells you otherwise is lying to you. Instead it takes many twists and turns. Our goal is to explain how a Florida shipwreck revealed its secrets to a determined group of scientists. This is not a story about a fabulous treasure of silver and gold; rather it is the story of how scientists "zig and zag" through their research, battle the elements, and battle treasure hunters and sometimes their own colleagues to reveal the past. We hope this will be something of a cautionary tale about how science is done, and how it should be done, as well as telling a little-known story about Florida history.

Those expecting a "site report" will be disappointed. That was written more than twenty years ago. Instead we seek to tell a story to you, the reading public, about how research is conducted in the face of the elements, litigious members of the public, and sometimes obstructive colleagues. We intend for this book to tell the "stories behind the story," the items that never make it into the scientific literature. We include not just the interesting untold items relating to the trials and tribulations incumbent in conducting historic archaeological research but the amusing, and sometimes bizarre, anecdotes that never make it into the general literature but are prime items for retelling at crew reunions. If we are successful in any of these, we hope that you will come away with some of the same passion we have had for a footnote in American colonial history. Hold on: the trip from "*Fowey* Lost" to "*Fowey* Found" is about to begin.

Acknowledgments

This book would never have been written without the prodding of David Brewer, state historic preservation officer for the Virgin Islands. For more than a decade after the 1983 project Dave was witness to the continued degradation of HMS *Fowey*. With each incident he said, "You guys know this story and it has to be told!" Here it is David: thank you for pushing us and for reviewing the manuscript throughout its lengthy creation.

We also wish to thank director Meredith Morris-Babb, editor-in-chief John Byram, and acquisitions editor Eli Bortz at the University Press of Florida for their encouragement and support for the telling of this story. Their patience and guidance are gratefully acknowledged.

The final version of this book benefited greatly from the once anonymous reviews of past Society for Historical Archaeology president J. Barto Arnold, formerly Texas state marine archaeologist and now at the Institute for Nautical Archaeology, and Dr. John Broadwater of the Monitor National Marine Sanctuary. Their extensive background with British and Spanish colonial era vessels and experience dealing with bureaucracies and legal issues made them an ideal selection as reviewers and made their insights all the more valuable.

Others also thought the *Fowey* story needed to have its day.

The late Denis Trelewicz of Key Largo, Florida, gave us information provided to him by the National Park Service.

Richard E. Johnson of Tallahassee read and commented on earlier drafts of the manuscript and dug into the dusty recesses of his memory to recall the heady days of 1979–1983.

Another member of the original team who read the manuscript, commented on it, and helped us with the collections associated with the Legare Anchorage wreck held at the Southeast Archeological Center is Richard H. Vernon, supervisory museum specialist, National Park Service.

Michael Pomeroy, divemaster on the 1983 project, offered helpful comments on an early version of the manuscript.

We wish to thank John E. Ehrenhard, retired chief of the Southeast Archeological Center (SEAC), for providing access to the documentary and material collections from BISC-UW-20.

Thanks are also extended to Chief Ehrenhard for seeking the preparation of an administrative history of the Southeast Archeological Center. Prepared by Cameron Binkley and entitled *Science, Politics, and the "Big Dig,"* the history helped us understand what happened to the Legare Anchorage site and to the underwater archaeology aspect of SEAC. Those seeking corroboration will find it in the pages of this important and extremely revealing publication. We thank him for this history. As he said to us, "I came, I saw, I reported . . . and I am glad it is useful." It was in many ways a smoking gun.

We also wish to thank Dr. John Seidel and Larry Murphy for generously sharing their 1996 Conference for Underwater Archaeology (CUA) paper. It helped us greatly in preparing the final chapter of this book.

Dr. Charles Ewen of East Carolina University and Dr. George F. Bass of Texas A&M University helped us find many references.

Thanks also to William J. Gladwin, Jr., and Rebecca A. Donnellan, attorneys for the State of Florida and the U.S. Department of Justice, who kindly shared their memories of the court case and checked the accuracy of our account.

Ole Varmer, attorney-advisor to the National Oceanic and Atmospheric Administration's International Law Office, kindly reviewed parts of this manuscript. He regards the *Fowey* case as a landmark and watershed in shipwreck litigation and has frequently used it in cases with which he has been involved. We thank him for his enthusiastic support of our work.

Michele Aubry, archaeologist with the National Park Service (now retired), generously reviewed portions of the manuscript. She provided valuable guidance and advice on matters relating to law, regulation, and practice that we had forgotten or that had developed since we were active in those areas. Michele observed that litigating *Fowey* today would be a far different matter than it was twenty-five years ago.

We wish to thank Dale Durham, retired regional curator for the Southeast Region of the National Park Service, for his helpful commentary on parts of the manuscript.

Thanks to Dr. Ann Millard and Dr. Isidore Flores of Edinburg, Texas, who provided lodgings during the initial writing of this book. Thanks also to the Edinburg Public Library for computer access and interlibrary loan. The College of Behavioral and Social Sciences and the Department of Anthropology and Psychology at the University of Texas–Pan American extended visiting scholar status during the fall of 2005.

We would like to thank another old sea-dog, Karl Lueck of San Jose, California, who helped us with the manuscript. Thanks also to Kathy Lewis, who edited our manuscript and made it far, far better.

The excellent index in this book was created by our dear friend Anita Cohen-Williams. Her expertise as a librarian, archaeologist, and historian was exactly the final touch that this manuscript deserved.

The participants in the 1983 project were Richard "Old Grog" Vernon, assistant field director; Ken Wild, crew chief; David Brewer, crew chief; Carl Semczak, conservator and photographer; Michael Pomeroy, divemaster; John Broward, dive technician; Diana Barrera, Ken Hoeck, Greg Toothman, Kate Lowell, J. P. Montegut, and Karin Hutchinson, crew members; and Matt Fischer, crew member/mechanic. Walt Woodside, George Bookmeister, Randy Bidwell, and Jenny Bjork from Biscayne National Park served as boat captains, as armed security, and in a myriad of other capacities.

The dangerous lifting, removal, and preservation of 3,000 pounds of coral-encrusted gun was made possible with the help of the late Herbert Bump, historic conservator, Florida Department of State, Bureau of Archaeological Research, Conservation Lab; and Gregg Stanton, Florida State University Marine Lab. We also wish to thank Gregg for the creation of the video and photo-mosaic in 1980. Conservation of the materials recovered during the project was conducted by Jamie Levy and Frank Gilson at the Bureau of Archaeological Research. Many of the original artifact drawings were made by Frank Gilson and Teresa Paglione of SEAC.

Final closing down and preservation of the site was aided by Peter Steuer and Richard Rodrigues, volunteers, and William Garrett of Seascape Technology, Inc., whose donation of fifty units of Seascape aided in the attempted restabilization of the site.

Help in the interpretation of the architecture and some artifacts was provided by the personnel of the following projects, historic ships, and maritime museums: the late Richard Steffy, Texas A&M University; John Broadwater and Harding Polk, Yorktown Project; *Dove*, St. Mary's City, Maryland; USF *Constellation*, Baltimore, Maryland; Salem Maritime National Historic Site, Salem, Massachusetts; Flagship *Niagara*, Eire, Pennsylvania; HMS *Rose*, Croton, Connecticut; *Beaver II*, Boston, Massachusetts; USS *Constitution*, Charlestown Navy Yard, Boston, Massachusetts; Independence National Historical Park, Philadelphia, Pennsylvania; the Maritime Museum of Philadelphia, Pennsylvania; the Peabody Museum of Salem, Massachusetts; and the National Museum of American History, Smithsonian Institution, Washington, D.C.

Special thanks are extended to Cathy Bray and Oliver Denison of the Mystic Seaport Museum, Mystic, Connecticut, for their time and documentation of naval architecture. In Canada, archivist Eric Krause of Parks Canada at Louisbourg, Nova Scotia, provided access to the park's extensive eighteenth-century document holdings. Thanks also to Brenda Lacroix of Halifax, who offered friendship, directions, work, and rest space while Skowronek visited the Citadel, the Maritime Museum of the Atlantic, and the Nova Scotia Public Archives.

Past research in Great Britain during the fall of 1981 provided baseline information on the Royal Navy and HMS *Fowey*. Again we must thank the staffs of the HMS *Unicorn*, Victoria Dock, Dundee, Scotland; the HMS *Victory*, Portsmouth; the British Library/Museum, London; the National Maritime Museum, Greenwich; and the National Archives (previously known as the Public Records Office), Kew, Richmond.

We would like to thank Captain Leslie J. Skowronek (U.S. Navy, retired) and Lieutenant Commander Lester J. Skowronek (U.S. Naval Reserve, retired) for their editorial comments on the manuscript and others regarding naval terminology and presentation of information in chapter 1. Lieutenant Commander Skowronek also did research on the uniforms of the Royal Marines in the 1740s. Ian MacGregor, archive information manager for the Met Office of the National Meteorological Archive in Berkshire, United Kingdom, provided information on weather conditions in Portsmouth, Hampshire, and the south of England in December 1748. Special thanks are due to the late David J. Lyon (1942–2000), curator of Naval Ordnance, and Christopher J. Ware, historian at the National Maritime Museum, for their help in the 1980s. National Maritime Museum staff members Doug McCarthy, Jeremy Michell, Caroline Wykes, and Liza Verity were kind enough to provide information on current research procedures in Greenwich and the Public Records Office.

Thanks also to Duncan Mackenzie, Fowey's local historian, and Arthur Credland, maritime historian and keeper of Maritime History at the Hull Maritime Museum: both freely shared their information and expressed sincere interest in bringing the *Fowey* and its story home to England.

We also thank Barbara Lewellen, our vicarious friend from the Internet, who has always generously shared information that she has discovered on

HMS *Fowey* and its crew while doing research on her ancestor Policarpus Taylor.

Cynthia Bradley and Leanna Goodwater, librarians at Santa Clara University's Orradre Library, helped obtain rare books and materials. We are also greatly indebted to Elwood Mills from Santa Clara University Media Services, who was responsible for producing the excellent photographs and illustrations that fill this book. Eric Loewe (Santa Clara University, class of 2002) conducted excellent research on the construction of *Fowey* and helped organize transcriptions of the ship's logs. Nicholas Fussell (Santa Clara University, class of 2007) worked on organizing *Fowey*'s logs, muster books, and associated documents. Finally, Skowronek wishes to thank Dr. Diane Jonte-Pace, vice-provost for faculty development, for her support of some of this research. The final aspects of this project came together with funding from a Faculty Development Research Grant during the summer of 2006.

Through the years more than a thousand professionals, interested laypersons, and undergraduate and graduate students in Florida, Michigan, Indiana, and California have attended lectures or actually worked on aspects of the project. At Santa Clara University hundreds of students have worked on creating transcriptions of documents relating to HMS *Fowey*. They include the following individuals:

Winter 2000: Meta Anderson, Ryan Auffenberg, Elizabeth Barrett, Sandra Benavidez, Karin Bencala, Keith Candau, Noel Dittmar, Meghan Francis, Thomas Garvey, Alexander Hanley, Christoph Holl, Nicholas Horwath, Stephanie Howe, Shelene Huey, Willy Khiang, Eric Loewe, Chet Lumor, Brent Maloney, Karie Marlin, Victoria Mayes, Ryan McKay, Robert McLaughlin, Anne Melson, Christopher Miller, Anne Montgomery, Melissa Muntz, Michael Paustian, Nicholas Thomas, Christina Uremovic, Jenny Wong.

Winter 2001: Anthony Ampi, Eleanor Anderson, Nicholas Ascolese, Victoria Bennett, Jeremy Black, William Brown, Erin Chambers, Natasha Dolginsky, Farah Evans, Grant Hughes, Anne Johnson, Stephanie Kreutter, Chris Madrid, David Mallen, Charlotte Matthews, Kevin Murray, Sarah Naumes, Christina Newell, Katrina Osland, Jelena Fanta Radovic, Willie Ronan, Daniel Schuet, Timothy Sutton, Nicole Thomsen, Kathleen Watt.

Spring 2002: Andres Adauto, Rene Bahena, Alison Bettles, Jessica Boyd, Stephanie Brunton, Robin Chapdelaine, Shana Clevett, Stacey Crespo,

Devlin Croal, Laurie Cvengros, Liane Dallal, Andrew Deller, Jacqueline Douglas, Lindsey Ganahi, Vanessa Garcia, Laine Gasparich, Meghan Hanratty, Kathryn Harrison, Charles Hernandez, Yessica Islas, Geoggrey Katsuhisa, Desiree Khu, Megan Kinnear, David Lando, Tianen Liu, Diana Mah, Melissa Moore, Rebecca Naumes, Megan Nelson, Alexandra Perazzelli, Manuel Perez, Nina Fanta Radovic, Mary Romley, David Stegemeier, Kimberly Thomas, Kelly Wendorff, Bonnie Young, Raul Zamudio.

Spring 2003: Daniel Alvarado, Cord Anderson, Adeel Baig, Stephen Batey, Denise Bertucelli, Carly Bird-Vogel, Brynn Booras, William Bouzek, Jacob Calvani, Kendall Craver, Steven Cronin, Abigail Fox, Charles Gilfillan, Adam Harper, Alexander Hazlehurst, Alexandra Lasch, Jeffrey Lopus, Russell Mangan, Shannon McCabe, Keith Stephon McGrew, Kendra Middendorf, Lesley Miller, Michelle Newman, Vinicio Oliver, Katrina Orbe, Daniel Orlicky, Coanan Phan, Elizabeth Rosenbaum, Angela Saldivar, Jamieson Suriyakam, Kirsten Tanner, Meena TePas, Lehuamakanoe Verkerke, Lindsey Washburn, Jillian Williams.

Fall 2003: Catherine Adinolfi, Daniel Albers, Trevor Basta, Harry Beckwith, Ranya Botros, Paul Breucop, Astra Bruff, Jamie Campbell, Kendyl Eriksen, Christina Estrada, Nicole Fox, Christina Gonzalez, Jennifer Gottschalk, Jennifer Grisaitis, Samuel Infantino, Emily Johnson, Michael Lange, Liz Lueders, Kellan McConnell, Elizabeth Menefee, Denis Moreno, Piper Phillips, Shuryn Riggins, Darby Riley, Carmen Rosas, Lissette Ruiz, Adam Saucedo, Patrick Sauls, Brian Sullivan, Jr., Linda Urbonas, Lindsay Westby, Michael Wiesner, Jennifer Woldrich.

Fall 2004: Stephane Alcantara, Darren Brazil, Robert Campbell, Stephanie Cope, Chandice Cronk, Brigid Eckhart, Catherine Finigan, William Foley, Drexel Harris III, Meaghan Hicks, Emily Houdeshell, Melissa Hunt, Stacey Ince, Kristen Jaber, Jonathan Joe, Melissa Johnson, Kaitlin Kelty, Thomas Knowles, Landis Lau, Mark Litchman, Kathryn Lum, Tanner Lund, Zachary Mershon, Christina Mogren, Edgar Morse IV, Tara Murray, Joseph Novotny, Briana Pelton, Robert Perry, Leslie Santikian, Cassandra Schwartz, Ferheen Siddiqui, David Skiver, Bradford Speers, Peter Sullivan, Rachel Terry, Kate Tryon, Megan Wahl, Elizabeth Woods, Devon Zotovich.

Winter 2005: Kristin Anderson, Mayra Arellano, Nicole Brand-Cousy, Laura Brown, Kristi Cabot, Anne Cung, Jennifer Cushing, Kellie Dunn, Michael Early, Stephanie Edwards, Ricardo Estrada, Devin Farnsworth, Lauren Feeney, Robert Flores, Cristal Friesen, Tammara Hanna-Anansi,

Jeremy Herb, Veronica Jacquez, Lisa Kinslow, Lauren Klepacki, Marci-anne Lewandowski, Rachel Lintott, Amanda Lowrey, Amy McGrath, Sean Moreau, Donna Nguyen, Henry Nguyen, Griselda Renteria, Julian Reyes, Johnathon Riggs, Angelica Rodriguez, Olivia Sorrell, Erin Taylor, Kara Taylor, Morgann Trumbull, Masayo Yamada.

Winter 2006: Sophia Aboitiz, Dennis Avilucea, Jessica Barnett, Carrie Clark, Jesse Clark, Ryan Cole, Cassie Conching, Eleni Ellenikiotis, Nicholas Fussell, Ryan Griffiths, Patricia Guzman, Conor Harding, Erika Hight, Michelle Johnson, Anthony Lara, Geraldine Linarte, Stephen Lindgren, Conor Murnane, Heather O'Hare, Brett Propersi, Robert Raymond, Peter Schumacher, Jessica Sekovski, Shanna Singh, Brittany Storey, John Tully, Ryan White, AnnaLisa Wilson.

Winter 2007: Christinah Barnett, Kelly Benson, Michael Bicos, Meredith Brown, Marisela Cardona, Maria de Lourdes Cervantes, Karen Chapski, Heather Clayton, Sarah Concklin, Margaret Doar, Samuel Fitzgerald, Gabriel Giannini-Covarrubias, Aaron Greene, Robb Hutchins, Brigid Kelleher, Jessica Mattioli, Christopher McNamara, Lauren Mitcheom, Jeanette Moritz, Mary Northey, Anthony Pastore, Elizabeth Perry, Kelly Richmond, Jillian Roehl, Robert Rosser III, Colleen Sinsky, Margaret Spicer, Christopher Tower, Jason Tran.

Our respective families have suffered our rants through the years. Nancy and Peg, Matt and Olga, we thank you for always being there for us when we were very far away in the world of academia, conservation, science, and fair play. May this book be the balm that heals a wound that has festered for some three decades.

As we look back on this work with some thirty years of perspective we realize that a job worth doing is worth doing right and that in the end inclusiveness trumps selfishness every time.

1

HMS *Fowey* Lost

It was December 5, 1748. The six-pound gun signaling the opening of the court-martial boomed from the forecastle of HMS *Anson*, a fourth-rate sixty-gun two-deck ship of the line. Its mushy, flat report echoed weakly through the rain-filled skies and across the gale-tossed waters of Portsmouth Harbor, Hampshire, in the south of England. The month was shaping up to be rain-filled and windy. In the great cabin of the flagship of the Blue squadron sat the court, sailors all, who would pass judgment on the loss of HMS *Fowey*.

In the half-light of the upper deck a red-coated private of the Royal Marines stood watch outside the cabin. Armed with the short sea pattern Brown Bess musket and wearing the distinctive marine grenadier-style cap of the era, he eyed the captain, first, second, and third lieutenants, master, two master's mates, two quartermasters, and carpenter's mate of the *Fowey* as they nervously awaited the opening of the court. No doubt they spoke in hushed voices. Their faces were slicked with perspiration, not due to the mild temperature but in fear of the outcome of the hearing. When the word was passed that court was now in session, the marine snapped to attention; the butt of his Brown Bess musket slammed against the deck as the first witness, *Fowey*'s captain, strode into the great cabin. In front of him, behind a table, sat seven officers of King George II's Royal Navy—his peers, jury, and judges.

Presiding over the court was Rear Admiral Charles Watson; his fellow judges and jurors were Captains William Farmer, Jervis Porter, James Gambier, Justinian Nutt, Molineux Shuldam, and John Storr. This would not be the trial of just any captain in the Royal Navy: the commander of the lost ship was the great-great-great-grandson of Thomas Drake, brother of Sir Francis Drake. Francis William Drake was the third son of the fourth baronet, Sir Francis Henry Drake of Buckland, Devonshire. He had been promoted ten months earlier on January 29, 1748, to the rank of post cap-

Figure 1.1. The only known portrait of Francis William Drake, rendered some three decades after the loss of HMS *Fowey*. (Originally published in Elliot-Drake 1911.)

tain. HMS *Fowey* was his second command. Born in 1724, Captain Drake was twenty-four years old (figure 1.1).

From the semidarkness of the middle deck the cabin was ablaze with candlelight and, through the stern windows, filtered the weak, migraine-producing gray light of a late autumn day in Portsmouth, England. As the captain entered the room, he tucked his hat under his left arm and came to attention. A single chair sat in the center of the cabin. The rest of the *Fowey*'s crew stood silently just inside the cabin door.

As Captain Drake settled into the chair, his mind spiraled back in time. For more than a decade the only life he had known was that of the sea. As a child in Devonshire he had grown up in the long shadow cast by the great Sir Francis Drake in the age of Elizabeth I as well as other family members such as Captains John and Francis Drake and his own uncle, Captain Duncomb Drake. The Drakes had made their name and earned their peerage at sea, and the tradition had continued through Francis William, who was known as William. He was the third of four sons, all whose first names were Francis. Henry, the eldest, born in 1722, became the fifth baronet in 1740 upon the death of their father. William never knew his elder brother Duncomb, who was named for his uncle, because Duncomb died shortly after his birth in 1723. Younger siblings Ann, Samuel, and Sophia were added to the family between 1726 and 1728.

As the surviving second son, William was sent to sea as a young teenager in the late 1730s. Through the influence and patronage of his father and uncle, William had learned the ropes as a "captain's servant." Captain's servants, known also as "volunteers," "young gentlemen," and later midshipmen, were the captain's apprentices. In this position William would have learned navigation and about life at sea in a Royal Navy vessel. As a midshipman William would have learned of his father's horrific death, gasping for air, coughing up blood, and burning with fever on January 26, 1740. His death had left his mother, Anne Heathcote, as the guardian of his eighteen-year-old brother Henry, the fifth baronet (Elliot-Drake 1911).

Naval regulations stipulated that to attain the rank of lieutenant an individual needed to pass an examination created by admirals and captains that focused on navigation and seamanship. The other necessary part was six years of active duty. On May 28, 1745, at the age of twenty-one, William passed the test for lieutenant and was assigned to HMS *Dreadnought*, a fourth-rate sixty-gun ship of the line, as its third lieutenant. Seven months later, on January 26, 1746, he transferred to HMS *Suffolk* as its third lieutenant. Fifteen months later, on April 28, 1747, he was appointed commander of *Dreadnought's Prize*, a captured sloop (ADM 6/17 p. 446).

It is important to remember that rank went with the ship. While the term "captain" was applied to anyone who commanded a ship, of any rank, rank within the navy system of ship rates becomes important vis-à-vis command. For example, sixth-rate ships mounted twenty to thirty guns and were captained by an individual with the rank of commander. Fifth-rates with thirty-two to forty-four guns were commanded by post captains, who sported a single gold epaulet. Fourth-rates of fifty to sixty guns and larger ships were commanded by full captains. Once an individual had commanded at a certain rate, he would never be assigned to anything lower. Lieutenants usually commanded vessels of fewer than twenty guns, which were generically called sloops-of-war. After commanding *Dreadnought's*

Prize, a sloop by all accounts, Drake had jumped in eight months' time from a lieutenant's billet or command past the rank of commander to post captain of HMS *Fowey*. Perhaps this discrepancy was simply due to the exigencies of war, or perhaps it was due to influence and patronage. Suffice it to say that he was named captain of the fifth-rate *Fowey* on January 29, 1748 (ADM 6/17, p. 446).

HMS *Fowey* was a relatively new vessel (figure 1.2). Part of the proposed naval establishment of 1741, it was one of eight named fifth-rates built at the beginning of the decade. Its sister ships were *Looe, Torrington, Lark, Anglesea, Roebuck, Pearl, Mary Galley, Ludlow Castle,* and *South Sea Castle.* Each was built at a different shipyard but with similar dimensions. For example, *Looe* was built at the Snelgrove yard in Limehouse and was 124 feet in length with a 36-foot beam, whereas the *Torrington* was built in Southampton by Rowcliffe and was 126 by 36 feet. *Fowey* was built at the Blaydes shipyard in Hull and was 127 feet long with a 36-foot beam. It carried forty-four guns capable of firing six-, nine-, and eighteen-pound shot. Named for the town of Fowey in Cornwall, HMS *Fowey* was the fourth vessel to bear this name since 1696.

Fowey had been a lucky ship for its first commander, Post Captain Policarpus Taylor. During the three years of his command, *Fowey* had captured a valuable French ship, the *Mentor*, in 1745 and in 1746 was credited with sinking the *Griffin*, a twenty-six-gun ship under the mounted guns of a French shore battery in the Bay of Feschampe in Normandy. Later that year, in consort with its sister-ship the *Torrington, Fowey* was sent to North America. First it convoyed troops to the recently captured fortress of Louisbourg in Nova Scotia and then patrolled off Virginia in the summer and Jamaica in the winter months. On November 3, 1747, Taylor went to a new command, the *Warwick,* a fourth-rate ship with sixty-four guns, and later the *Elizabeth.* For three months *Fowey* was commanded by Thomas Innes, past captain of the *Aldborough,* another fifth-rate. Less than three weeks before Drake took command, Innes and the *Fowey* captured a French vessel off the coast of Jamaica on January 11, 1748. On January 27 the last French prisoners were discharged at Port François, Guadeloupe, and on January 28 Innes was promoted to command HMS *Warwick,* Taylor's old command. The next day Drake left the fourth-rate *Canterbury,* to which he was temporarily attached, and took command of *Fowey.*

The five-month duration of Drake's command was largely uneventful. *Fowey* cruised the Caribbean, hunting for Spanish and French ships. On

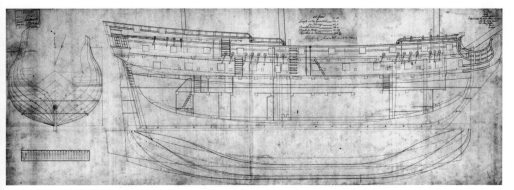

Figure 1.2. Builders' lines from the *Establishment* of 1741 for fifth-rate ships, including HMS *Fowey*. (Copyright by National Maritime Museum, Greenwich London.)

June 3 in the Bay of Campeche it fell upon the *St. Judea* (aka *Judah*), a twenty-gun Spanish ship bound for Havana from Caracas, Venezuela. The *St. Judea*, crewed with 108 men, carried a cargo of cocoa, indigo, and some sixty thousand pieces-of-eight. Those were happy days.

Drake snapped back into the reality of his situation when Rear Admiral Watson called the court to order. Admiralty had requested the enquiry "into the cause of the loss of His Majesty's Ship *Fowey* upon Cape Florida." Captain Drake made his deposition.

After the capture of the *St. Judea*, *Fowey* and the prize, with Lieutenant Robert Middleton serving as "prize" captain, sailed through the Gulf of Mexico toward their summer station off the Virginia coast. While heading north they fell in with two merchant vessels, the *Jane*, a "snow" from New York under the command of Captain Abraham Kittletash, and the brig *Mermaid* from Rhode Island, under Captain John Collins. Snows were the largest type of two-masted sailing vessels to carry square sails on both masts. Immediately behind the mainmast was a trysail mast used for setting fore-and-aft trysails. Brigs were smaller two-masted sailing ships with square sails. They carried a trysail or small fore-and-aft sail set on a boom on the mainmast. Because England and Spain were at war, Captain Drake agreed to convoy the vessels through the hostile waters of Spanish Cuba and Florida to British North America.

On the morning of June 26, 1748, the convoy under the protection of *Fowey*'s guns was off the north coast of Cuba. At 6 a.m. in the morning watch "Keysal [*sic*]" (Cay Sal or Salt Key) Bank was sighted. Four hours later, with an east by north wind pushing them, the bank lay some seven leagues away to the convoy's east-southeast. Steering a north by northeast course and with the leadsman finding no bottom on his half hour soundings, the convoy sailed up what they perceived to be the center of the Florida Straits. Twelve hours later the convoy was becalmed. Just after midnight on the morning of June 27 a southeasterly wind arose. Two hours later, after the 2:30 a.m. sounding found no bottom, a gun from Captain Collins' brig was fired, signaling that *Mermaid* had gone aground.

Drake quickly came on deck and assessed the situation. He cut the tow line to the *St. Judea* and ordered the masters and quartermaster's mates to tack eastward away from the brig. In the darkness, as they began to set their staysails and main sail, *Fowey* slammed onto the reef with a grinding lurch. As quickly as the sails went up, they were furled. The ship was in danger of being holed on the sharp edges of the coral and anything that would cause that (such as the sails) had to be eliminated. Sunrise came early on June 27. In the water surrounding the stricken ship were its cutter, barge, and longboat and the prize's launch. They were sounding for deep water and were laying their stream anchor and the *St. Judea*'s best bower in an attempt to pull themselves free. At 6 a.m. in the morning watch the brig floated free of the reef. Fearing that *Mermaid* would sail off and leave them, Drake dispatched Third Lieutenant James Kirkpatrick and seven men to assure Collins' compliance with his orders to remain on station with the stricken *Fowey*.

As the morning wore on, *Fowey* remained stuck on the reef. The pulling of the boats' crews and the tugging on the anchor lines were not enough to lift the ship free. To lighten the vessel the topmasts and yards were struck and thrown overboard. While the main battery of nine- and eighteen-pound guns was moved aft to raise the bow of the ship, two six-pounders mounted on the forecastle were disabled and hove overboard. Finally, they began to dump their heavy barrels of drinking water and started to work the pumps. At 11 a.m., just before the end of the forenoon watch, the snow *Jane* was sighted and signaled regarding their distress. One hour later, at noon, the daily latitude reading was shot. Marking the beginning of June 28, they were at 25 degrees 25 minutes north latitude on or near Ajax Reef in waters ranging from zero to twelve feet in depth. For three more hours the crew worked the pumps and continued to try to pull the ship off. At 3 p.m., during the afternoon watch, in a final act of desperation five more guns (two six-pounders, two nine-pounders, and an eighteen-pounder) were disabled and thrown over into the shallows on the reef. Meanwhile the *St. Judea* had similarly grounded on the reef.

At 5 p.m. both *Fowey* and the *St. Judea* floated free of the coral's embrace. After more than twelve hours of captivity on the reef the relief would have been palpable. Unfortunately, it would also be short-lived: almost immediately both grounded again near Long Reef. This time *Fowey* was "stove in" or bilged, and the water began to rise in the hold. All of *Fowey*'s hands, eighty Spanish prisoners, and fourteen seamen from the *Jane* worked to bail and pump the ship out. For twelve long hours they labored, until 4 a.m. at the beginning of the morning watch. With two feet of water in the hold, Drake called his officers together to ask their opinion. Without reservation, all agreed that *Fowey* was lost. They determined that it would be better to drive the ship higher onto the reef rather than allow it to sink in four fathoms of water, where lives and provisions might be lost. Drake ordered the stern cable cut to the prize's best bower anchor that held *Fowey*. The ship's sturdy construction must have awed Drake as it scraped right over the reef, lost its rudder, and continued to drift northward. In an attempt to steer the sinking hulk, Drake put out sweeps (oars) and set topsails and small sails. They drifted for some distance until they let go the sheet anchor, their last. In three and a half fathoms of water *Fowey* began to settle on its starboard beam. Drake ordered the carpenter to cut away the bowsprit and foremast and to open the seacocks to scuttle the ship. The guns were to be spiked, and all of the small arms, except thirty-three muskets, were thrown overboard.

The *Jane*, with Captain Kittletash, was anchored some three leagues or seven to eight miles away. Nearby, Collins' brig *Mermaid*, with Lieutenant Kirkpatrick onboard, beat back and forth, as it had no anchor. In their launch, cutter, and longboat the two hundred men of HMS *Fowey* were slowly ferried to the waiting merchant ships. Additionally, nineteen of the elite and therefore most likely to be ransomed Spanish prisoners were moved to those ships. The remaining eighty were returned to the *St. Judea*'s boats and, having given their parole, sailed to Havana. There was no succor on the *St. Judea*, as it too was lost on the reefs.

HMS *Fowey* was last seen on the morning of June 28, 1748; it was lying on its starboard beam ends as it slipped beneath the waters. One life was lost in the disaster, a Spanish prisoner Juan "Caseant [*sic*]," along with all of *Fowey*'s stores. A week later, on Wednesday, July 4, the *Jane* and *Mermaid* arrived in South Carolina. Captain Collins and *Mermaid* reached Newport, Rhode Island, on July 22, 1748, and had their version of the incident reported in the August 1, 1748, issue of the *New York Weekly Journal* (no. 763, p. 2):

> *Newport, Rhode Island, July 22*
> Yesterday arrived here Captain Collins from Jamaica . . . he put away thro; the Gulph [*sic*], where he met the Fowey Man of War with a very rich Spanish Prize Ship of 20 guns and 108 men in tow both of which soon after lost on the Florida Keys. Captain Collins, with a New York Snow, then in company, took out all the people, and 70,000 dollars, which they landed at South Carolina. After the ship stranded, the Spaniards informed them, that the prize had 190,000 dollars more on board, under the lading, which consisted chiefly of cocoa and indigo; but the truth of this, is much doubted by many.

Fowey's survivors spent the torrid months of the summer at Port Royal, South Carolina. Port Royal is located just south of Beaufort and is now the entry to the U.S. Marine Corps Recruit Depot on Parris Island. In 1732 Fort Frederick had been built at Port Royal. Its garrison manned patrol boats used to scout for the attacks of Indians, pirates, and other hostile forces. There *Fowey*'s crew lived on food requisitioned from nearby plantations (ADM 354/141/17). In September most of them were reassigned to HMS *Warwick* and HMS *Rye* (ADM 36/1187). A month later, in October, *Fowey*'s captain, commissioned officers, and warrant officers left Port Royal, South Carolina, and returned to England for the court-martial (ADM 36/1187).

Drake, after making his deposition, left the witness chair and stood to one side of the cabin. He had a good crew. In his mind they all had done everything they could to save the *Fowey*. The rest of the crew cleared the cabin and were called in individually to be examined under oath.

Robert Middleton, *Fowey*'s first lieutenant and the commander of their prize, the *St. Judea*, had lost the most. He had served on the *Fowey* since its commissioning in 1744 and had been at sea for fourteen years. At thirty years of age he was older than Drake but lacked the family connections to fast-track his naval career (ADM 107/3, p. 475). Command of the *St. Judea* might have been his chance to earn an independent command. Instead the prize was gone, *Fowey* was lost, and there he stood in this court-martial. Loyal to Drake, he stated that everything possible had been done to save the ship. When asked how the currents had set, Middleton succinctly replied: "To the northward according to my observation. It might probably set to the westward too, or the ship could not have been where she was." The court probed further: "Do you think you steered a proper course?" Middleton replied, "I do." When asked "What do you think was the cause of the ships going ashore?" Middleton replied: "I attribute it to the currents only."

James Mackey, second lieutenant of HMS *Fowey*, took the stand next. He too was queried about the conditions. "What think you was the occasion of the ships going ashore?"

"The current," he answered. It set to the "West North West or Northwest by West" and "I believe [at] more than three knots."

James Kirkpatrick, *Fowey*'s third lieutenant who had boarded the Rhode Island brig, was called next. He was twenty-seven years old and had been at sea some fifteen years (ADM 107/3, p. 425) "Pray, when you took your departure on the 26 June last from Keysal do you think the course you steered was a proper one to keep clear of all danger?" "I do," replied Kirkpatrick. And in response to the question "What do you imagine was the occasion of the *Fowey*'s going ashore?" he answered: "A strong western current."

Fowey's master's mates John Beezley and John Montgomery and quartermasters Wilfred Inman and Robert Taylor all agreed that a proper course had been steered and that it was a current to the northwest that had caused the demise of the warship.

The one man who should have had the most to say about the grounding and loss of HMS *Fowey* was its master. By the 1700s the Royal Navy had warrant officers, distinct from commissioned officers. They were seamen but not "officer gentlemen." Warrant officers were subordinate but independent officers, craftsmen, and experts, responsible for their departments. These included the purser, gunner, cooper, carpenter, sailmaker, blacksmith, armorer, surgeon, and master. Under the command of the captain, the master was in charge of navigating the ship as well as provisions, rigging, and trim. Masters were the only source of hydrographic information for the admiralty and were ordered to note shoals, rocks, and water depths in their journals. A wise captain took care that he had a good master, if he had a choice.

Fowey's master was Robert Bishop. He would gain fame in the second half of the eighteenth century for the publication of navigational charts and books based on several decades' experience on ships of the Royal Navy (Bishop 1763: 65, 80; Romans et al. 1799: 45, 52). When he entered the great cabin of the *Anson* on that December day, Robert Bishop was probably subdued, and (as will be shown) for good reason. He was thirty years old, had been at sea for a decade, and had been the master of two other naval vessels, the *Sheerness* and the *Looe* (ADM 107/3). After he was sworn into the proceedings, Bishop was asked, "Pray Sir, where was you [sic] the 26th of June in the morning?"

"I was sick in my cabin."

"Did you know what course was steered?"

"I enquired and was told that she never went to the westward of the North all night."

"Do you think that was a proper course to carry you clear of all danger?"

"In my opinion it was."

"What do you think might be the occasion of your going ashore?"

"An uncommon current setting to the NW." So ended Bishop's deposition.

Of course today we know the current described by Bishop is the Gulf Stream. By the eighteenth century it was known to many mariners. Benjamin Franklin is credited with noting as early as 1724 that the water temperatures in the Gulf Stream were some twenty degrees warmer than the surrounding Atlantic waters. Nearly fifty years later, in 1770, he published a map showing the oceanic "river." In fact, Walden Hoxton had charted and named the Gulf Stream in 1735, thirteen years before *Fowey* was lost. The name became more popularly known in the 1760s when William Gerard De Brahm, surveyor-general of the Southern District of East Florida, compiled his observations of the Gulf Stream for publication. Clearly, in the 1740s the Gulf Stream was little understood by the *Fowey*'s master.

Seventeen years after the loss of *Fowey*, Bishop (1765: 53) noted that there were strong currents in the Straits of Florida that were the result of tidal flow through the barrier keys and the Gulf Stream but that 100 fathoms of water could be found "with the bushes just in sight from the poop of a 40 gun ship, and distant from the reef 6 or 7 miles." He added that "in latitude 25 degrees 30 minutes North are other rocks, where the *Fowey* was lost." On the next page he noted that the Florida peninsula "does not go north, as has been formerly imagined, till you arrive in the latitude of North 25 degree

40 minutes." In an appendix to this book (1765: 77) is a letter he wrote to Governor James Grant of East Florida regarding the loss of *Fowey*. It was republished in Romans et al. (1783: 49). In it he stated:

> The purpose, says my letter, I had in seeing the Florida shore, was, that in the last war, I being Master of HMS *Fowey*, Captain Drake, was cast away in the latitude of 25 degrees 25 minutes* North and got over the reef in three fathoms of water, after our bottom was very much beat to pieces, and all our anchors gone, and being left without the reef, and we drove to the northward in 5 or 6 fathoms water, for 5 leagues. At the same time wished for less depth, that we might keep our men and prisoners dry; but at last were obliged to let her stay in that depth, for fear of being drove out into the Gulf. (* There is an error of 10 minutes in this observation, the Fowey Rocks being in 25 degrees 35–40 minutes North.)

If hindsight is 20/20 at least one contemporary, Bernard Romans, an accomplished cartographer, was critical of Bishop's observations as early as 1775. In *A Concise Natural History of East and West Florida* he stated: "These remarks of that gentleman are very judicious, and indeed most of his performance tho' strangely unconnected is generally pretty just, *but his charts bad* [emphasis added]. I will however (often asking his pardon) endeavor to rectify a few of his annotations, which seem rather crude or too hastily penned down" (1775 [1962]: xlviii). In subsequent pages Romans pointed out several errors in Bishop's work. Some observations were charitable: "Mr. Bishop mentions the depth within the reef at 4 or 5 fathoms, which is more than double the quantity found. This is, I suppose, an error of the press" (1775 [1962]: li; Romans et al. 1783: 28 footnote). Others are damning: "The distance from the Fowey rocks to Cape Florida is 15 leagues, as Mr. Bishop observes, but he makes an *egregious mistake* [emphasis added] in calling it only 3 from the Cape to Key Loo [*sic*]; for upon supposition that the south end of the reef before the Matecombe islands, be the true cape, the distance there to Key Loo is above 20 leagues on a W S W course; . . . I therefore guess him to have been misinformed with respect to the local situation of the loss of the Loo" (1775 [1962]: l; Romans et al. 1783: 28 footnote).

Robert Bishop was anything but "misinformed" regarding the *Looe*, because he had been the *Looe*'s master when it went ashore on February 4,

1743, less than five years before the *Fowey* was lost. The situation was eerily similar. *Looe* was cruising off Havana, had captured a prize, and was heading to the Carolinas. During the day they identified Double Head Shot Key in the western end of the Salt Key Bank (or Keysal) and began heading north. Robert Bishop was on deck for the midwatch, midnight to 4 a.m., and was casting the sounding lead every thirty minutes. At 1:15 a.m. he was surprised to see white water. As its captain came on deck, the *Looe* ran aground, lost its rudder, and was lost. They had thought they had come ashore on part of the Salt Key Bank until morning, when they realized they were on the Florida Keys (Peterson 1955: 22). The crew was rescued by a passing merchant vessel and carried to succor in South Carolina. On May 31, 1744, the court-martial found that the officers of the *Looe*, including Bishop, "did in no way contribute to her going ashore, but that it was owing to some unknown accident, it appearing to the Court, that the course the ship steered was a good one, and must have carried her thro the Gulph [*sic*] of Florida, with all safety had not some unusual current rendered the said course ineffectual" (Peterson 1955: 27).

Did the court know that Bishop had lost another fifth-rate at nearly the same location a few years earlier? Did anyone really know where *Fowey* had sunk? Did Drake or his officers know? Unfortunately, the answers to those questions remain unknown. It is certain, however, that they breathed a collective sigh of relief when they reentered the great cabin. It was the opinion of the "Court that they and all of them be acquitted." Yet there is evidence of some retribution. After the *Looe* court-martial, an exonerated Captain Ashby Utting was posted to HMS *Gosport*, another fifth-rate. It may be argued that experienced captains were needed in a time of war. Captain Francis William Drake and the *Fowey*, however, were a different matter.

Influence and patronage may well be the key words to describe how history came to be rewritten for this scion of a peer of the kingdom. Yet it should be remembered that patronage was a common aspect of the Royal Navy during the Georgian era (Rodger 1986: 273–302). Shortly after the court-martial, Captain Drake was given a new command. HMS *Mercury* was a sixth-rate warship with twenty-four guns: a ship appropriate for an individual with the rank of commander, *not* post captain. In subsequent publications (e.g., Charnock 1798: 61; Elliot-Drake 1911: 262; Marx 1983: 216) it is said that he moved to the *Mercury* from the *Fowey*, "a vessel of the same description" (Elliot-Drake 1911: 262). Drake would continue to serve in sixth- and fifth-rate ships for the next decade. Ultimately, at the age of fifty-four, he had survived long enough on the captain's list to be promoted to the rank of rear admiral in 1778. As for HMS *Fowey*, the next vessel to bear that name was launched on July 4, 1749, and was a sixth-rate warship armed with twenty-four guns (ADM 180/3, p. 353 [368]). All previous ships had been fifth-rates (ADM 180/2, p. 480 [291]). The family name had been protected in history, and *Fowey* was lost.

2

When Dreams Become Nightmares

Treasure Hunters and the Tragedy of Gerald Klein

The new year had started, and it appeared to be a good one for Gerald Klein and his family. The seemingly ever-expanding Florida population of refugees and retirees meant steady employment for this heavy machine operator. His wife's restaurant, Joan's Galley, was doing well. Some day there might even be a Joan's Galley Too to further situate the family. Of course, a successful "treasure hunter" might not have to worry about money. He had read about the success of Art McKee Jr., Kip Wagner (Burgess and Clausen 1976; Wagner 1966), Mel Fisher, and others in Burgess' *They Found Treasure* (2000 [1977]), in Martin Meylach's *Diving to a Flash of Gold* (1971), or in the pages of *National Geographic* (e.g., Wagner 1965; Lyon 1976). You could hardly open a newspaper in south Florida in the 1960s and 1970s without reading about recovered gold and silver. Now Gerald Joseph Klein, of Perrine, Florida, was poised to go down in history as another of the fortunate fortune finders. Or so he dreamed.

Four years earlier Klein had found "his" shipwreck about twelve miles south of Miami and some twenty miles due east of Homestead. There it lay, a mere thirty feet down in eighty-degree water, three miles off Elliot Key in Legare Anchorage. It looked just like the pictures in *National Geographic*. He saw cannons and cannonballs, swords, bottles, spoons, and other debris: all his for the taking, if he followed the law and requested title to the site. Others had done it, and now it was his turn. Perhaps dreams did come true after all.

The Birth of Treasure Hunting

At the end of World War II the "Greatest Generation" returned to the United States with new skills, new technologies, and a healthy dose of both optimism and contempt for following orders. These were the men who had experienced the grinding realities of the Great Depression and were part of the great mobilization that defeated the Axis. They had returned to a country that was beyond the wildest dreams of the 1930s. The GI Bill and an expanding economy meant that the "Levittowns" would be filled with prosperous families and the streets with new cars.

Some of these GIs chose a different route to their dreams. Perhaps they remembered Errol Flynn as Captain Blood in the movies of their youth, or perhaps as soldiers or sailors in transport they had read one of the "new-fangled" paperback pocket book novels about pirates, undersea adventure, and lost treasure. James Michener's *Tales of the South Pacific* no doubt resonated with many. The war also brought people together from around the country. They all had their own skills and stories. New Yorkers had their Captain William Kidd, the Tar Heels of North Carolina their Blackbeard; people from the bayous of Louisiana and Mississippi had stories of Jean Lafitte; and the Atlantic coast of Florida had not only stories but treasure! Now that the war was over, they could make their dreams into realities.

During the Depression and later during the war, many had learned to "scrounge" and "make do" while being trained to operate a myriad of technologies, including small and large engines, sonar, metal detectors, aircraft, and underwater breathing apparatuses of many kinds. As the armed services began to demobilize and mothball its fleets and armies, not only did the sailors and soldiers return to civilian life but the materials that had been so carefully made and warehoused were being sold at bargain-basement prices in Army-Navy surplus stores across the nation.

Florida, unlike neighboring states to the north or even northwest, is nearly surrounded by warm, clear, and shallow water and enjoys a salubrious year-round climate. It was a place that beckoned to those dreaming of riches, a place where Cuba and the Bahamas were just a short boat or plane ride away. Ernest Hemingway did for the Florida Straits what Michener did for the South Pacific. He described a wide-open, wild-west sort of place where gangsters and rum-runners and fishermen and beachcombers were the norm. During the war, naval air squadrons flying out of Pensacola, Jacksonville, and Key West would hunt the Nazi U-boats by day and haunt the Complete Angler Hotel in Bimini and the Hotel Nacional and Sloppy Joe's in Havana and Key West after dark. This was a place in the United States where freedom was writ large: a place where the beer was cold and no one (usually, that is) was shooting at you.

Figure 2.1. The Treasure Island store and museum in St. Ignace, Michigan, was decorated with an anchor from a wreck site in the Atlantic. (Photograph by Russell Skowronek.)

Along its littoral lay the remains of hundreds of ships claimed through the centuries by hurricanes, reefs, and commerce raiders. Now it was a beachcomber's delight. From Fort Pierce, where the *Urca de Lima* of the 1715 plate fleet was found in 1928, and Jupiter Inlet to Key Largo on the Atlantic side of the Florida Peninsula, winter storms had washed up black, oxidized, silver eight-reales, smaller "cobs" and coins, and the occasional piece of historic ceramic or gold. This was the siren's call to a new life.

Florida was rapidly becoming a vacation destination-point for all those returned GIs and their new families and cars, where the kids could frolic in the warm, clear water, Mom could relax, and Dad could read some Hemingway or Michener, sip a beer, and close his eyes to think about unrealized dreams. There they saw restaurants decorated with the flotsam of wrecks and surrounded by rusting anchors and cast-iron guns (figures 2.1, 2.2). Post-1949 tourism made the dream a tangible reality for all who made the drive down U.S. Highway 1 to Plantation Key in the Florida Keys and visited McKee's Museum of Sunken Treasure. There they could "See Sunken Treasure, Silver Bars, Gold Doubloons, Pieces of Eight" and visit the excavation of a genuine Spanish treasure ship, the *Rui* (aka *Rubi Segundo*), or view the *Capitana* (the flagship of the 1733 *flota*) from a glass-bottomed boat and even go diving on it (Burgess 1988: 26–27). Even today at Sebastian Inlet State Park near Vero Beach, Florida, visitors flock to the McLarty Treasure Museum. How did this phenomenon begin?

Popular (Mis)Perceptions of Treasure Hunting

Ask anyone today to define the term "treasure salvage" and you will immediately elicit far-away stares and stories of the fabled discoveries of valuable lost cargos. Some might describe the salvors themselves as adventurers who risked life and limb and became fabulously wealthy. For them, Mel Fisher's mantra "Today is the Day!" is the touchstone of this perception. Few remember that he spent sixteen years searching for the *Atocha* and the *Margarita* and repeatedly teetered between bankruptcy and bonanza.

Most have a Disneyesque mental image of a shipwreck as the archetypical broken ship of their childhood fish tanks with a skeleton at the wheel and sharks or giant clams rhythmically opening and closing their maws to protect a gold-filled chest. Few will remember the reflections and admonitions of those who have found treasure. Kip Wagner recalled: "I had a hard time matching what I saw underwater with my imagination's image of a treasure wreck. No timbers remained—probably all having long since

Figure 2.2. When retrieved from wreck sites in the Atlantic Ocean, these guns looked pristine. Without proper conservation they became unrecognizable masses of iron oxide. After being on display in St. Ignace, Michigan, these guns were thrown in a landfill in the 1980s when Treasure Island closed. (Photograph by Russell Skowronek.)

passed through the digestive tracts of . . . shipworms" (Peterson 1974b: 45; Wagner 1966: 72–73). On another occasion, after the auction of some of their finds, Wagner and his team considered the paucity of their returns after expenses were deducted: "Seems ironic as hell, we find a fortune in treasure estimated to be in the millions, but these few thousand dollars are all we're able to stuff into our pockets" (Burgess 1988: 122). Similarly, Robert Sténuit commented: "The sad truth is that most wrecks—even treasure laden ones—yield the finder far less net profit than expected. So the diver must always balance his possible find against the staggering costs of the expedition" (Sténuit 1974a: 181). Perhaps Mendel Peterson said it best: "Many treasure salvors put $10 or $20 into the sea for every dollar a few take out " (Peterson 1974b: 38). Nevertheless, treasure hunting conjures the romantic image of brave adventurers facing the terrible mistress that is the sea . . . images that have been more than a century in the making.

Beginning with the reduction of the North African Barbary States at the turn of the nineteenth century and continuing through the proclamation of the Monroe Doctrine and into the 1830s, the United States Navy worked assiduously to clear the Atlantic Ocean and Caribbean Sea of smugglers and pirates, while the Royal Navy did the same in Asia, following the defeat of China in the Opium Wars and the establishment of a British naval base in Hong Kong. As a result, the late-nineteenth-century world had radically changed. The rule of law as dictated by remote governments would regulate trade and thus regulate people's lives, which were already becoming increasingly regulated in the shift to wage labor in factories.

The pirates that were so much a part of the accounts of the early eighteenth century had largely disappeared by the mid-nineteenth century. In the West the growing strength of the state made many long for an earlier, freer time. Escape to that time would come through one of the benefits of life in the controlled world of the West—literacy. If there is a common denominator among successful treasure hunters, it is a childhood filled with dreams of pirates, lost treasure, and sunken ships. We are fortunate that Robert Burgess (2000 [1977], 1988) has interviewed many of the salvors about their childhood and youth and their personal path. Clearly, the tales found in Robert Louis Stevenson's *Treasure Island*, Jules Verne's *20,000 Leagues under the Sea*, and Mark Twain's *Adventures of Tom Sawyer* and *Huckleberry Finn* resonated with the likes of Mel Fisher, Art McKee, Robert Marx, and Kip Wagner. Robert Sténuit (1974a: 182) may have best characterized the difference between treasure hunters and deep-sea salvage companies. "They [the deep-sea salvage companies] are businessmen, with automatic weapons, not poets dreaming of long-lost doubloons and ducats."

Most of the famous treasure hunters came from fairly mundane backgrounds. Kip Wagner (1906–1972) of Miamisburg, Ohio, was a house builder by trade. He arrived in Florida after World War II and began searching the beaches south of Cape Canaveral with an army-surplus metal detector. Mel Fisher (1922–1998) was originally from Hobart, Indiana. After a hitch in the army during World War II he moved to California, where he started a chicken ranch and opened a dive shop. In 1953 he sold the ranch to devote his full attentions to diving. In 1964 he answered the siren's call and moved to Florida (Burgess 1988; Peterson 1974b; www.melfisher.org). Tom Gurr, who excavated the wreck of the *San José de las Animas*, part of the ill-fated 1733 *flota*, was an engineer by training (Peterson 1974b: 57). Art McKee, Jr. (1910–1977), of Bridgetown, New Jersey, and Robert Marx (b. 1935), of Pittsburgh, Pennsylvania, were oddities: they entered the world of treasure hunting through the gateway of commercial salvage (Burgess 1988).

For all of the romance, a deadly earnestness in the life of treasure hunters can make the story-line of Humphrey Bogart's *The Treasure of the Sierra Madre* seem almost tame in comparison. Mendel Peterson, the late curator of maritime history and historical archaeology at the National Museum of American History, Smithsonian Institution, once wrote: "I have yet to hear of a big treasure find that didn't end up in some kind of legal wrestling. Treasure hunting is a gamble, I would warn those lured to its adventure, or those tempted to invest money as backers. And even if gold and silver are found, they have a long history of arousing bitterness and discord among all who covet them" (Peterson 1974b: 58). The accounts of rival groups of treasure hunters who "poach" each other's wreck sites are well documented. During the excavation of the *Girona* in Northern Ireland, Sténuit and his team were attacked by twelve "amateur pirates," as he charitably termed them, armed with crowbars (Sténuit 1974b: 24). Art McKee, Jr., the acknowledged "grandfather" of treasure hunters, was repeatedly challenged by armed individuals both on site and in his museum (Burgess 1988: 29–35; Peterson 1974b: 43, 50–51). The authors of this volume experienced firsthand the dangers associated with shipwreck research during a project at Fort Jefferson National Monument in 1982. While diving on a wreck as part of a National Park Service archaeological project, we were shot at with automatic weapons by individuals who, when confronted by National Park Service rangers, said that they were "shooting at sharks."

The American public can be very fickle. They like to drive their SUVs and have cheap gasoline, but they do not want drilling in the Arctic National Wildlife Refuge. Still, when a "little guy" wins the lottery or finds a diamond, the general public is happy for these lucky few and genuinely puzzled if there is not a happy ending when third parties enter. When insurance companies or governments intervene, they are seen as unfair intrusion by the "bad guys." The dichotomy of bad and good seemingly strikes a primal note of fair play. Fifty years ago, "finders keepers" may have been common in the realm of childhood ethics; but once landowners and previous owners realized that they had potential claims the "finders" became "trespassers." In general, if something of value that may be defined as treasure is found on land simply lying on the surface, it is "finders keepers." If the object is embedded or buried in the ground, however, it belongs to the landowner. In that case, the "finder" must have permission from the landowner to disturb the property; otherwise a case of criminal trespass often results, with the "finder" now claiming a reward from an "unwilling owner." By way of example, we might consider a private home. An individual might one day decide to cut another person's lawn or shovel the snow from someone else's sidewalk or driveway and then demand payment for the labor. Because this person failed to ask for permission to do this job, the individual who is the titleholder is not obligated to pay and is deemed an "unwilling owner."

In the 1990s the SS *Central America* was found hundreds of miles off the coast of South Carolina. The salvors at the time thought they were home-free, since they were working in international waters on an abandoned wreck—that is, until the insurance companies got into the act. Even though they had historically paid off on the claims, a judgment found that the insurance companies were entitled to a share of the recovered treasure. This, of course, has created a tidal wave of similar claims based on concepts such as sovereign rights vis-à-vis "government-owned ships." Everyone is probably aware that most World War II naval vessels have been considered to be war graves and therefore the property of the sovereign state. To this day, the National Park Service has to walk (or swim) a narrow line at the USS *Arizona* Memorial in Pearl Harbor, for it is both a war grave and a national park. Recently, others have questioned the ethics of disturbing the Civil

War–era graves popularly known as the USS *Monitor* and the CSS *Hunley* by historians more interested in technology than in the men who sailed and died in them. Now Spain is exerting claims to its once-sovereign king's treasure on his ancient and wrecked flagged ships. Taken to its logical extreme, we might further confuse the situation by dragging in Christianity. A few years ago, salvors in Anguilla were trying to claim a Spanish wreck that had identifiable king's property. It had also been carrying some priests, with their accouterments and materials for mission work. This included a lot of small religious medals and relics, which nowadays have substantial material value. They could potentially be claimed as church property: would the claimant be the Roman Catholic Church, the pope, God? Perhaps that is the next step in these expanding and complicated questions of ownership.

Prior to 1987 the same argument could be made for submerged lands within the territorial waters of the United States. With the exception of federal preserves, adjacent state governments could claim a portion of the value of the discovered objects that were found on the surface of the seabed and within territorial waters (Burgess and Clausen 1976: 104). To understand a treasure hunter's point of view, we are obliged to understand our culture.

Americans like to see themselves as a different breed: a John Wayne or Atticus Finch sort of society that is slow to anger but stands up to fight injustice. They dislike thugs or governments who take advantage of underdogs. Americans imagine themselves to be like Zorro or Robin Hood or the Magnificent Seven, coming to the rescue of those less fortunate. They are as outraged about police on the take as they are about the mob extorting "protection money" from mom-and-pop store owners. Americans dislike muggers, thieves, and Enron entrepreneurs who take from the "little guys" not just because it is against the law but because it is not right. Yet this position is not always clear-cut in history. Today drug dealers and smugglers are vilified as law breakers and murderers. Three-quarters of a century ago Al Capone and other bootleggers were the law breakers and murderers. While television programs like the *Untouchables* left no doubt who the good guys were, many people in Cicero and in the suburbs of Chicago saw Capone as their Robin Hood because of the stability and safety he brought to their community. Similar things were said about the infamous Blackbeard (Edward Teach). Within the world of law-abiding citizens he was a murderous thug. Yet more than two centuries after Blackbeard's death Ben Dixon MacNeill (1958: 58–64) recorded a very different image of the man that survived on the nearby Outer Banks of North Carolina. The people had "a very lively belief that Captain Teach was a right considerable fellow." He was said to maintain a respectable house in Bath and to make gifts to the church and to the first library in North Carolina. Perhaps most important was that "he preferred the hospitality of the simple folk across the Inlet from Portsmouth to the brawling thieves who built their warehouses and defrauded" the local Hatterasmen. "And, anyhow, what if he was a pirate? He was a respectable pirate and a good neighbor when he was around the community" (MacNeill 1958: 61). Oral histories collected by MacNeill detail Teach's bravery and the unfair advantage of Lieutenant Robert Maynard's surprise attack. Teach died in the battle, and it is reported that his head hung from the bowsprit of Maynard's ship on its return to Virginia (Rankin 1960: 58–59). The accounts suggest that after the battle Maynard fled the region, fearing reprisals at the hands of the local inhabitants.

"'He slunk out of here,' an Islander would say, near two and a half centuries afterward, and he says it as if it happened no longer ago than last week" (MacNeill 1958: 63). It is against this backdrop that we must examine America's love affair with treasure hunters.

Phil Silvers as Sergeant Bilko, a man with eternal schemes for finding ways to get rich quick and make fools of his "superiors," epitomizes this aspect of the American psyche. And some things never change. Decades later, in the 1990s, the use of the Internet and the technology to copy music onto compact disks combined to make a so-called victimless crime of downloading music. People were stealing, yet it was justified as "fair use" or because the record companies and artists asked "too much" for recordings and tickets. As we can see, Horatio Alger–type stories about little guys making it big, in spite of the odds or government interference, are a cornerstone of this worldview. We need to understand, however, that the real world of treasure hunting has changed for many societal reasons.

It is fair to say that in the fifteen years following World War II no state protected cultural resources in its waters. For eleven years, from 1949 to 1960, Art McKee had a lease from the State of Florida for mining shipwrecks. He paid $100 per year and gave the state 12½ percent of his finds (Burgess 1988: 34–35). He felt betrayed when "claim jumpers" drove him off his sites and the state refused to uphold his claim because a certain wreck was three and a half miles offshore in *international* waters.

We should also recall that underwater archaeology did not exist until 1960, when Dr. George Bass (then of the University of Pennsylvania Museum and today professor emeritus at Texas A&M University) conducted the first scientifically driven underwater research project off the coast of Turkey. In that same year Dr. John Goggin (1913–1963) of the University of Florida published "Underwater Archaeology: Its Nature and Limitations" in *American Antiquity*. Prior to this time the underwater world had been left to the sport divers. In fact, many people in the scientific and historical communities had already come to recognize the value of underwater cultural resources from sport and professional divers. For example, in 1951 Mendel Peterson of the Smithsonian Institution learned how to dive and excavate from Art McKee, Jr., and others and "excavated" HMS *Looe* (aka *Loo*) (Peterson 1955, 1974a: 131). Robert Marx worked with John Goggin on a terrestrial project on Spanish colonial sites in Latin America in 1957 and 1958. Goggin would later represent the State of Florida and serve as both an interested advisor and friend to Kip Wagner. In the Old World the late Peter Throckmorton (1928–1990) and George Bass (b. 1932) learned about the sea's potential to provide insights into the past from sponge divers. The government of Greece had supported these divers *cum* salvors since the turn of the twentieth century (Throckmorton 1974: 105, 109). Bass still relies on the reports of sponge divers; but for more than forty years he has understood that it is easier to teach a scientist to dive than to teach a diver to be a scientist. And that is the issue that needs further exploration.

When we consider the development of the discipline of archaeology, it is fair to say that its roots lay in collecting ancient and exotic materials. In the eighteenth century Pompeii and Herculaneum were "mined" for statuary and mosaics for the homes of wealthy patrons in Naples and Rome. Egyptian obelisks, statues, mummies, and even the Rosetta Stone were later carried off to Paris, London, and New York. The most famous of these cases was probably the removal of the friezes from the Parthenon by Lord Elgin to England. These and countless other discoveries over the past two and a half centuries have scattered many of the greatest treasures of the world thousands of miles from their original homes. Today the home countries of these items are not only requesting their return but also attempting to restrict the export of other "national treasures" to modern and extremely wealthy collectors.

In the careless retrieval of many of these artifacts, many other incidental yet culturally and historically valuable objects may have been utterly destroyed. In any case, the primary context of the finds was certainly lost. "Context," in archaeological parlance, gives meaning to objects in time and space. To understand context we must know precisely where an object was found, both horizontally and vertically. If those facts are not known, an information-laden artifact becomes little more than a curio, with much-diminished intrinsic value. To demonstrate this, we can cite a genuine discovery.

During the excavation of one of the vessels from the Spanish 1715 plate fleet (the Douglas Beach site, 8SL-17), in the shallow waters off the Atlantic coast of Florida, salvors recovered all the detritus of shipboard life as well as "treasure" of silver, gold, and even an ivory tusk. There was a problem, however. The ivory tusk was not from a modern African elephant. It was from an elephant that had died during the last Ice Age (Murphy 1990), when sea levels were lower. Thousands of years later, an unfortunate ship sank and serendipitously came to rest on top of this paleontological site. This would never have been realized without contextual information, and the tusk would have been listed as, well, another piece of cargo.

Context not only can help us understand what happened first but also can help us understand past activities. Let us consider a modern example, which is analogous to a shipwreck. An armored truck leaving the Denver or Philadelphia mints may carry thousands of dollars in coins. They are freshly minted and are being carried to Federal Reserve Banks for distribution. These coins will be stored in bags or boxes and carried in the main cargo compartment of the vehicle. The driver may also have a pocketful or a cup full of coins to use for highway tolls or perhaps to purchase lunch. Those other coins will have a variety of dates and may even include a Canadian coin picked up in change. They are all coins, of course, but it is their context that can ultimately provide us with various insights into many aspects of our world. The size of the bags or boxes may tell us what the Occupational Health and Safety Administration limits are for acceptable weights to be lifted. If the coins are secured in a locked container or if they are only in the armored "container" we might learn about the level of concern regarding pilferage by guards. The presence of local and international currency in the driver's compartment would provide evidence on the circulation of coins and perhaps the proximity of national boundaries or of important trading partners. The presence of a single exotic coin might simply represent a curio or good luck item. The recent discovery of the SS *Central America* in the murky depths of the Atlantic Ocean off the coast of South Carolina provides a similar example of this.

Lost in 1855, the vessel was filled with freshly coined gold specie from the San Francisco mint. In addition to the cargo, the ship carried hundreds of recently wealthy miners from the gold fields of the Sierra Nevada who were transporting not only gold coins but also gold dust and nuggets and circulating silver coins. Their context on the wreck site can separate cargo from personal items.

Perhaps the most significant example of the significance of context in American archaeology came in 1927, when a fluted Folsom point was found lodged between the ribs of an extinct form of bison. This discovery provided the first unequivocal evidence for the presence of humans in the Americas during the Pleistocene epoch. What if an "arrowhead" collector had found this site first and collected the point but left the skeleton? Our knowledge of the age of the peopling of the Americas might have been set back for decades.

With these examples in mind we need to return to the perception that treasure salvors have been unfairly treated. More than thirty years ago Mendel Peterson (1974a: 147) noted that, at least in the Western Hemisphere, there were no degree-granting programs in underwater archaeology, perhaps only two dozen underwater archaeologists, and no "good" museum dedicated to underwater history. Today in the United States graduate programs at East Carolina University, Florida State University, the University of Hawaii, and Texas A&M are educating archaeologically trained scientists for the sea. Most of these programs came decades after the first collectors ventured into the water and decades after the passage of state laws (e.g., Florida, 1964; North Carolina, 1967; Texas, 1970) and the creation of state underwater archaeology programs to protect offshore historic resources. Furthermore, today there are many world-class maritime museums, including the Museum of Florida History in Tallahassee; the Graveyard of the Atlantic Museum in Hatteras, North Carolina; the Maritime Museum of Newport News, Virginia; and the South Port Museum in New York City, to name but a few. These changes over the years have occurred specifically because of the perceived success of the treasure hunters, the growing access to submerged sites, and a larger shift in the ethos of the American public toward the preservation of cultural resources.

In the decades following World War II the American countryside began to fill with new housing, and historic structures in America's cities were often destroyed to make way for new construction. By way of example, at

Cahokia Mounds in East St. Louis, Illinois, the largest Pre-Columbian site north of Mexico and today listed as a World Heritage Site by the United Nations, a thousand-year-old Mississippian Period ridge-topped mound was destroyed in the early 1960s in order to construct a retail store. This store subsequently went out of business and was demolished. But the great prehistoric earthen mound is also gone. In San Jose, California, at the end of World War II there were still some fifty adobe houses that dated to the Spanish and Mexican regimes. By the late 1960s, however, only the Peralta Adobe remained as the sole example of life in the Mexican pueblo in San Jose. By this time, though, there was also a growing interest in America's "roots," and both the public and preservationists saw those roots being un-ceremoniously dug up and dispersed without regard to their meaning to the larger public. A greedy few were benefiting at the cost of many. Perhaps the most eloquent defense for the protection of shipwrecks, and the difference between archaeology and treasure hunting, was written in 1979 by George Bass: "The Men Who Stole the Stars" is a scathing indictment of state-sponsored pilfering of historic sites, be they on land or under the sea. Repeatedly republished, it may well be cited as *the* seminal statement that led to the end of wholesale commercial treasure hunting within the territorial waters of the United States.

As a result, in the 1960s, 1970s, and 1980s both Democratic and Republican administrations passed a number of federal laws to protect historic properties on public lands and to promote their protection on private lands (1966: National Historic Preservation Act; 1969: National Environmental Protection Act; 1972: Executive Order 11593; 1979: Archaeological Resources Protection Act; 1988: Abandoned Shipwreck Act). Today every state and territory in the United States has a State Historic Preservation Office with oversight responsibilities.

Yet thirty years ago, when Mendel Peterson (1974b) wrote that any curtailing of the treasure-hunting business would be seen as an example of government interference with the "little guys," the case of Tom Gurr and the excavation of the *San José* (one of the 1733 fleet wreck sites) was often cited. It lay more than three miles off the coast and therefore not within Florida state waters. The State of Florida took Gurr to court and won a ruling that Florida state waters actually extended from the edge of the offshore reefs and not from the mean low-water mark of the shore. Although the federal government later challenged the state, Gurr ultimately lost, but not without garnering the support of fellow treasure hunters and much of the public's sympathy. When Mel Fisher won in court against both the State of Florida and the federal government over the remains of *Nuestra Señora de Atocha*, he and many other treasure hunters were lionized by the public for gaining the upper hand over the egghead academics and big government (Burgess 1980: 205). For archaeologists and other scientists, however, this was in fact an act of piracy of the archaeological and historical record. For the laws protecting shipwrecks are meant for the real "little guys": the people of the United States, who visit and enjoy the national parks and museums, children, older citizens, and others, including all those who have neither the will or the wherewithal to go "treasure hunting." The fear in the archaeological community by that time was palpable. Without protection, there would be complete uncontrolled destruction of wreck sites, both inside and outside the jurisdiction of the United States.

This takes us to a final question. Are treasure salvors the "good guys" or are they the thugs who take advantage of the "little guys"? Again, a comparison may illuminate this issue.

Studies of the Mafia in Sicily have shown that the mid-nineteenth-century ascendancy of the Italian nation-state with its unified civil and criminal codes played a significant role in shaping the perception of outlaws. The result was that outlaws or bandits were glorified or at least accepted in their native districts, while feared as raiders outside the area. These "Robin Hoods" would walk an ambiguous line between the poverty of their neighbors and the wealth of others. Successful bandits stand out as individuals who evolved from poverty to relative wealth and who acquired power in spite of existing government. The more successful they were as bandits, the more extensive the protection granted to them and the more they were able to make themselves respected.

Thus, in the years after Mel Fisher's courtroom victory, treasure hunting in Florida took on another visage. This case involved people who were above the law and who had "rights" that were not to be challenged. It was also during this period that the *Godfather* went from bestseller to the big screen, and everyone understood the significance of being a "legitimate" business owner with an attorney.

In October 1979 Gerald Klein retained the services of two law firms: Corlett, Merritt, Killian & Sikes of Miami and David Paul Horan, a Key West–based lawyer with considerable experience in treasure salvage cases. On October 4 Horan & Sireci, on behalf of their client, filed an *in rem* complaint in United States District Court, Southern District of Florida, requesting title or alternatively a liberal salvage award to "a wrecked and abandoned sailing vessel within the Legare Anchorage" (Case No. 79-4627-Civ-CA). The wreck was initially described as lying forty feet down in waters under the jurisdiction of the State of Florida. It was further described as dating to about 1740. If everything went according to past experience, Gerald Klein would be awarded a salvage contract. The case was brought within the Admiralty and Maritime Jurisdiction of the court, as a claim to salvage an "unidentified and abandoned vessel" under the Admiralty Salvage Act of 1912. This act was a codification of earlier English common-law practice that permitted the salvage of abandoned vessels and their imperiled cargos and liberally rewarded anyone who risked life or limb in the rescuing of those vessels or their cargos.

There was one problem, though. Klein's wreck lay within the boundaries of a federally protected park, Biscayne National Monument (established on October 18, 1968, and reestablished as Biscayne National Park on June 26, 1980), which meant that the federal government would be the claimant or the "unwilling owner" in this case. In November the United States government intervened as a defendant seeking title to the wreck. In Klein's favor was the fact that, while the wreck lay within the boundaries of the monument, it was still very close to the three-mile limit of national sovereignty claimed by the United States. Could federal preserves extend beyond territorial waters? And could the 1906 Antiquity Act supersede the Admiralty Salvage Act of 1912?

Today, with a quarter of a century of hindsight, the outcome of this lawsuit might seem obvious. In that era of early historic preservation awareness, however, Admiralty Law still saw salvage as a means of rescuing imperiled cargos, be they two weeks or two hundred years old (see appendix 1). This was long before the 1987 passage of the Abandoned Shipwreck Act, which gave title and jurisdiction over all shipwrecks with the territorial waters of the United States to the adjacent state governments. It was also long before the recognition of the perpetual rights of foreign nations to wrecked vessels. While that practice had been observed vis-à-vis World War II–era ships as war graves, it was never actively applied to "historic" wrecks dating from the early modern era until July 2000, when the Fourth Circuit United States Court of Appeals in Virginia ruled against treasure hunter Ben Benson and Sea Hunt, Incorporated, finding that Spain owned two warships, *La Galaga* (1750) and the *Juno* (1802) (Broad 2000; U.S. Court of Appeals for the Fourth Circuit N. 99-2035, 99-2036). This was later codified in the

Federal Register (2004: 5647–5648) to include protection for sunken vessels owned by the governments of France, Germany, Japan, Russia, Spain, and the United Kingdom.

On January 6, 1980, within months of the filing of Klein's "complaint," the United States District Court granted temporary custody of the site to the United States. In March, as a result of this order, Gerald Klein was required to surrender his collection of some two hundred artifacts from the site to the National Park Service. Federal marshals and an archaeologist—George Fischer—from the National Park Service's Southeast Archeological Center came to Klein's restaurant to collect the materials. The Park Service would analyze and stabilize the materials and eventually (or so he hoped) return them to Gerald Klein.

On New Year's Day, 1982, forty-seven-year-old Gerald Klein turned his car off 186th Street into the parking lot of his wife's restaurant, Joan's Galley. The future probably seemed limitless when he opened the door and stepped across the threshold into—an armed robbery. One moment, he stood between a robber and the door. The next, his body lay between a murderer and the door. His treasure hunt was over.

3

Rumors of a Wreck

The Archaeologist

It was one of those picture-perfect late October days in Tallahassee. The torrid humidity of the summer months had passed, and the trees were beginning to change color. Automobiles in the capital city were sporting a new bumper sticker that read "Strive for Five—Gig the Gators." Old Sol, "FSU's Number One Fan," was the darling of the co-eds, just as football coach Bobby Bowden was for the alumni. Yes, there was a different feeling in the city and at Florida State University. Three decades had passed since Florida State College for Women was transformed by returning GIs into FSU, home of the Seminoles. It was now a Research 1 institution, albeit not quite yet on the scale of the University of Florida at Gainesville, but it was "going places." President Bernie Sliger (whose Ph.D. was from Michigan State University, a land-grant university) understood service learning and research. Florida State was not going to be just another "southern" university. Connections to the community were going to be created, and the opportunities would be used to drive faculty and student research. One of those connections was with the Southeast Archeological Center of the National Park Service (NPS).

Founded during World War I (hence the well-known Smokey the Bear campaign hats that are still a standard part of its uniform), the National Park Service was created to be the steward of the nation's battlefields, monuments, parks, seashores, and trails. The National Park Service Establishment Act of 1916 states that these are not just "public lands" but federal reserve lands, each set aside by an act of Congress or presidential proclamation for a specific purpose. Briefly, the purposes articulated in the Organic Act are "to conserve the scenery and the natural and historic objects and the wildlife therein and to provide for the enjoyment of the same in such manner and by such means as will leave them *unimpaired* [emphasis added] for the enjoyment of future generations." These are lofty and sometimes contradictory goals; but when conflicts exist, preservation should prevail. This stewardship includes plants, wildlife, vistas, and cultural resources. In fact, decades before the establishment of the National Park Service, the federal government recognized that the nation's treasures had to be protected from those who would despoil them for private gain. Enforcement on park lands was originally in the hands of the U.S. Army. Other public lands, however, contained more resources than could be "protected" with a policing force. For instance, in the vast distances of the American Southwest were the well-preserved ruins of thousands of prehistoric and historic settlements. At the end of the nineteenth century some of these sites were "mined" by foreign and domestic museums and collectors, and the materials were often carried away with total abandon. As a result, the first great conservationist president, Theodore Roosevelt, signed into law the Antiquities Act of 1906 that "protected" archaeological sites on public lands from unauthorized excavations (Lee 1970).

During the first twenty years of its existence the National Park Service was largely relegated to a caretaker role. This role was greatly expanded during the Great Depression and included care, maintenance, and long-term planning to protect both natural and cultural resources while at the same time affording access to the public. As a result, arborists, architects, biologists, engineers, historians, and archaeologists joined the ranks of the archetypical "rangers" of the modern National Park Service. At the same time, many of today's most popular destinations (such as the Blue Ridge Parkway, Ocmulgee National Monument, and Mammoth Cave National Park) were originally developed under the auspices of the Works Progress Administration and the Civilian Conservation Corps and subsequently placed under the protection of the NPS.

In the post–World War II era the expanding economy and more leisure time meant that thousands more people were able to travel and visit America's parks. These visitors in turn requested and required expanded amenities from roads to restrooms to campgrounds and visitor centers. Each addition had the potential to have an adverse impact on the very resources that the National Park Service was charged to protect. As a result, the planning offices for the NPS were divided into a number of different geographic regions where local specialists could be concentrated and thus make the overall planning process more streamlined and efficient. It also meant that these highly trained regional specialists could specifically use their expertise where it would have the most relevance.

Cultural resource management at the parks now required a wide array of specialists, including archaeologists, historians, curators, and conservators. American archaeology had been transformed during the Depression from the limited world of relic-hunting antiquarians working mostly in exotic foreign locales and at only a few North American sites to a more "democratized" endeavor focused on the Great American Experience. As a result, hundreds of prehistoric and historic sites were excavated, and dozens more historic structures, buildings, and birthplaces were stabilized and are now part of the National Park Service system. Millions of artifacts were collected, with tens of thousands of drawings, notes, and photographs documenting those excavations. These collections are now mainly housed in regional Archeological Centers and offices in Oakland, California; Tucson, Arizona; Lincoln, Nebraska; Philadelphia, Pennsylvania; Tallahassee, Florida; and elsewhere.

Many of the people who were in charge of these projects went on to important university positions after World War II. Their students used the collections and associated reports for graduate research and then filled the hundreds of new positions for archaeologists that developed as a result of these activities in universities as well as in federal and state government. Those who continued with the NPS realized that their archaeological skills were being honed through their various interactions with colleagues in the universities. They feared that being housed in remote park settings could lead to a schism between the academic and applied world. Furthermore, by drawing upon the resources of many eager part-time, cheap, and academically trained student employees and hungry assistant professors, the Park Service could more efficiently carry out its mandate. It would save the public's money, while at the same time ensuring the highest-quality work.

Archaeology for the National Park Service's Southeast Region followed this pattern. Immediately after World War II the Southeast Regional Office's archaeological experts and activities were located in Richmond, Virginia, in the NPS Southeast Regional Office. Later known as the Southeast Archeological Center (SEAC), it relocated to Ocmulgee National Monument in Macon, Georgia, where the late John W. Griffin (1919–1993) became the original director. Early in his career Griffin had worked with Charles Fairbanks (1913–1984) first at FSU and later at the University of Florida and with his classmate from the University of Chicago, Hale G. Smith (1918–1977) of Florida State University, on a number of sites in Georgia and Florida. These were pioneers in the new field of historical archaeology who, with John Goggin (1916–1963), William Sears (1920–1996), and Gordon Willey (1913–2002), had blazed a broad archaeological trail through Florida in the years before and immediately after World War II. When the opportunity came in 1972, Hale Smith, then chairman of the fledgling Anthropology Department, with the backing of President Stanley Marshall, brought the Southeast Archeological Center to the campus of Florida State University. The Memorandum of Agreement brought the center to the heart of campus, with offices in the basement of Montgomery Gymnasium and the ground floor of the navy-built classroom complex known as the Bellamy Building.

One of the archaeologists to make the move from Macon to Tallahassee was George Fischer. Tall and slender, with a full beard, he was a dead ringer for Tsar Nicholas II or King George V. Something of a renegade in the National Park Service, George was both wise and a wise-guy, beyond his thirty-five years. George's childhood and youth were anything but mundane. He and his sister, Helene, were the precocious children of a U.S. Forest Service Ranger, George A. Fischer. They grew up with a great reverence for nature and an abiding respect for history. The area where they lived was one of the points of entry for a branch of the Immigrant Trail and also the site of the Modoc Indian War, one of the last such conflicts. George's father managed a large ranger district and helped guard the Modoc National Forest from Japanese balloon-borne firebombs during the war and the far more mundane but not necessarily less lethal lightning-induced forest fires. Sometimes he would come across the detritus of abandoned supplies scattered along the old trail in the forest. One of those finds was a well-worn ox shoe that he gave to his son. George valued that artifact; and decades later, relying on the skills that he picked up doing archaeology, he conserved it and returned it to his father as a sign of his respect for the past and the role that his father had played in teaching the son about the importance of preserving it.

People sometimes wonder how a native Californian, who grew up in the very rural high desert in the northeast corner of the state, ended up at the farthest point across the country doing underwater archaeology in Florida. It is kind of a complicated story, which nobody could have predicted as it developed. In retrospect, however, it makes a certain amount of sense.

George Fischer was born in Susanville, a small town in very rural Lassen

County, California, in 1937. The family lived some distance out in the surrounding Lassen National Forest, in a small government compound. His father's employment with the U.S. Forest Service in those days was as much a way of life as a job.

George A. Fischer was born and reared in the Palouse country of eastern Washington. He had wanted to be a cowboy, but his father had made him go to college, where he majored in forestry, with a specialty in range management. One summer he obtained a job doing a range reconnaissance and assessment, on horseback, in the Plumas National Forest in California. He loved the country, John Muir's "Range of Light," and figured that was about as close as he was going to get to being a cowboy, so that is what he decided to do with the rest of his life.

When George the younger was four, his father was offered his own ranger district in the Modoc National Forest, a relative coup at that early stage of his career. That became his own fiefdom—eventually nearly a hundred square miles of diverse and beautiful country. This again entailed a move to a yet smaller place, Tulelake, a very rural community immortalized by Zane Grey in the book *Forlorn River*. There the family, including George and his sister, Helene, lived for the next sixteen years.

George's mother, Ruth Isabel Robertson, also a native of Washington, was a schoolteacher and quite dedicated to the education of young people. She saw to it that the children had a lot of exposure to culture, so she often would read the family poetry or Shakespeare on winter nights when the wind whistled and snow swirled outside. She was also very much a liberated self-actualizing woman, long before anyone ever described it as such. Although she might cover it up by acting helpless and hopelessly female a lot of the time, she could do about anything when left to her own devices, including pushing the younger George toward academic successes in which he was not particularly interested.

Shortly after the Fischers moved to Tulelake, World War II broke out. There was a great deal of fear and apprehension about the West's substantial Japanese population, which led to the massive and infamous Japanese-American "internment." Tulelake, being about as far from anywhere as you could get, was selected as one of the sites of an internment camp. George's mother was very upset about all the American children of Japanese descent who had been uprooted from their homes and schools and crowded into tar-paper-covered barracks. She mobilized the local women she could find who had teaching credentials, and they quickly signed on to work in the camp. This created the problem of what to do with George. As he was only five, the Tulelake elementary school would not have him, and there was no other alternative. His mother enrolled him in school in the military section of the place (Camp Newell) but soon discovered that she had to go through considerable security (two sets of gates and checkpoints) to deposit him and then get back to her teaching post. An elementary school within the camp, a few buildings away from where she was teaching high school chemistry, was willing to have George. That is where he started his elementary education, in the midst of a forcibly and unjustly incarcerated population. George was large for his age and thus integrated into the group fairly well, other than having blond hair and blue eyes. Even at the age of six those kids knew that bad things were happening to them and to their families and that Caucasian-featured individuals had something to do with it. George's mother nonetheless figured that it was a good opportunity for him to learn about the injustices of life firsthand and at an early age. He soon gained acceptance, however, and joined the rest of the kids throwing stones at the guards during recess. It is always a conversation stopper when people get on the subject of their summer camp experiences and George mentions that when he was a kid his mother sent him to a concentration camp.

As the son of a schoolteacher, George was expected to express himself in an educated manner. He learned to write well and read all the classics—including *Treasure Island, Tom Sawyer, Huckleberry Finn*, and *20,000 Leagues under the Sea*. He was perhaps one of the few in the area to read the stories of far-off lands in the pages of *National Geographic*.

George's appreciation for other cultures also stemmed from family stories and personal experiences. His grandfather, Dr. J. Benjamin Robertson, had been a teacher/missionary among the Igorot tribe in the Philippines shortly after the Spanish-American War. He brought home a number of native artifacts and stories of life among the Filipinos.

Tulelake was a pretty nice lifestyle, as far as George was concerned. The hunting and fishing and similar activities were incredibly good, and George's father saw that he had a lot of opportunity. In those prelitigious days the Forest Service encouraged active-duty personnel to take their sons with them in the field. That created a safety factor not present when they were off in the wilds alone, and the youngsters were also very useful in opening gates, filling water canteens, and carrying out duties of that sort. The U.S. Forest Service also figured that this had some long-term recruiting value for legacies. So George went out with Dad a lot, opening gates, collecting "arrowheads," and making the world a safer place by shooting all the porcupines, rattlesnakes, and jack rabbits he could find with his .22 rifle.

Over the years George found the social situation and opportunities in Tulelake very attractive and enjoyable. When he graduated from high school he was a fairly successful and well-adjusted juvenile delinquent. At that point he would have been happy to have stayed there and become a cowboy or potato farmer, but his parents and a couple of his teachers who took some interest in his future tried very hard to disabuse him of those intentions and divert him toward college. George applied and was accepted at Stanford, which was kind of a family thing. As his interests and experience seemed to point to some sort of field science, he was guided to a major in geology. After the unrestricted life in Tulelake, George did not adjust well to an urban environment and soon discovered that geology was not his calling, so he rattled around uninspired and unmotivated for a couple of years.

George had a good friend from his freshman year, Land Lindbergh, son of the famed aviator Charles Lindbergh. While they were rooming together, Lindbergh started taking some anthropology courses and some field archaeology, which looked interesting to George. He gave it a try and discovered that anthropology really appealed to him. He had kept in touch with one of his high school teachers who had shown some interest in him and wrote her that he had a new major. She immediately wrote back and urged him to apply for summer work as an archaeologist with the National Park Service in the Southwest, which she thought would really fit him, considering his experiences growing up in the Forest Service. He did so and ended up with a summer job at Mesa Verde National Park in Colorado.

It was an epiphany. George loved the Southwest and found working in the NPS a job that provided a rich opportunity for cultural and natural resource management and preservation. But public education, involving an exposure to all those things, and cultural relativity were really his thing, so he made up his mind then and there that this would be his career. George returned to school with a new focus and developed a plan for a career with the NPS as an archaeologist in the Southwest, forever—or so he thought.

George went on to graduate school to refine his education, avoid the draft, and maintain a proximity to Miss Nancy, with whom he'd had an off-and-on relationship since he met her as a seventeen-year-old freshman. She had a few more years to go, and unfortunately his absence had not made the heart grow fonder.

George completed his course work for an MA degree, Nancy graduated, they married, and he got a summer job at Wupatki National Monument in northern Arizona. It was much different than Mesa Verde, but he loved that too. George feared that Nancy was developing misgivings about the lifestyle: she was deposited in a well-worn 28-foot house trailer surplused from the Bureau of Indian Affairs, fifteen miles from a real road but with an excellent view of the Painted Desert. All the while he was wandering around the park doing rangerly things, leaving her at home to bake in the trailer in the wilderness.

To keep his parents and in-laws from thinking that he was too profligate, George applied for a permanent job with the NPS, although his secret intent was to go to Mexico for a while as an itinerant archaeologist.

At that time the Park Service was one of the more difficult federal agencies to join, exceeded only by the Federal Bureau of Investigation and the State Department. There were only thirty-two archaeologists in the entire U.S. government then, all in the NPS, with a couple on loan to other agencies. When George applied, he specified that he wanted a job a grade above entrance level (because he believed that his graduate work qualified him) and good housing, remembering the 28-foot trailer. That was unheard of audacity. But there happened to be five vacant positions in the Southwest because of transfers to a large road project at Ocmulgee National Monument in Georgia, so it turned out that he was the only qualified person on the Civil Service list. George received an offer from Montezuma Castle National Monument in central Arizona. He had never been there, and it sounded interesting. The offer also included housing in a nice apartment and the requisite higher grade level, so he accepted, figuring he would try that for a few years then go to Mexico.

After eighteen months George was promoted and transferred to Ocmulgee National Monument in Macon, Georgia, as park archaeologist. Never having been east of the Mississippi, he thought he would give that a try to broaden his experience then return to the Southwest and his career plan. Suddenly, though, he had to learn a lot of southeastern prehistory and history, which was a new challenge. Macon was a much different place than any he had known, but eventually he grew to like it. Today, in retrospect, he sometimes wonders why. Maybe it was that cultural relativity thing. He arrived there in April 1964, just as the civil rights movement was coming into full bloom, which made for an interesting time, particularly driving around town in a vehicle prominently marked as U.S. government property, wearing a government uniform, and speaking with a nonsouthern accent. George sometimes felt like he was the only California Yankee in town, and he probably was. He weathered it well enough, though, and ultimately was sorry to leave.

Following Ocmulgee, instead of going west, however, George was offered a staff position with the NPS Division of Archeology in Washington. He thought that this job would provide him an opportunity to gain some insight into how the government worked, which he took advantage of. It was an interesting situation, since he worked and acted under the authority of the Office of Chief Archeologist of the National Park Service, which was kind of a heady thing. For most of his time there he had an office overlooking Pennsylvania Avenue, from which he could see the White House, three blocks down the street, the riots following Martin Luther King's assassination, protests against the war in Vietnam, the bomb threats following Watergate, and a lot of other nifty stuff. It was supposed to be a short-term thing but evolved into much more.

One day the chief of the Office of Archeology and Historic Preservation, Dr. Ernest Connolly, the assistant-director level boss, walked in and asked Dr. John Corbett, the chief archaeologist, what the National Park Service was doing in underwater archaeology. Dr. Corbett answered that they were not doing a thing but had for some years been keeping up with developments in the field and might be considering applications in the NPS. About a day later Connolly came in again and asked why they were not doing anything.

George overheard this and began to nurture some ideas. He had always been very oriented toward things aquatic, a legacy from his mother (an ex-lifeguard and avid swimmer), who kept him wet as often as possible. He had considered diving in his youth and tried (unsuccessfully) to make a couple of different ad-hoc diving apparatuses. He had even given some thought to doing some archaeology underwater when working on a Native American site with bedrock mortars submerged in the Mokelumne River in California while doing fieldwork for his MA thesis, but time and resources had not allowed. This new development, however, piqued his interest.

George started going around the office mentioning underwater archaeology and related things as often as he could. He took Dr. Corbett out for one of his favorite lunches, multiple martinis, and steered the conversation in that direction. Shortly thereafter Corbett called George in to tell him that he'd had this great idea to do a study of both the needs and potential for underwater archaeology in the Park Service and he wanted George to do it. The seeds had fallen on fertile ground.

George soon was enrolled in a SCUBA certification course and was researching the field as thoroughly as he could. This was not particularly difficult, because at that time it was so new that there was very limited activity, and even fewer publications. He established a relationship with Mendel L. Peterson, curator of maritime history at the Smithsonian Institution Museum of History and Technology, a real pioneer in the field, and Peterson took him under his wing to help get things rolling. George was soon on one of Peterson's projects on the 1733 Spanish plate fleet galleon *San José de las Animas* in the Florida Keys.

The result of these activities was the publication of a *Prospectus for Underwater Archaeology* in the National Park Service (Fischer and Riggs 1968a). The director read it and liked it and said to implement it, so Fischer suddenly became the underwater archaeologist for the National Park Service.

In 1968 the NPS was steward over many national seashores, monuments, and parks that had extensive submerged cultural resources. At that time most diving worldwide was being conducted in fairly shallow and clear blue waters. The cold, turbid waters off Cape Hatteras, Cape Lookout, and Gulf Islands National Seashores, Fort Moultrie, Fort Sumter, and Fort Pulaski National Monuments, and many other park areas had protected hundreds of wrecks from the colonial era, American Revolution, Civil War, and world wars.

But in 1968 the National Park Service added Biscayne National Monument to its stewardship (figure 3.1). This huge new parcel would consist of about 4,000 acres of fast lands and some 175,000 acres (95 percent) submerged lands, located just south of Miami. Its clear waters contained the northernmost coral reefs in the Atlantic Ocean and the remains of many shipwrecks, including the two northernmost wrecks from the Spanish 1733 plate fleet—*Nuestra Señora del Pópulo* and *El Consulado* (figure 3.2). The monument/park was authorized by Congress to include southern Biscayne Bay, the extreme northern portion of Card Sound, and the waters east of

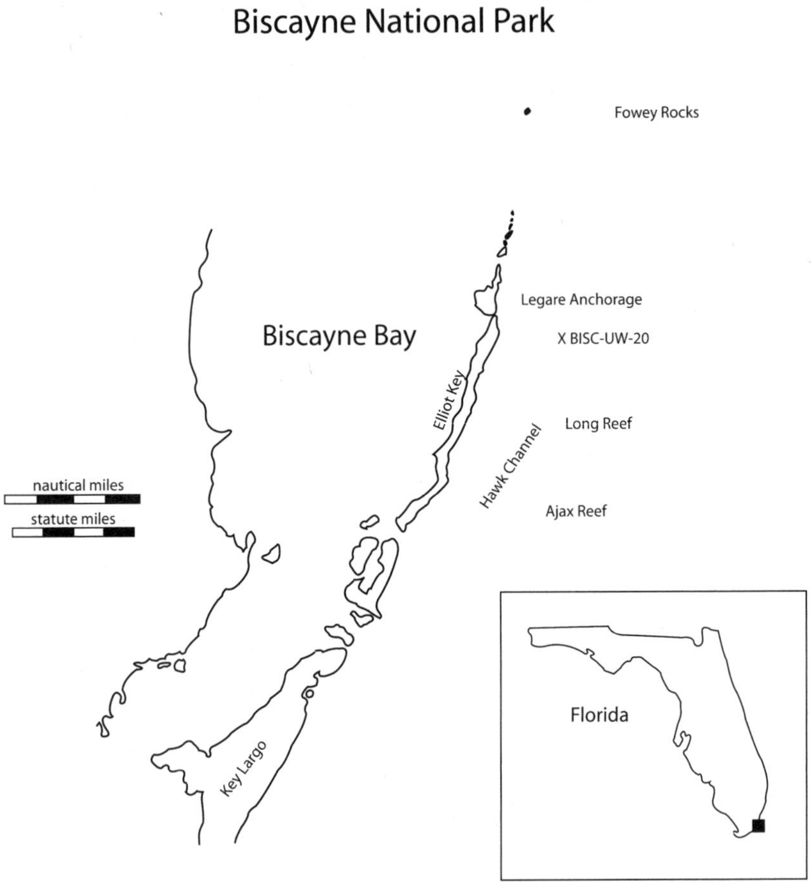

Biscayne National Park

Figure 3.1. Map of Biscayne National Park with the site of the Legare Anchorage indicated. (Courtesy of the National Park Service/Southeast Archeological Center.)

Elliot, Old Rhodes, Sands, Totten, Swan, and Adams Keys, including Hawk Channel and the coral reefs, seaward to a depth of ten fathoms or sixty feet.

The park was first inhabited by Amerindians of the Glades tradition who arrived in the area at least two thousand years ago. They subsisted by fishing, hunting both land and marine mammals, alligators, snakes, and other creatures, collecting plant foods, and gathering shellfish.

Juan Ponce de León traveled along the coast of this area in 1513. Later in the sixteenth century a Spanish mission was established near the mouth of the Miami River, but it was abandoned shortly thereafter. The historical

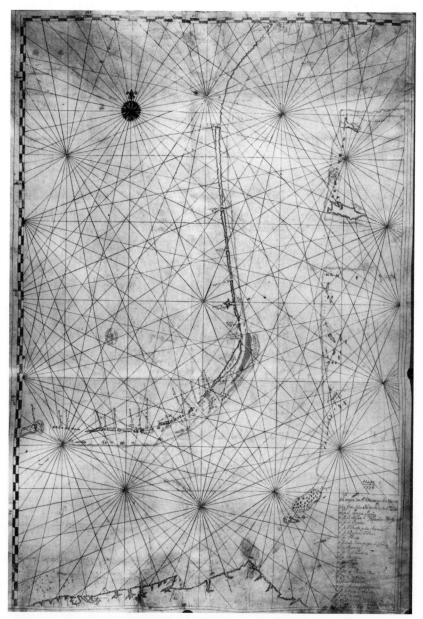

Figure 3.2. 1733 salvage map of the Upper Florida Keys, indicating the approximate locations of the wrecks of the *flota*. The two most northerly sites (numbers 1 and 2) are respectively *Nuestra Señora del Pópulo* and *El Consulado*. (Courtesy of the British Library.)

record is largely mute regarding south Florida over the next two hundred years. Disease, slave raids, and the movement of displaced Muskogean-speaking peoples into the area from Georgia finally eradicated the local Tequesta culture. The few Europeans who did venture into what would become Biscayne National Park were not permanent residents. Some came to log, others to capture turtles, and still others to salvage shipwrecks. Salvaging shipwrecks along the Florida Keys was a big business from the seventeenth century on, well into the beginning of the twentieth century.

Other illicit activities are reported in this area. Black Caesar, an African American pirate, is said to have operated out of Elliot Key. During the Prohibition era the keys in the monument were used as staging areas by rum-runners from the Bahamas and Cuba (and are still used that way in support of illicit narcotics trafficking). At the same time, in the 1920s the Coco Lobo Club on Adams Key was developed by presidential friend Bebe Rebozo as a retreat for the well-heeled. Among the visitors to the club were Presidents Warren G. Harding, Dwight Eisenhower, Lyndon Johnson, and Richard Nixon, who became Bebe's "buddy" and a frequent visitor while in office.

As a property under the stewardship of the National Park Service, Biscayne National Monument's cultural and natural resources had to be inventoried and evaluated in order to make wise management decisions. Park personnel might begin to collect basic resource information, but it generally falls to the Park Service's specialists to compile more exhaustive and authoritative data to compile a comprehensive management plan. For Biscayne, that specialist in cultural resources was George Fischer.

In 1970 Fischer was part of an advanced planning team sent to the area before it had yet been transferred from the State of Florida to the National Park Service. At that time he began compiling information on known and potential shipwreck sites in the park. Among these data were recurring rumors of the existence of a probable eighteenth-century vessel in an area called Legare Anchorage. George Sites, at that time employed by the state but later the first ranger at Biscayne National Monument, sent Fischer a base map that he had compiled, which contained a dot in the center of Legare Anchorage. In 1975 Fischer wrote an archaeological assessment and compiled a preliminary archaeological base map of Biscayne, which included a dot in Legare Anchorage, among forty-six other sites, representing an unidentified shipwreck site allegedly dating to the eighteenth century (Lenihan 2002: 101). This assessment and the Historic Resource Study by

T. Stell Newman (1975) were the first government efforts at identifying Biscayne's historic resources.

As a result of the assessment, the Southeast Archeological Center was provided funding for "ground-truthing" or locating and describing some of the tentatively identified sites. In July 1975 Fischer returned to Biscayne with Martin Meylach to accomplish just that. Marty Meylach was a hirsute, well-built man, whose shaved head was decades ahead of its time. An avid diver and contracting consultant, he was the author of *Diving to a Flash of Gold* (Meylach 1971). He brought his magnetometer to help with the month-long search. A magnetometer is an instrument for measuring variations in the magnetic field of the earth. It involves a sensor towed behind a motorized vessel. In the limestone environment of south Florida fluctuations in the magnetic field are generally caused by the presence of vast concentrated quantities of iron. Shipwrecks may have iron fittings, guns, and ballast. Even the smallest wooden ships used in trans-Atlantic transport in the colonial period probably carried a minimum of a ton of iron in the form of nails, spikes, through-hull fittings, and other structural elements and equipment. After they are located, magnetic anomalies can then be checked or "ground-truthed" by divers. As a form of remote sensing the use of a magnetometer is cost efficient but requires careful navigation to ensure adequate coverage. In the shallow waters (twenty-eight to thirty feet deep) of Legare Anchorage this meant that the boat towing the magnetometer would have to follow a tight grid, with "runs" separated by roughly thirty meters. Any larger spacing would miss the target.

During the thirty days of the project Fischer and Meylach made two passes through the two-square-mile area named for the USS *Legare,* the U.S. Navy ship aboard which the first modern chart of the area was made in 1855. More than forty sites had been identified in the park. In Legare Anchorage the sporadic and limited magnetometer work failed to identify any presence of a "target." But it was a big area, and the wreck rumored to lie therein waited for a more systematic approach.

It was a quiet Friday afternoon in the Bellamy Building. The hubbub of life on a college campus was lessened because of the approaching weekend, and most of the graduate students, and more than a few of the faculty, were over at the Pastime Tavern enjoying the beverages of their choice. At the Southeast Archeological Center everyone was looking forward to the weekend and enjoying the absence of the chief, Richard "Pete" Faust. In his absence George Fischer was acting chief. George recalls:

The center chief was off somewhere, and I had been appointed acting chief in his stead. That mostly meant I got to sort the mail and route it to wherever it should have gone, and, if it was the second Thursday, sign the time sheets for our couple of dozen employees. Otherwise it was just a titular sort of responsibility, one that mostly involved reading, writing, and signing things, and talking on the telephone. I anticipated it would be a quiet and peaceful time when I had nothing special going on and could catch up on some backlog work.

In his paneled office in Bellamy, down the hill from Montgomery Gym, George sat in his large brown leather chair (figure 3.3). On his desk was a large ashtray filled to the rim and patted flat with fine gray ash and a sign that read: "Feel Free to Smoke." His walls were lined with filing cabinets and bookshelves and his desk and credenza, as usual, were littered with papers. It was October 26, 1979. Classes had been in session for a month. George was taking advantage of the quiet to put his notes together for Monday's lecture. Since the center had moved to Florida State he had made some valuable connections and contributions to both the university and the Park Service. His university class "Introduction to Underwater Archaeology" usually attracted two dozen or more students. He also worked with the FSU Marine Lab and Academic Diving Program, co-instructing classes on scientific diving techniques, and sat on many MA committees in the Department of Anthropology. As any of the graduate students will attest, these were exciting times at Florida State. Although they were students, no one was playing at archaeology. Anyone who would think otherwise did not appreciate the deadly serious and cold-blooded earnestness of the archaeology program at Florida State in those days, first under Hale Smith and later under Kathleen Deagan. A number of these students went on to do important underwater and terrestrial archaeological research.

One of these was Daniel Lenihan, now retired head of the National Park Service's Submerged Cultural Resources Unit, commonly referred to as SCRU (and today as the Submerged Resources Center), in Santa Fe. Dan had entered the Florida State University anthropology graduate program a few years earlier, after graduating from Guilford College with a degree in philosophy. George had hired him as a GS-4 "archaeology technician," and he had participated in a project at Gulf Islands National Seashore in west Florida prior to his graduation in December 1973.

Figure 3.3. George Fischer in his SEAC office in the Bellamy Building in his traditional posture. (Courtesy of George Fischer.)

Another was Chris Hamilton. After graduating from Florida State and earning a Ph.D. in anthropology at Penn State University, Chris was in charge of the excavation of the pirate ship *Whydah* off Cape Cod. Today he is an archaeologist with the U.S. Army at Fort Benning. Martha Zierdan of the Charleston Museum, Richard Vernon and Kenneth Wild of the National Park Service, and David Brewer, senior territorial archaeologist for the U.S. Virgin Islands, all took George's class.

The crop of graduate students in 1979 was a promising and interesting lot. There were three "Yankees" in the group, who all had archaeological experience. Rich Johnson had been exposed to underwater shipwreck investigation by Professor Dave Switzer of Plymouth State on the wreck of the American Revolutionary War vessel *Defence* in Penobscot, Maine. He learned about underwater survey working with Warren Reiss in his search for the *Angel Gabriel*. Rich was a returning student, enrolled in the interdisciplinary graduate program in anthropology, history, and geography. Charlie Ewen, now a professor at East Carolina University, knew archaeology. In addition to that he could dive and was as sharp as a tack. Russ Skowronek already had six years of archaeological field experience and had gained extensive experience with the law of the sea as a student at the University of Illinois. There was potential in this group.

Just after noon the silence was broken when George's intercom buzzed. He figured that the secretary, Wilma Clark, was calling to tell him she was leaving for the day. Instead she told the "acting chief" that she was going to transfer a call from Curtiss Peterson, then the Conservation Laboratory director for the Florida Division of Archives, History, and Records Management (the forerunner of the Bureau of Archaeological Research). Curtiss was breathless and obviously excited. He and Wilburn "Sonny" Cockrell, state underwater archaeologist, had just come from a meeting in Judge's Chambers in U.S. District Court, Southern District of Florida, in Miami. David Paul Horan, a prominent attorney for treasure salvage interests, had been informing the court (and them) of a series of alleged shipwrecks on which he and his clients were filing suit for salvage rights. "Arresting the wreck" was the somewhat bizarre legal terminology. Horan said of one such wreck: "This will be of interest to the National Park Service." The alleged location was within what was then Biscayne National Monument, shortly to be elevated in status to Biscayne National Park. The long-anticipated event of the NPS becoming involved in a treasure shipwreck case was suddenly upon us.

George immediately called the NPS assistant director at the Regional Office in Atlanta and notified him of the new development. He passed it on to the Southeast Regional Directorate and Interior Department Solicitor's Office in Atlanta, so they could initiate appropriate action, and the word then was spread to the park itself and elsewhere as appropriate.

This development had long been anticipated, but George was far from eager to see it arrive. As treasure salvage of historic shipwrecks had developed and increased in the mid-twentieth century, the cases had almost exclusively involved state jurisdictions. He knew that inevitably the time would come when attempts would be made to extend the cases to federal jurisdiction and beyond that, specifically to the reserve lands administered by the National Park Service. He happened to be there when it happened. And thus began a great adventure.

4

Reflections on the First Salvo

Legal Wrangling, 1979–1980

At the time there was considerable confusion, misunderstanding, and misinformation regarding the Legare Anchorage Shipwreck and the litigation relating to it. This pertained to perceptions of the situation among the public, within the profession, and within the NPS in general. Although not lawyers, we will reconstruct the story as best we can. The legal minutiae are preserved in the various court proceedings of *Klein* v. *Unidentified Wrecked and Abandoned Vessel, Her Tackle Apparel and Armament* (Case No. 79-4627-Civ-CA). The following details are from the records of the National Park Service and the memory of George Fischer.

Fischer initiated the National Park Service's program in underwater archaeology in 1968, while an assistant to the chief archaeologist in Washington, D.C. One of the first things he needed to do was a thorough background study. He undertook a comprehensive analysis of the Park Service's potentials, responsibilities, and requirements in the field. This included an assessment of potentially pertinent legal issues. Dr. John M. Corbett, then chief archaeologist, had been considering the subject since the early 1950s. He had a sensitivity in particular to legal issues relating to archaeology and in fact used to say occasionally, not entirely in jest, that—if he had to do it over again—he probably would have pursued a degree in law rather than a doctorate in anthropology, as it would have served him better in his position. With that in mind, he had earlier encouraged Fischer that he should try to flesh out the information in a notebook that he had on that subject in order to make sense of the confusing mass of law, regulation, and policy relating to archaeological resources. That project got out of hand and became an end in itself. It eventually received limited publication in 1969 as *Legislative and Related Guidelines for Archeological Programs* (Fischer and Riggs 1968b) and proved to be very useful in applications to underwater archaeology, since there did not seem to be much help from the legal profession.

On several occasions Dr. Corbett had requested opinions and advice on jurisdiction over submerged cultural resources from NPS Counsel, the Department of Interior Solicitor's Office, and the Justice Department. Their responses to Corbett, and later to Fischer, were invariably nebulous. Because there were no legal precedents, the lawyers, in lawyerly fashion, were very reluctant to be pinned down with anything specific. Very little case law existed on the subject. Their opinions in general were that shipwrecks within national parks were probably the property of the federal government unless a legitimate claim could be made by a previous owner. Not entirely satisfied, Fischer asked NPS historians to look into the matter, and they researched the treaties and agreements under which various submerged lands had come under U.S. jurisdiction. Their scattered and somewhat nebulous nonlegal opinions were that in some cases questions could, and would, be raised over jurisdiction and ownership. George would have to live uneasily with this ticking time bomb for a decade, before it would finally explode in the waters off Florida.

The facts are as follows. In October 1978 Gerald Joseph Klein was diving with his son south of Miami. While spear-fishing, he found a shipwreck in Legare Anchorage. In the following months Klein returned to the site at various times with some friends and began collecting artifacts.

A year later, on October 4, Gerald Klein filed a "Complaint in Admiralty" in the U.S. District Court for the Southern District of Florida, Miami Division, claiming "An Unidentified, Wrecked and Abandoned Sailing Vessel, Her Tackle, Apparel and Armament" (believed to have sunk in 1740) in Legare Anchorage. His complaint was entered into the docket of the court.

Almost three weeks later, on October 22, U.S. District Judge C. Clyde Atkins heard Klein's complaint and the attached request to be named substitute custodian of the wreck. Anyone involved in legal issues related to shipwrecks might have considered that the State of Florida, and perhaps even the federal government, might be an interested party in this case. As a result, Atkins stated that he would not issue a warrant appointing Klein the substitute custodian of "an ancient sailing vessel, sunk in 1715 [*sic*]" until Klein contacted both federal and state officials. Atkins assigned the Case Number 79-4627-Civ-CA and set a date for a follow-up hearing for October 26, 1979, at 9:30 a.m.

On Friday, October 26, Klein returned to the District Court, at which time Judge Atkins ordered Klein be named the "Substitute Custodian" of the wreck until the state and federal government responded. Pending their response, the court would decide later how any and all recovered finds would be divided. In the interim, this ruling gave Klein the right to continue salvaging the wreck. The ruling was reported the next day in the *Miami Herald* (Crankshaw and Voboril 1979) and on October 29 in the *South Dade News Leader* (Swalm 1979). The wreck was described in the *Herald* as an "almost intact Spanish treasure galleon."

That Friday, October 26, Curtiss Peterson, conservator for the Florida Bureau of Historic Sites and Properties (today the Bureau of Archaeological Research), called the Southeast Archeological Center in Tallahassee and spoke with Fischer about what had occurred in court. He informed him that the court had noted that both the state and federal governments might be interested in this case.

It should be understood at the outset that national park areas are not just "public lands" but federal reserve lands, each set aside by either an act of Congress or presidential proclamation for a specific purpose and administered under the National Park Service Establishment Act of 1916 (http://www.nps.gov/legacy/organic-act.htm). Briefly, the purposes articulated in the Organic Act (as cited earlier) are "to conserve the scenery and the natural and historic objects and the wildlife therein and to provide for the enjoyment of the same in such manner and by such means as will leave them unimpaired for the enjoyment of future generations." These are lofty and sometimes contradictory goals for preservation and use; but when conflicts exist, preservation should prevail, so that use of the resources may continue into the future. The Justice Department was very concerned about the implications of this action for the national park system in particular and federal lands in general and therefore put considerable effort into pursuing the case. As those familiar with the system know, in admiralty court, any potential salvor initiates legal action as plaintiff against the shipwreck site (the "defendant"), in effect suing the wreck itself. In this case, the federal government became involved in the litigation as "defendant intervenor." This particular lawsuit was no secret. It was plastered all over the *Miami Herald* and elsewhere, so it was not as if anyone was keeping it confidential.

Things moved ahead quickly after that hearing. On October 29, 1979, Gerald Klein turned over his salvaged collections to U.S. marshals and was told to catalogue and turn over all subsequent finds. Based on the news reports, that same day George Fischer reported in an internal Southeast Archeological Center memo his suspicions that the wreck could be either the *Consulado* or the *Pópulo*, both members of the 1733 *flota*. He also noted that William J. "Bill" Gladwin, Jr., would be the counsel representing the State of Florida. Bill was very interested in archaeological resources and had in fact been a classmate of Fischer's in a course on historical archaeology at FSU, so Fischer was very pleased and relieved about his assignment to this matter.

On November 1, after checking the location of the wreck site, the Southeast Archeological Center informed the Regional Solicitor's Office for the U.S. Department of the Interior in Atlanta of a "possible treasure salvage effort in Biscayne National Monument." That would be a violation of the Antiquities Act of 1906. Three weeks later, on November 21, Rebecca A. Donnellan, attorney for the U.S. Department of Justice, Land and Natural Resources Division, called Gerald Klein's counsel, David Paul Horan, and asked if Klein had conducted any salvage on the wreck and whether or not he had either "sought or obtained" permission from Biscayne National Park. Horan confirmed that salvage had occurred and that only the court had given permission to conduct salvage.

With that information, six days later Donnellan requested a temporary restraining order and a preliminary injunction. She also requested that all artifacts be turned over to the National Park Service. By that point the case had been moved to the court of District Judge Alcee L. Hastings. The next day, November 28, he permitted the United States to "intervene as defendant" for the wreck against Klein's claim. Citing the Antiquities Act of 1906 and the newly enacted Archaeological Resources Protection Act of 1979 and the fact that Klein did not have a permit for any activities within the Biscayne National Monument, Donnellan requested that a restraining order be issued against Gerald Klein. At 1:30 p.m. Hastings placed a temporary restraining order on Klein and all salvage activities.

Two weeks later the case was back in the court of Judge C. Clyde Atkins. There, on December 12, he met with Bill Gladwin, attorney for the State of Florida, and David Paul Horan, counsel for Gerald Klein. The parties agreed that a representative of the State of Florida would be present during all salvage and that proper conservation methods would be followed (No. 79-4227-Civ-ALH).

A week later, on December 19, David F. McIntosh, an attorney with Corlett, Merritt, Killian & Sikes, who also represented Gerald Klein, submitted a "Memorandum of Law" that stated: "The National Park Service is completely unable to preserve the wreck site from unauthorized salvors (pirates) who would not respect the Court's Order." The memorandum further argued for "the predominance of Admiralty and Maritime law over the regulations of the NPS." This, of course, was the presumptive essence of any long-feared test case of federal antiquity laws.

During the next ten days Klein's lawyers searched to try to find any local archaeologists who would support their research. Fortunately, none agreed to do so.

At the beginning of January Rebecca Donnellan argued for a preliminary injunction. One of the witnesses for Gerald Klein was the most famous of all treasure salvors, Mel Fisher. Nevertheless, Donnellan prevailed: the court granted her motion, naming the secretary of the interior as the substitute custodian. The court also ordered Klein to turn over all salvaged materials to the National Park Service and directed the government of the United States to locate and protect the wreck, which put the ball firmly in our court.

The last directive was slightly problematic, because the National Park Service did not know exactly where the wreck was. This twist was obviously not lost on the members of the press who witnessed the hearing. On January 12, 1980, the *Tallahassee Democrat* (hometown paper of the Southeast Archeological Center) gleefully printed an article titled "Federal Agency Is Proud Owner of Spanish Galleon It Can't Find."

While the senior staff of the Southeast Archeological Center was developing a research strategy for finding the wreck, the staff members of Biscayne National Park, acting independently and before the judge had issued his written opinion, began searching for the wreck themselves. This kind of unilateralism became typical of the case.

Luckily, before any damage could be done to the government's case, the park's staff members were told by the Regional Office to cease and desist from their efforts. As the result of the litigation to that point, SEAC was provided funding for a precise and exhaustive survey of the area, using a sophisticated microwave positioning system to locate the subject site. A two-week window for the project was established by the Park Service's Southeast regional director, on the basis of available funding (as well as apprehensions about Fischer camping down there for the whole summer). The project was also limited to one square mile, lest they try to survey the whole park.

On March 19 George Fischer went to Miami to receive the recovered artifact collections from Gerald Klein. These collections were awarded to the NPS, with no restrictions. Fischer and an attorney from the U.S. Department of Justice and a U.S. marshal were originally to meet Klein at Joan's Galley. When they arrived at the restaurant, they found it filled with Klein's friends, who were not happy about the court's ruling and were in the process of staging some sort of demonstration. The attorney told Fischer to stay outside and told Klein to bring the collection to the courthouse. Thus a potentially ugly confrontation was averted.

5

Finding the "4th of July Wreck," 1980

How can you protect a shipwreck if you don't know where it is? This was the problem faced by the staff of Biscayne National Monument in the spring of 1980. A few months earlier, in October 1979, Gerald Klein had filed the claim in admiralty court for title to a certain shipwreck in Legare Anchorage. Since that time the staff members had felt under siege. Their job was to protect the park's resources. To do that they felt that they had to enlist the support of the general public, because the park was large and the staff (and operating budget) was small.

As the New Year began the staff members were faced with fighting a losing public relations battle. It was the old image of "big government" beating up on the little guy: on January 6 the United States District Court issued a preliminary injunction and granted custody of the wreck to the United States. Two months later Gerald Klein complied with the preliminary injunction and surrendered his collection of artifacts to the National Park Service as a representative of the United States. In addition to the artifacts, the court required Klein to provide the National Park Service with his coordinates for the site. For Klein, this was anathema, akin to publishing a verified treasure map or opening the doors of a bank and telling people to help themselves. He would show them who knew what. Compliance with the law can come at many levels, and he was not going to make their jobs any easier after all the work he had done. As a result, Klein provided the absolute minimum amount of information and told the Park Service that the wreck was somewhere within 3,000 yards of a given point of latitude and longitude—an area of 9.2 square miles (figure 5.1). This is a traditional locational description in admiralty arrests. If the Park Service could find the site on its own, that was not his problem. In fact, if it could not find the wreck, that might strengthen his case for "rescuing" the site.

Almost everyone knows the problems associated with living on a fixed income. When emergencies arise, reserves are put to the test to meet these

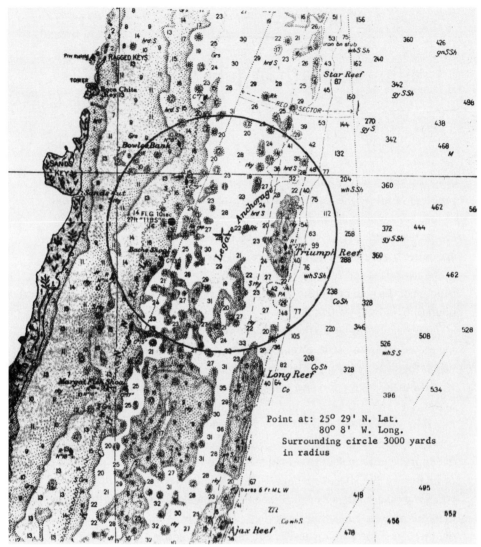

Point at: 25° 29' N. Lat.
80° 8' W. Long.
Surrounding circle 3000 yards
in radius

Figure 5.1. Navigational chart of the survey area based on information provided by Gerald Klein. (Courtesy of the National Park Service/Southeast Archeological Center.)

needs. Funding for the National Park Service since its earliest days has always been bare bones. Deferred maintenance is the operating rule. When an emergency threatens the park, its resources must be redirected to protect what it is meant to safeguard. The first attempt to find Gerald Klein's wreck would be done on the cheap. Rangers from Biscayne National Park were directed to find the site based on the broad generic coordinates provided by Klein. Repeated intensive searches by their divers failed to locate the site. After all, it is a big ocean, and Biscayne Bay is still a big bay. Even more precious resources were then redirected, and a small magnetometer and a positioning system were purchased. The search continued and again ended without results. It was no longer simply an issue of law enforcement. Identifying the wreck site would take the expertise of an archaeologist.

In the spring of 1980 the Southeast Archeological Center was asked to conduct a survey, utilizing equipment with greater sensitivity and accuracy than the equipment available to park staff. In charge of this survey was George Fischer, the archaeologist who had conducted the earlier survey of Biscayne National Monument with Marty Meylach back in 1975 and wrote the archeological assessment that precipitated that field research (Fischer 1975). This needle-in-a-haystack survey would not be an easy undertaking, as the repeated failures of the park's staff, who knew the waters well, had demonstrated. As anyone who has ever conducted research at sea will attest, Murphy's Law lurks at every step of the endeavor. This project would be made even more difficult, because it was conducted under unusual pressure for performance, not with the usual island-time leisure of standard academic research. The site had to be found. The reputations of both the field of archaeology and preservationists of the National Park Service hung in the balance. If the archaeologist could not find it, then perhaps the treasure hunter would have a case that he was "rescuing" a site that the NPS neither knew about nor seemed to care about before his admiralty case.

The little red hen syndrome was certainly more than alive and well in the Park Service in 1980. A lot of people suddenly had a lot of ideas on how to find the wreck. These included even a deputy regional director, who insisted that sextants be used horizontally to maintain position control, as he had done during a hydrographic survey in Katmai National Monument in Alaska in the 1930s.

The deputy regional director resourcefully obtained sextants from the Corps of Engineers (now readily available since they did not use them for positioning anymore, of course—as Fischer undiplomatically pointed out to him in an unguarded moment). Everyone in the Regional Directorate, the park superintendent, and those down the line seemed to have a theory that they thought was better than Fischer's, and a heated debate ensued. George stuck with a then state-of-the-art magnetometer survey with a highly accurate computer-interfaced microwave positioning system—accurate and also highly expensive. He finally won the argument and arranged for the loan of a Geometrics G-806 magnetometer from the Corps of Engineers office in Savannah, the instrument of choice at that time. From the Corps of Engineers office in Jacksonville he arranged to use a survey boat with precise positioning capability and contacted a private contractor with experience in operating these systems to serve as the survey technician. This would be the first electronically positioned shipwreck survey in the state of Florida and the first by the National Park Service. It is interesting to note that what was a highly sophisticated, complex, and expensive system in 1980 can now be obtained at a price that almost anyone can afford and carried in your pocket—science lurches on.

Just when it seemed that things were all falling into place, the Justice Department decided that the survey should be an all-NPS effort for security reasons, lest the specific location become known outside the circle of the government employees involved with the case. Fischer protested, asking: keeping it secret from whom? It seemed like the NPS was about the only entity involved that did *not* know where the Legare Anchorage Shipwreck was located. The SEAC chief told him that the situation was non-negotiable, and there it rested.

So Fischer had to go back to the drawing board. The NPS Submerged Cultural Resources Unit in Santa Fe, New Mexico, was the obvious alternative. SEAC initially had been told that the unit was otherwise committed at that time; but considering the exigency of the situation, it had to become uncommitted.

Any underwater archaeological project is a team effort, because of the complexity and specializations required. This particular project was a pioneering effort as far as the National Park Service was concerned and in some elements was unique in underwater archaeology at that time. Considering the mounting pressure for success, George knew that he had to field a crack team to find the site. It was down to that: find that ship, or maybe catch one of the recent Mariel Boat Lift vessels on its return and defect to Cuba.

The key players on Fischer's "dream team" were found equally in the ranks of the National Park Service and in the halls of Florida State University. Looking back on that and subsequent underwater projects, these individuals, who on the surface represented two distinct mental makeups, in fact had very common origins.

Larry Murphy, an archaeologist with the Submerged Cultural Resources Unit, was selected to serve in the project as the principal operator of the electronic equipment. He had previously worked as a technical field representative under Wilburn "Sonny" Cockrell, Florida State underwater archaeologist, as a salvage and exploration field agent, overseeing treasure salvage activities relating to the 1715 Spanish plate fleet shipwrecks. Larry had known George for several years and had some experience in precise electronic surveys. On April 21, 1980, Richard Faust, chief of the Southeast Archeological Center, made a request of the Southwest Regional Office to loan Larry's services to be a key member of the team, agreeing to pay his salary and expenses for the duration of the project and for a week in Texas before the project to learn how to use the system.

Dan Lenihan of the Southwest Regional Office, chief of the Submerged Cultural Resources Unit and Larry's boss, had been hired for the National Park Service by George Fischer in 1973. Dan volunteered to come at his own program's expense for the opportunity to participate and obtain experience in this type of survey system and to be a part of this landmark project. He proved to be an invaluable member of the group. Upon his retirement Dan wrote about this project among others in a retrospective book chronicling his career (Lenihan 2002).

Although the Submerged Cultural Resources Unit participants were of tremendous assistance throughout the survey, it was still funded and directed by the Southeast Archeological Center.

Gregg Stanton, research diving coordinator for Florida State University's Academic Diving Program, was a marine biologist and master diver. He and George had cooperated for several years, teaching scientific diving techniques at Florida State University and conducting many small research projects in National Park Service areas and elsewhere, directed and accomplished by students in training.

Gregg had worked off Looe Key, just south of the park, for years, studying reef life through the seasons. He had participated in the prestigious Scientists in the Sea program and had experience in underwater habitats, working under the ice in Antarctica and in other demanding programs in underwater scientific research. In his position at the Academic Diving Program at Florida State University, Gregg had taught hundreds of students and faculty in marine biology and underwater archaeology about safe, efficient, and effective research. He had learned about underwater archaeology just as Dan Lenihan did, mostly from working with George Fischer.

The last member of the team was a newcomer to the ranks, Richard Johnson. Rich was a decade younger than Fischer and had come to Florida

State University and the Park Service via a circuitous route. A native of New Jersey, Rich was raised south of Newark in Roselle Park. He graduated from Kent State University with a degree in fine arts and got a "safe" job with Lockheed Electronics in 1968. Six months later Uncle Sam's call overrode the "safe" job. A few months after that, "Sky Soldier" Sergeant Johnson of the 173rd Airborne was off to Vietnam, where he was eventually awarded a Bronze Star. Graduate school at Kent State got him an "early out" at the end of 1970. There he married Barbara Wisniewski of Cleveland, and the young couple began a quiet life, teaching at local middle schools. During the summer of 1975 they moved to Plymouth, New Hampshire. There Rich pursued a master's degree in counseling while he taught fifth and sixth grades at a local elementary school. One of the sixth-graders showed him a "lead marble" that his father had found. His father was David Switzer, who was excavating the American Revolutionary War ship *Defence* in Penobscot, Maine. Rich was invited to work with them during the summer of 1978. There he met Roger Smith, Warren Reiss, Sheli Smith, Charlie Mazel, and Peter Throckmorton—all luminaries in the field of underwater archaeology. Rich fell in love with archaeology. Roger Smith, his mentor, suggested that he follow his dream at either Florida State or Texas A&M. A major artist headed this program at Florida State, so Rich chose to go there. He and Barbara moved to Tallahassee in January 1979. There he matriculated at the same time in two graduate programs—one in art education and the other in the social science interdisciplinary program administered through the departments of anthropology, history, and geography.

That winter and spring Rich immersed himself in art and archaeology while taking classes through the Academic Diving Program with Gregg Stanton. He met George Fischer that spring and was in his class on underwater archaeology in the fall of 1979, when Gerald Klein filed his claim. Just as he had recognized Dan Lenihan's potential six years earlier, Fischer saw that Rich Johnson had what it takes to excel and hired him as an archaeology technician for the National Park Service in the spring of 1980.

Eleven days, from June 26 to July 6, were allocated to find the wreck. The length of this period was mainly dictated by budgetary constraints and not by the court order. Nine of those days would be dedicated to the actual survey. The survey was conducted from one of Biscayne National Park's 25-foot patrol boats operated by park staff. The park provided a great deal of assistance and support throughout the field survey phase of the project. To find and locate the wreck a Geometrics G-806 Marine proton magnetom-

Figure 5.2. The survey equipment used in 1980 in operation: George Fischer at the Geometrics G-806 Proton Precession Magnetometer, the Hewlett Packard Computer, and real time x-y plotter, with the Decca Autocarta Microwave Positioning System's Distance Measuring Unit beneath the table. (Courtesy of George Fischer.)

eter was interfaced through a computer with a Decca Autocarta microwave positioning system (figure 5.2).

The magnetometer is a sophisticated electronic instrument that operates on the principle of nuclear magnetic resonance to produce a measurement of the total intensity of the earth's magnetic field. Areas of significant difference within this field are normally caused by the presence of concentrations of ferrous material and are commonly referred to as anomalies. When anomalies are encountered, their size is indicative of the amount of ferrous material present and thus can be used for general identification of the size of submerged targets. Signal strength diminishes by the cube of the distance from the instrument to the anomaly. Years later, for instance, Robert Ballard used a magnetometer to identify the remains of RMS *Titanic* some two and a half miles below the surface. From the reports of survivors and rescue ships he knew the generalized area where the ship sank. He also knew the tonnage of the historic ship and the depth of the sea in that area. With that information he was able to limit his search area and to predict the size of an anomaly consistent with the size of the historic *Titanic*. When an anomaly was encountered, it was "ground-truthed," and the ship was found. A similar system was used at Biscayne.

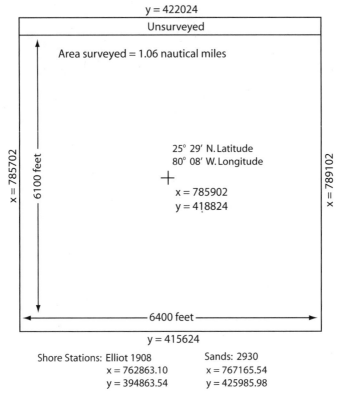

BISCAYNE NATIONAL PARK
Legare Anchorage Shipwreck Survey Grid

x-y coordinates
Florida East Zone Transverse Mercator Projection

y = 422024

Unsurveyed

Area surveyed = 1.06 nautical miles

x = 785702   6100 feet

25° 29′ N. Latitude
80° 08′ W. Longitude

+

x = 785902
y = 418824

x = 789102

6400 feet

y = 415624

Shore Stations: Elliot 1908   Sands: 2930
                x = 762863.10   x = 767165.54
                y = 394863.54   y = 425985.98

Figure 5.3. Area surveyed during the 1980 project to locate the site. (Courtesy of the National Park Service/Southeast Archeological Center.)

Gerald Klein had provided the court with general information regarding the location of the site. In adherence to their directive, the survey team projected a one-mile-square box around Klein's coordinates as their operating area (figure 5.3). Rather than using a 5,280-foot statute mile, however, which may have been what the regional director had in mind, the box was established with an international nautical mile of 6,076 feet. In order to maintain the proper lane spacing at the end of magnetometer runs, generous turn lanes were established outside the square so the boat could adequately reposition the towed "fish" of the magnetometer sensor, following about 100 feet behind the boat, after each run. This provided an actual survey area more comfortably about 1.5 square miles in size.

Unlike the case of the *Titanic,* there was no information regarding the size of this sunken vessel or the probable quantity of ferrous material. As a result, the spacing of the survey transects had to be a prime consideration in the design of the survey. If they were too far apart the wreck would be missed. Archaeologists elsewhere (Clausen and Arnold 1976) had determined that a colonial-period shipwreck could be detected using fifty-meter lane spacing if there were enough large amounts of ferrous material such as anchors and guns. The National Park Service knew that one gun was present on the site from Klein's deposition but knew nothing more. A lane spacing of thirty meters or about one hundred feet was chosen, in the event the wreck site had very little ferrous material.

The survey system was such that the crew had confidence that any historic shipwreck situated within the target area would be found. Nevertheless, there was no small amount of apprehension over the possibility of suffering a breakdown of the complex and delicate electronic systems or completing the assigned survey area in a technically perfect manner without locating the target.

Survey operations were carried out day and night, beginning on June 27. Participants recall the presence of large, aggressive barracudas and frequent and explosive bouts of seasickness. George Fischer, Larry Murphy, and Mark Schoneman of Decca Survey Systems handled the electronic equipment. A buoy was dropped when the magnetometer indicated the presence of ferrous material, and the survey team continued its search. Another boat carrying a team of "bounce" divers would search the area where the buoy was dropped. They were known as bounce divers because they would bounce in and out of the water, pursuing anomalies to verify them as historic or modern garbage or as "unknown." Dan Lenihan was in charge of these divers. Joining him were Jack Morehead (superintendent of Everglades National Park), Richard Curry (Biscayne's park oceanographer), and Rich Johnson. Rich recognized that he was a rookie, but he took in all the stories that Lenihan and Murphy told about underwater archaeology, Mel Fisher, and the treasure hunters.

On July 4, 1980, the eighth day of the ten-day project, the crew was looking at another long day of searching. Despite flagging morale, mounting disappointment, and fatigue, the team continued to work from dawn until dusk on the water and then late into the night on logistics and data analy-

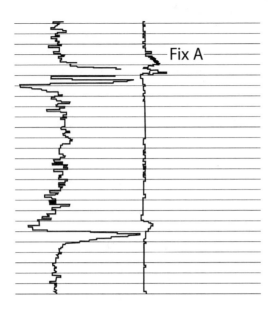

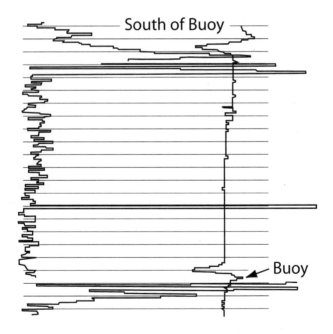

Figure 5.4. In the 1980s tapes captured the dramatic magnetic devia-
tions of 80 and 100 gammas read by the magnetometer. (Courtesy of
the National Park Service/Southeast Archeological Center.)

sis. That morning a large magnetic target was located, and divers were deployed (figure 5.4). As the search boat systems were working perfectly, it continued survey activities. Those operating the magic machines were all but overcome with curiosity over the cryptic snatches of radio conversation being intercepted from the dive boats. In early afternoon Dan Lenihan, unable to contain himself further and with no prearranged code on a project that had been clouded in secrecy, radioed: "I believe the eagle has landed."

That sounds a little melodramatic now, but at the time it did not seem so at all. Despite an uncooperative computer that was recalcitrant in its own esoteric language, batteries that would not hold charges, and a generator that ran on its own schedule and then nearly blew up a boat (and Larry Murphy) when being refueled while underway, a historic shipwreck of the first order of importance was found.

The next three days were a whirlwind of activity. The bounce divers had observed guns, shot, wooden ship elements, and other artifacts and features undoubtedly from a shipwreck. They also saw a lot of evidence that the site had been seriously disturbed. The presence of a makeshift grid system, shallow craters, and a modern lifting sling still attached to one of the guns made it apparent that the site was probably partially salvaged and most likely to be the site in question (Lenihan 2002: 100).

Following the initial reconnaissance by the team, a systematic investigation was begun, which included a thorough diver investigation of the entire site and surrounding area with documentation of observations through photography, sketch maps, and other notes.

A thirty-minute videotape was made by Lenihan on the last day of this investigation, not only to document the appearance of the site but for the purpose of providing nondivers (lawyers, NPS managers, and others) with a perspective on the nature and current status of the site. This record of the environment of the site also would be useful to managers for documenting areas of sand and grass, sea life, and exposed areas of the wreck. Dan narrated the tape while he made it, which required the use of a specialized diving mask known as a Kirby-Morgan that would allow him to speak while diving. Although Dan sounded like Darth Vader, the video did a credible job of documenting the site's condition (figure 5.5).

This video later proved to be invaluable in demonstrating the exact nature of the site to NPS managers and others. One of the questions often asked was whether we were going to "bring the ship up." Despite being provided with explanations, many still expected to see a mythical ship that

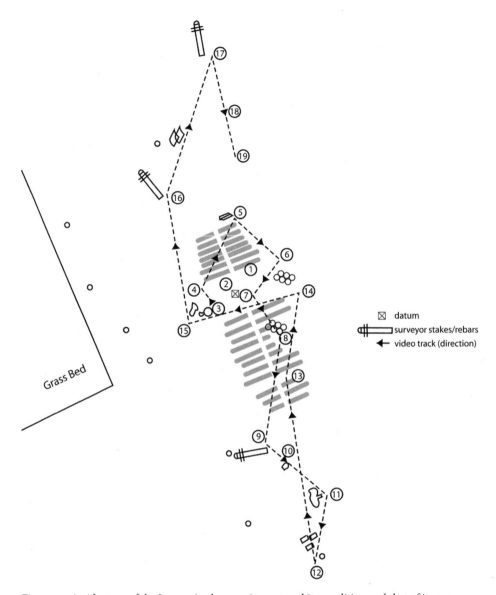

Figure 5.5. A videotape of the Legare Anchorage site captured its condition and that of its surrounding environs. It played an important role in the court case that followed. This map shows the route followed by archaeologist Dan Lenihan in 1980, with nineteen features indicated: *1*, bottle base; *2*, datum; *3*, strap for deadeye; *4*, rigging hook; *5*, pig iron ballast; *6*, cannonball aggregate/rebar; *7*, hull timbers; *8*, brick and ballast aggregate; *9*, cannon #1; *10*, lead scupper; *11*, cannon trunnion (?); *12*, survey stake/cannonballs; *13*, keel; *14*, main concretion/pry bar; *15*, lead sheeting/scupper; *16*, cannon #2; *17*, cannon with sling; *18*, mast hoop; *19*, ceramic. (Courtesy of the National Park Service/Southeast Archeological Center.)

resembled the fish tank ornaments. Instead it was possible to demonstrate through the video a very fundamental fact regarding historic shipwrecks. They are usually like an airplane that crashed and burned. The remains represent perhaps only 10 or 20 percent of the original fabric, and that is badly damaged by chemical and biological activity and scattered or obscured by sea action.

Controlled stereo photographs were also made on July 6 to provide a detailed map and systematically record the appearance and feature of the site. The 250 photographs were taken in a grueling eight-hour session on July 6 by Gregg Stanton and Les Parker, both of the Florida State University Academic Diving Program. Gregg and Les stopped by for a visit while working on their own project but abandoned other plans and joined the team when their timing coincided with discovery of the site. Obtaining the photographs required laying eleven transects, made of yellow polypropylene line marked at one-meter intervals, across the site. Each photograph was taken from the height of three meters above the seabed. Exact height and positioning was made possible by using a small weight, attached to the camera with a transparent monofilament line. As Gregg "flew" over the site, he touched each mark on the transect lines with the weight and then snapped a photograph. His support boat crew had several Nikonos underwater cameras. When Gregg gave them a camera that had exhausted its film, they would reload it and hand back a camera that was loaded. A photo-mosaic was made from these photographs later by painstakingly tearing their edges and taping them together to form one large master photograph, which was then itself photographed and reproduced to make full-sized prints and quarter-sized copies for publications. This not only provided archaeologists with a lot of data on the site but demonstrated to nonarchaeologists what the shipwreck really looked like (figure 5.6). A detailed hand-drawn map was later made from the photos (figure 5.7).

Finally, a limited controlled surface collection of twenty-one diagnostic items was recovered from the wreck. The precise provenience of the objects was recorded in order to recover any potential information relating to context or their in-site positioning. Artifacts included fragments of ceramics and glass, bricks, ballast stones, a cannonball, and fragments of a pewter spoon, a brass candlestick holder, and a brass buckle.

With this information in hand George Fischer and Rich Johnson returned to Tallahassee. They had found the wreck, but their job was just beginning. Now they had to attempt a positive identification of the wreck.

Figure 5.6. Photo-mosaic of the Legare Anchorage site made by Gregg Stanton and Les Parker. This demonstrated to nonarchaeologists what a historic shipwreck really looked like. (Courtesy of the National Park Service/Southeast Archeological Center.)

By January 1981 they had completed a draft report (Fischer and Johnson 1981). It was never finalized. Due to the pace of the litigation at the time and subsequent studies that superseded the original conclusions, this initial report has remained a draft to this day. Considering the high profile of the project, the report was very broadly reviewed; as was the case in so much of what we did, a dozen or more opinions were obtained from the NPS staff as to what should be included, excluded, or changed, many of which were mutually incompatible. A more important factor, however, was that management wanted the archaeologists to provide a solution to a major problem that was complicating their lives. Ultimately, there was no quick fix, and for each question we were able to answer we posed several more.

Twenty-two years later Dan Lenihan (2002: 100–102) recalled his 1980 dive on this site with amazing clarity. It may be true that hindsight is 20-20, because that first summer's findings were anything but certain. Some of the artifacts had been misidentified as Spanish-made in the field, and certain other tell-tale features had been overlooked or dismissed. Sometimes you just have to lay out what you have and then return for further clarification—this is how science progresses. And it was no different with the Legare Anchorage site.

According to Gerald Klein, there were four visible guns at the site. During the hectic days at the end of the project in July 1980, only three guns had been located. Their surfaces were obscured with coralline concretions, disguising any potential identifying marks. The SEAC survey team also

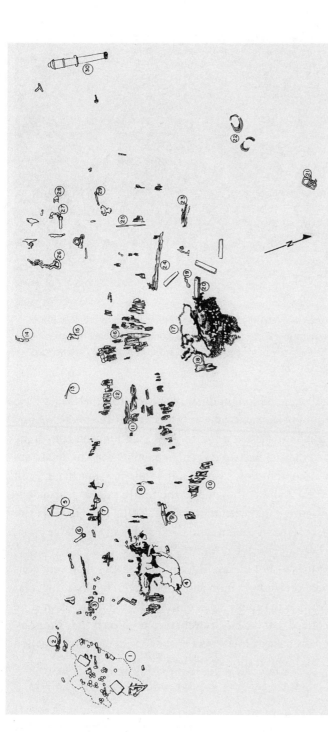

Figure 5.7. A plan map was created from the 1980 photo-mosaic. It was the basis of the grid that was established in 1983. A number of artifacts were identifiable, including: 1. Brick, tile, shot, rigging artifacts; 2. Chain; 3. Brick scatter; 4. Large aggregate rising three–four feet above the sea floor composed of brick, ballast, shot, and timbers; 5. Cannon (partially buried); 6. Lead scupper; 7. Timbers; 8. Timbers; 9. Unidentified artifact; 10. Timbers; 11. Timbers; 12. Timbers with bottle base; 13. Unidentified artifact (possible rigging pin); 14. Unidentified artifact; 15. Unidentified artifact; 16. Timbers; 17. Main aggregate of wreck (bricks, cannonballs, cannon); 18. Rebar or surveyor's rod; 19. Eyebolt (rigging); 20. English pig iron ballast; 21. Unidentified artifact; 22. Coils of lead sheeting; 23. Timbers; 24. Possible keelson; 25. Rebar or surveyor's rod; 26. Straps for deadeyes; 27. Lead scupper; 28. Large spike (protruding two feet above the sea floor); 29. Unidentified artifacts; 30. Cannon; 31. Rigging strap or fitting; 32. Cannon with sling. (Courtesy of the National Park Service/Southeast Archeological Center.)

Figure 5.8. A large concretion later determined to be composed of iron ballast blocks and cannonballs towered some six feet above the sea floor. It was home to a green moray eel who watched over us and the site. (Courtesy of the National Park Service/ Southeast Archeological Center.)

had noted several concreted longitudinal blocks of iron that could have represented a form of permanent ballast. Inspection of the photo-mosaic and other photographs suggested a fourth gun. Rich Johnson and Gregg Stanton returned to the site for two days in September 1980 to obtain accurate measurements of the guns, search for the "missing" fourth gun, and further investigate the ballast. They found the fourth gun and made another important discovery in the heart of the site. Rising more than six feet above the sea bed, covered in sea fans and coral and home to a large green moray eel, was a heap of concreted iron (figure 5.8). Dan Lenihan (2002: 99) had identified it as a shot locker. The rounded shapes that were concreted together were certainly cannon shot, but they were obscuring a far more important feature: an orderly stack of iron ballast blocks. Upon close inspection Rich noticed that the blocks were pierced at each end. The guns' measurements and the ballast blocks were encoded with much information that could lead to the identification of the wreck.

6

Narrowing the Possibilities, 1980–1983

To the uninformed the identification of a shipwreck might seem to be a simple task: you just dive onto the wreck and read the name off the name board or stern of the wreck. Of course, that might work with recently lost vessels, where there are still remains identifiable as a specific part of the structure of a vessel. In the twentieth century ships were increasingly constructed using iron and other metals, fiberglass, and plastics, with less and less wood. These more modern materials had certain qualities that made them attractive to their owners, including strength and durability and lower production costs. With the Industrial Revolution came mass production, however, and shipbuilding was no longer in the hands of master shipwrights, who crafted each vessel according to the materials on hand and the general specifications of the owner. Instead the parts were made to exact specifications and then were pieced together in assembly-line fashion, according to exact plans. Thus ships of the older individualized and various style, and the resulting wrecks, from before the heyday of the Industrial Revolution pose greater challenges in identification, for many reasons.

The coast of southwest Florida has been the scene of extensive maritime activity from the period of early Spanish exploration to the present. Inevitably, it has also been the scene of many shipwrecks. During the early portion of the historic period wrecks were common, due to extended voyages by unseaworthy vessels and an absence of accurate and reliable navigational information on the Straits of Florida. These problems lessened as time passed, and the number of ships sailing through the Straits increased considerably. In addition to the natural increase in shipping with the growth of commerce in the New World, by the end of the seventeenth century it had become evident that the Straits of Florida were superior to the Bahama Channel as a route for exiting the Gulf of Mexico, propelled by the Gulf Stream, and then catching the prevailing westerlies for the return route to Europe. The Straits of Florida became the favored return route. Greater use of this route, and thus increased traffic, offset the advances that made the trip safer and resulted in significant changes in the annual volume of shipwrecks from the beginnings of navigation past the peninsula to the present.

We cannot put an exact date on the beginning of the Industrial Revolution. Some might put it in the middle of the nineteenth century, with the expansion of steam power. Others might point a century earlier to Josiah Wedgwood's mass production of ceramics. Yet even that could only have come about through the development of canals and the movement of bulk quantities of raw materials, a process that dates to the beginning of the eighteenth century. When we consider shipbuilding from this era, we are looking at more of a craft than an industry.

Until the Industrial Revolution the most complex machine known to humans was the ship. Their construction required the marshaling of great numbers of resources and great numbers of artisans. First came the selection of sources of timber and its peculiar harvesting for just the right-shaped frames. Timbers would then have to be moved to shipyards, where they would be seasoned and, years later, shaped by shipwrights. The finished frames and planks were then put together. Below the waterline the fastener of choice was the treenail, a wooden pin or peg, with the hole for each of thousands individually drilled by hand. Once driven into place, it would swell on contact with water and tightly lock the parts together.

Above the waterline, treenails or other metal fasteners of iron or bronze could be used. But most metal fasteners had certain shortcomings. First, use of iron involved the problem of oxidation. Next came the cost. Metals had to be mined and the resulting ores refined and sometimes combined with other metals. This, of course, required fuel for smelting and other aspects of fabrication. The fuel was initially wood that had to be cut and then burnt into charcoal. Coal was later used as a fuel, but it too had to be mined and transported. Once iron pigs and bar stock were formed, smiths could work them into fasteners. As the costs associated with the fabrication of metals fell, they began to play a greater role in ship construction. At the beginning of the eighteenth century cast iron even began to be used for ballast, and by mid-century sheet copper was being produced in sufficient quantities to be used for sheathing the bottoms of ships.

Ships also required the work of farmers and weavers. After being harvested hemp and flax were transformed into line and sails in rope houses, first by cottage weavers and later at factories. Others, such as foresters, collected pitch and turpentine from pine trees and fabricated preservatives for the wooden ships; thus they were termed "naval stores."

When the ship was launched, its complexity as a machine was evident: from its pulleys to its pumps, all the parts had to work together. The crew was also made up of specialists, who not only could operate the machine (that is, sail it) but could repair it as well, even while underway. To keep the machine operational required ongoing maintenance; and without it any ship was doomed. Obviously, maintenance ended when a ship sank, and the parts were transformed to a state of entropy. Organic materials were consumed by living organisms. Inorganic substances such as glass and ceramic were broken through mechanical actions, and metals were oxidized until they too either were lost or became encapsulated with coralline concretions that halted their breakdown. As a result, the remains of wooden sailing vessels are often sparse, disconnected, or simply gone, which can make their identification difficult.

Rich Johnson knew that the Legare Anchorage wreck represented the remains of a wooden sailing ship. The question was: which one? Over the last five hundred years hundreds of wooden sailing ships have been lost in Florida's waters. When each sank, it represented a time capsule of sorts. Encoded in the surviving material remains of the vessel was evidence that could point to its age, function, and cultural affiliation. Many vessels sank in the shallow waters that surround the peninsula. As a result the survival of crew members was not uncommon. Also, parts of the wrecks might protrude from the shallows for years. This meant that the approximate locations and names of some shipwrecks have been known for hundreds of years. Of course, many ships were lost due to the presence of navigational hazards such as reefs. Those reefs often claimed many vessels through the centuries. Some were even named for ships that crashed into them. In the Florida Keys a number of these navigational hazards were named for Royal Navy ships, including Looe Key; Ajax, Carysfort, and Triumph Reefs; and Fowey Rocks.

As Johnson reviewed the literature he found a number of candidates for the Legare Anchorage wreck site. Although he was a rookie at this kind of historic archaeological analysis, it appeared to him, based on the presence and absence of certain identifiable features, that the wreck dated to the first half of the eighteenth century. Throughout that period a number of Spanish and English ships were known to have been lost in the vicinity of what would become Biscayne National Park (Marx 1969: 47; Meylach 1971: 21).

For instance, on July 13, 1733, twenty-one Spanish ships cleared Havana, Cuba, and embarked on the final leg of their return journey to Spain. Filled with coins and silver and gold bullion, majolica (also called maiolica and mayólica) and porcelain ceramics, dyewoods, and silks, the *flota* was bringing these Asian and New World valuables home through the Straits of Florida. Two days later, while navigating the Straits, the fleet was caught by a hurricane. Most of the ships ran aground or later foundered after striking the offshore reefs. The loss of lives, ships, and their cargos was great and would deal a crippling blow to the Spanish Crown. Nonetheless, making their way home, the survivors informed Havana of the tragedy, and salvage teams were quickly dispatched to the scene. The wrecks were emptied of their treasures, curiously yielding, according to some, more treasure than had originally been registered on the manifest. The hulks were then burnt to the waterline to remove valuable metal fittings and guns. A chart was produced by the Spanish salvage team, which identified each of the wrecks (figure 3.2). This chart is now part of the holdings of the British Library in London. Many of the wreck sites were relocated more than two centuries later by modern salvage teams, who carried out illicit excavations, with considerable destruction of the historical information that the wreck sites had the potential to provide. These included the wrecks of the *El Rui* and the *Capitana*, found by Art McKee, and the *San José de las Animas*, found by Tom Gurr. Both ships sank south of Biscayne National Park.

Two smaller vessels of that fleet, the "pink" (sometimes spelled pinque) *Nuestra Señora del Pópulo* and the *aviso* or courier ship for fleet communications, *El Consulado*, were thought to have been lost within the park boundaries. The northernmost Spanish site (that of the *Pópulo*) on the Spanish chart is located east and slightly south of the first break or cut in the offshore islands, which would have been visible to the Spaniards. Although the map describes the island as Key Largo, it has been interpreted as their misconception of the extension of Key Largo into Elliot Key. The cut illustrated on the chart west and a little north of the purported wreck site of the *Pópulo* is thought by many in the local treasure salvage community to be Sands Cut. As this chart has proved to be otherwise accurate in locating wrecks of the 1733 *flota*, it suggests that the Legare Anchorage wreck was also the northernmost member of the 1733 fleet.

The *Pópulo* has been described as a small sloop-rigged warship or pink (Meylach 1971: 18). It is reported that the *Pópulo* was an English-built ship that had been sold to the Spanish. This was a common practice for the period, whether purchased or captured as prizes and later resold. Some ships of the 1715 fleet had also been purchased, and excavation revealed that as much as 20 percent of the recovered material culture was English in origin (Burgess and Clausen 1982: 80). As a naval support vessel the *Pópulo* would not have been carrying any cargo items other than victuals and water for the crew, although it was also reported to have been carrying a small cache of religious items. The Florida Master Site file maintained by the Bureau of Archaeological Resources lists a shipwreck in Legare Anchorage as 8Mo148 (also designated 8UW55) and describes the wreck as the *Pópulo*, as reported by Jack Haskins, a Florida treasure hunter.

El Consulado (the *aviso*) was another member of the 1733 fleet. It too was an armed, sloop-rigged scout vessel. Marty Meylach, the renown Miami area shipwreck hunter, claims to have salvaged the *Consulado* in what is now the southern portion of Biscayne National Park before its establishment as Biscayne National Monument in 1968 (Meylach, personal communication, 1975).

Besides these members of the 1733 Spanish fleet, there were two other British candidates. The first, for which there is very little evidence, was HMS *Wolf*. A sloop-of-war, it was lost somewhere along Florida's Atlantic coast in 1741 (Marx 1969). "Somewhere" is a very big place. Sloops were small, lightly armed fore-and-aft-rigged vessels. There seemed to be an awful lot of material lying in the heap on the bottom of Legare Anchorage for it to be a mere sloop. That left one other possibility, the *Fowey*, but at the time that also seemed to be a long shot.

Tradition had held that Fowey Rocks, a navigational hazard some five miles north of Legare Anchorage, was the final resting place of HMS *Fowey* (hence the name). Even if *Fowey* had merely hit Fowey Rocks and then drifted to its ocean grave, it was considered unlikely that it drifted southward, against the Gulf Stream. When experts at the National Maritime Museum in Greenwich outside of London were contacted, they said the traditional explanations of Fowey Rocks and the Legare Anchorage site were both incorrect. According to their research, HMS *Fowey* had sunk five miles to the south of Fowey Rocks.

In the fall of 1980 George Fischer called on his old friend Mendel Peterson (1918–2003) to help settle the issue. Peterson had retired in 1973 from the Smithsonian Institution. During his quarter-century in the National Museum of the United States, he had served in a number of capacities, including being curator of the Division of Historical Archaeology, curator and chair of the Department of Armed Forces History, curator of the Department of History, and director of underwater exploration. Mendel Peterson was one of those people who had forgotten more than most people ever learn. George had met "Pete" when he was stationed in Washington, D.C., at National Park Service headquarters in the Department of the Interior. Peterson had participated in numerous underwater projects with the salvage and research communities, including work with Art McKee and Tom Gurr on the 1733 fleet and on HMS *Looe*. He had written a number of books and articles on this work and was such an overflowing font of information that it began to flood and even drown the research focus at hand. As we came to see, Peterson knew too much.

Peterson was told about the iron ballast blocks. He accurately noted that he had found similar ones on the *Looe* and also pointed out that they were normally associated with British ships built in the first half of the eighteenth century. He went on to note that Spanish iron guns were not known to bear founder's marks on their trunnions. Other items from pewter spoons and plates to brass buckles, fragments of glass, and a number of navigational tools were examined. Many were noted as being similar to ones he had seen in collections from the *San José* and *Capitana* of the 1733 fleet or from Spanish wrecks such as the *Guadalupe* and *Tolosa*, both lost in 1724, or the *Matanzeros*, lost in 1741. When handed a concretion-covered copper gunpowder barrel hoop, Peterson said authoritatively: "There is a Broad Arrow under this." Moments later, following a light tapping with a small soft hammer, the stated Broad Arrow—a mark signifying ownership by the British Crown—appeared. Peterson felt that the evidence was clear. The ship was Spanish and part of the 1733 fleet. He noted that an eyewitness had reported that eleven of the ships were of English origin; thus the Broad Arrow and several others were of non-Spanish construction as well. The expert had spoken, and he felt that there was a "95 percent probability" that the Legare wreck was indeed the *Pópulo*. Therefore the prophecy was fulfilled: it was Spanish—or was it?

Rich Johnson was in a quandary over the probable identity of the site. It gnawed at him that everything that had thus far been found by Klein or by the Park Service was undoubtedly English in origin. Why would it have to be Spanish? In a memo written to SEAC chief Richard Faust and dated 12 December 1980, Johnson expressed his uneasiness about the Spanish identification. He also noted that Peterson had said there was a remote chance it was a British privateer. Johnson felt that the National Park Service needed "to explore the possibilities of the Legare wreck being British."

A few weeks later, at the beginning of January 1981, Rich was attending the Society for Historical Archaeology/Conference on Underwater Archaeology annual meeting in New Orleans. Discussions with archaeologists and associates from the salvage community hinted strongly that the vessel in question was British and was HMS *Fowey*.

When Rich later reported this to George Fischer, there was a moment of silence and growing paranoia. Klein had publicly stated that he had a Spanish galleon. Attorney David Horan and his client Mel Fisher had gained notoriety for their claims on and salvage of Spanish shipwrecks. Now the definitive talk on the street was that the wreck was a British warship. Why? Could it be a setup, intended to make the National Park Service look incompetent? It was time to have other experts examine the evidence and settle the issue.

Sometimes we see what we want to see even when there is evidence to the contrary. Self-fulfilling prophecies can haunt even the most objective researchers, and it was no different in Tallahassee. The Park Service "wanted" to find a Spanish ship from the 1733 treasure fleet. Could the Legare wreck be made to fit the profile?

During the winter and spring of 1981 Rich Johnson worked with Dennis Finch of the Southeast Archeological Center on the Klein collection and the other artifacts and information retrieved the previous summer and fall of 1980. Finch was convinced that it was Spanish (a position he would later recant), but others were consulted. Anyone that Rich could pull into his lab space in the Bellamy Building was asked to examine the collections. Dr. Kathleen Deagan, then a professor at Florida State, looked at the ceramics from the site. She noted that some of the French-made tin-glazed faience matched vessel forms found at St. Augustine and dating from 1730 to 1760, but none of the ceramics were positively identified as being either Spanish or Spanish-colonial in origin. Another visitor, Dr. Nicholas Honerkamp of the University of Tennessee–Chattanooga, looked at the rest of the material culture. Dr. Honerkamp had conducted extensive excavations at Fort Frederica on the Georgia coast. The English fortified-town site had been occupied during the second third of the eighteenth century. He noted that many of the glass and ceramic artifacts from the wreck had identical counterparts at Frederica.

Another piece of information appeared in a letter dated June 18, 1981 (H42-SER-OC; Q 6177), when N. A. M. Rodger, then assistant keeper in the Search Department of the Public Record Office (today the British National Archives), weighed in on the issue. The Southeast Regional Office of the National Park Service had contacted the British consul-general in Atlanta, who forwarded the letter to the British naval attaché in Washington and then to the Naval Historical Branch in England. Ultimately the query was passed on to Rodger, who would become the authority on the Georgian navy in later years with monumental works such as *The Wooden World* (1986) and *The Command of the Ocean* (2004). In regard to the possibility of the *Wolf* sloop he wrote:

> ... you may ignore [it]; it is clear from the court martial of her captain (ADM1/5274) that she was wrecked in the Caicos Islands. The *Fowey* remains a possibility, but I consider it an unlikely one. . . . Unless you have some strong reasons for thinking that you have found the *Fowey*, I conclude that your Spanish identification is far more likely.

Hmm, more contradictory information was coming to light.

Johnson was mystified as to how Peterson had arrived at his identification. Nothing had been identified as Spanish or Spanish-colonial in origin. The objective artifactual evidence did not fit those conclusions. He turned to one last person to look at the collection: Russ Skowronek.

Skowronek was one of the Yankees who had sat next to Rich in Fischer's class in the fall of 1979. A graduate of the University of Illinois, he had been working on archaeological projects since 1973. Skowronek had grown up reading *National Geographic* and watching Jacques Cousteau on television. His father, brother, and sister were all navy veterans, which meant he grew up in a world of Hornblower novels and *Victory at Sea*. The summer before, as he matriculated into the anthropology graduate program at Florida State, his sister, then an officer in the U.S. Navy, gave him a copy of Robert Marx's book *The Underwater Dig* (Marx 1975). She had written in it: "Perhaps this will open a new area for you." Little did she know!

Skowronek was one of Kathy Deagan's students and had been charged with analyzing information from the 1733 *flota* that was stored at the Florida Bureau of Archaeological Research in Tallahassee. The ceramics from the *San José* had earlier been analyzed by Patricia Logan (1977). Skowronek (1982, 1984b), however, considered all the recovered materials and written data in his study.

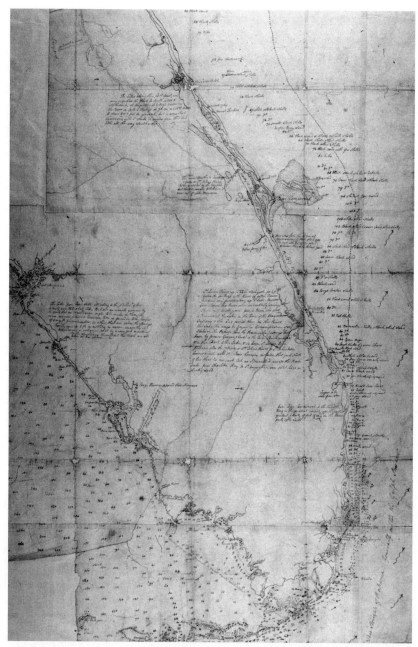

Figure 6.1. Dating from 1771–1774, this draft of the Bernard Romans Map of East Florida from St. Augustine to Tampa Bay was crucial in identifying the wreck site. (Clinton map 331; no. 645; Guide to manuscript maps in the Clements Library; courtesy of William L. Clements Library, University of Michigan.)

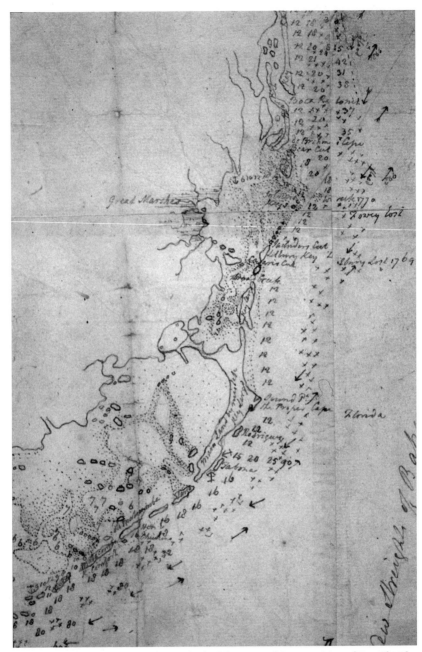

Figure 6.2. Detail from the 1771–1774 draft of the Bernard Romans Map of East Florida from St. Augustine to Tampa Bay. Note that "Fowey Lost" is near the Legare Anchorage site. (Clinton map 331; no. 645; Guide to manuscript maps in the Clements Library; courtesy of William L. Clements Library, University of Michigan.)

When Skowronek finally saw the Legare Anchorage collections, he asked one question: "Where are all the sherds of majolica and olive jars?" Every one of the seven ships he had studied had been littered with those ubiquitous ceramics. That fall Skowronek was going to be traveling to London. He had planned on visiting the British Library anyway, to obtain a copy of the chart showing the 1733 fleet wreck sites. Rich Johnson asked him to visit the Public Records Office as well, to see what he could find on HMS *Fowey*.

That October Skowronek arrived in Britain and found the logs, muster books, and court-martial proceedings for HMS *Fowey*. He returned to Tallahassee with copies of the documents and proposed a new candidate for the Legare Anchorage wreck. According to an eyewitness account the *Fowey* had grounded about five miles south of Legare Anchorage, probably near Ajax Reef. After twelve hours it floated free but was still sinking. Twelve more hours would elapse before the ship finally sank at an unrecorded location. Given the northward flow of the Gulf Stream, it appeared only logical that the point of sinking had to be somewhere north of Ajax Reef.

Then Rich made a fortuitous discovery with the help of librarian Marian Donnell in the maps department of the Strozier Library at Florida State University: a photostat of a draft of Bernard Romans' 1775 map of Florida. The original of this draft chart is housed at the Clements Library at the University of Michigan (figure 6.1). It was marked "Fowey Rocks," and just below that entry at a location some five miles to the south was "Fowey Lost" (figure 6.2). That all-important descriptive notation on the draft chart did not appear on the published version of the map.

It appeared more than likely now that *Fowey* was another candidate for the identity of the Legare Anchorage site after all.

Perhaps Rich Johnson was no longer such a rookie. He had studied the evidence and reached a conclusion that fit the historic and archeological record, based on the facts. Although it was contrary to the views of his mentor, George Fischer, and the expert Mendel Peterson, it was solidly reasoned. Fischer studied the evidence and concluded that facts had indeed trumped the emotional tug of finding a Spanish treasure ship. They might actually have a British man-of-war. Only further work could answer that question.

7

Testing and Evaluation of the Legare Anchorage Shipwreck

A warm subtropical breeze blew in off the shallow waters of south Biscayne Bay. It was a little after 7 a.m., and Biscayne National Park's dive locker, pier, and dive boats were swarming with the twenty-odd Park Service and Florida State University researchers sent to investigate the Legare Anchorage Shipwreck. As they wiped the sleep and the sweat from their eyes and drained the dregs of their coffee or sodas, each wondered what the day had in store. All had an individual reason to be there. Some were learning firsthand about underwater archaeology, others were polishing their diving skills, and still others were engaged in answering the questions posed by the court while trying to conduct serious scientific research. The group included the boat captain, various Park Service representatives from Biscayne and Everglades National Parks, a conservator, a dive master and safety officer, a small machine operator, the crew, and the archaeologists. It fell upon the archaeologists to orchestrate the team and still make it efficient and safe.

Several factors limited daily operations in late May and early June 1983. First, the project relied heavily on a variety of the park's boats to conduct the project. These boats were only available during the work week, not on weekends. That limitation was largely self-imposed, because Biscayne National Park was a popular destination for Miami's boating public. Every weekend the waters of the park would be filled with boaters, divers, and snorkelers. Both rangers and boats were needed to monitor, rescue, and enforce the laws among this teeming horde of recreational individuals, and it was feared that any attention focused on an archaeological project would bring in not only the curious but those intent on misdeeds as well. Work was also limited to daylight hours and generally calm days. To optimize working conditions, the project was scheduled for late May and early June

1983, before the serious hurricane season really began. The daylight constraint was also tied to the travel time associated with the location of the wreck site, some seventeen miles from Convoy Point. Seven miles from the headquarters the boats had to negotiate the shoals and shallows of Caesar Creek, past the historic dock of Rebozo's old Coco Lobo Club. It was a historic dock indeed: on December 31, 1972, "President Nixon fired [NPS director] George Hartzog for eliminating Bebe Rebozo's docking privileges at Biscayne NP" (Binkley 2007: 198). Then they passed through the south end of Elliot Key. From there it was another eight miles down Hawk Channel, then two more miles eastward to Legare Anchorage. On a good day the average one-way trip took an hour. Once the boat arrived, it was moored to a permanent anchor set in the bottom, rather than simply "dropping anchor," to avoid detrimentally affecting the fragile marine life and cultural resources from repeated anchorings.

Making that trip at extreme low tide or in poor light was not an option. Once the team was at the site, water conditions were usually very good, with twenty-five to fifty feet of visibility. If conditions were poor, the Legare Anchorage would be wave-tossed, and the water would be murky from sediment and often have running currents. Six-foot seas and ten-foot visibility were not optimally conducive to good science. Nonetheless, no one was ever put in harm's way. When it was over, 372 dives had been completed over 23 days. All told, nearly 500 hours of underwater research had been conducted without injury, accident, or incident. This can be attributed to the project's strict compliance with the regulations, policies, and procedures of the diving practices of both the National Park Service and the Florida State University's Academic Diving Program. All of the participants were certified SCUBA divers, who also met the additional qualifications and requirements of one or both of these agencies. Three females and eleven males, with varying degrees of archaeological and diving expertise, formed the core of the project's crew. As the project demonstrated, they truly epitomized the George Bass adage that it was easier to teach an archaeologist to dive than to teach a diver to be an archaeologist.

The routine never changed. Five days a week, the crew members awakened early in their rooms at the Sea Glades Motel in Homestead, had a hurried breakfast, took their Bonine to prevent motion sickness, lathered on a layer of sunscreen, grabbed a bag with personal items, and were off for the fifteen-minute drive to Biscayne National Park's Headquarters at Convoy Point.

The project equipment and artifacts were stored under lock and key at the park's dive locker. This was the era of both the Mariel Boat Lift and an influx of unhappy Haitians into metro Miami. It taught boat-owning Floridians to lock everything down, and the Park Service was no different. This facility had an air compressor for filling tanks and storage locker areas. Every diving day, 2,000 pounds of diving equipment were transferred from the dive locker to the dock via a waiting pickup truck. The truck was repeatedly driven to the pier, where the equipment was unloaded and passed down a human line and onto the NPS's 45-foot work boat (figure 7.1). The process would be repeated at the end of each day in reverse, when a bone-weary crew would then have to fill tanks, wash and repair equipment, catalogue finds, and plan the next day's work.

In addition to the 45-foot work boat, the project used a number of other vessels at different times as safety boats, as screening and excavation platforms, and for towing the magnetometer. They included 16-foot, 17-foot, and 25-foot boats. We had the tools: now we had to answer the questions.

Before the project left Tallahassee the Southeast Archeological Center had prepared a "Section 106 Statement" and a research design. The "106 Statement" is derived from Section 106 of the National Historic Preservation Act of 1966 (CFR 800, as amended), which stipulates that any federally funded undertaking on sites listed on or eligible for listing on the National Register needs to be both planned and peer-reviewed to ensure the feasibility of the project and to consider any adverse affects that might result from it. For the uninitiated, this is essentially a justification and plan for a project, similar to the more familiar environment impact statement. In this case, the goal was to assess the site for individual significance to determine its eligibility for the National Register of Historic Places and to meet Biscayne National Park's management goals of preserving the site, as well as determining the best means of providing long-term protection and interpretation. It would be a minimally invasive operation that would yield a detailed map of exposed ship's architecture, artifact scatter, and other features. Certain diagnostic artifacts would be collected from the surface that might provide information on the age, function, and cultural affiliation of the wreck. A limited amount of subsurface excavation would be carried out to make a determination regarding the integrity of the site. The most important concern was to maximize our information about the site while at the same time disturbing it as little as possible. In the end, exposed organic portions of the wreck were to be reburied, and the site was to be

Figure 7.1. Every inch of the main deck of the 45-foot boat was used to get dive teams in and out of the water. (Courtesy of the National Park Service/Southeast Archeological Center.)

monitored over time for changes in the biological and archaeological setting. The project's research design was finally approved, and it was deemed ultimately not to have an overall adverse effect on the site (or at least the information necessary for planning would outweigh the effects of the minimally invasive scientific investigation). All told, a mere $30,000 had been allocated for the project, including $9,500 for salaries for six people over a six-week period. The rest was for logistics: lodging, meals, and other project costs for twenty-odd people. In-kind donations of equipment, and personnel were being made by the Southeast Archeological Center, Biscayne National Park, and the Department of Anthropology at Florida State University, among others. Many of the participants were earning credits at FSU for a course titled "Anthropological Fieldwork: Underwater Archaeology." Given the limitations posed by the scope of work, and the fiscal limitations of the budget, this project was wildly successful.

George Fischer had fielded an excellent team for this project. In the early 1980s Florida State's graduate program in anthropology had jelled. Students from across the country had come to Tallahassee and made it one of the preeminent programs in historical archaeology in the country. This particular cadre of graduate students knew their stuff and worked well together.

When one left, another could step up and fill the slot. The logical choice for the position of director of the Legare Anchorage site was Rich Johnson. He had been involved in the project since its inception in 1979. But, as the saying goes, time and tide wait for no one. By the spring of 1983 Rich had completed his degree and was in the Everglades on another National Park Service archaeological project. Into the breech stepped Russell "Skowdog" Skowronek.

Skowronek brought a wealth of knowledge and enthusiasm to the position. By 1983 he had already been involved in archaeological research for over a decade. During his four years at FSU he had completed master's degrees in both anthropology and history. Russ knew his stuff. Not only had he learned many of the alchemical arts of conservation from the staff of the Florida Bureau of Archaeological Research, but, serendipitously, he had written his master's thesis on the material culture of the 1733 Spanish *flota*, most of which had wrecked in the vicinity of Biscayne and the Upper Keys. On top of that, in 1979 he had prepared much of the background legal information on the Legare Anchorage wreck as a paper for Fischer's underwater class and in 1981 had initiated research in Great Britain on one of the potential targets—HMS *Fowey*.

The other key players were Richard Vernon, the assistant field director, and field crew chiefs David Brewer and Ken Wild, commonly referred to as Frick and Frack or "the boys." Vernon was another well-seasoned terrestrial archaeologist, who had also learned to dive while in graduate school at Florida State. A graduate of Southern Methodist University, he had worked on archaeological projects from Oklahoma and Texas to England. In England he had worked with David Barker, the renowned ceramicist, and his astute knowledge of Spanish and English material culture had repeatedly earned him a position as a field school supervisor for Kathleen Deagan in St. Augustine. Brewer and Wild were returning students. Brewer had once been a carpenter and Wild a bricklayer. Those experiences, combined with their knowledge of diving and archaeology, made them the "go to" team for getting the job done. These three and Skowronek were everywhere on this project. To ensure the best archaeological work possible, at least one of them would be on every dive—and they were.

Two other key players were Carl Semczak (a look-alike for Michael Stipe of REM) and Michael "the Man of Iron" Pomeroy. Semczak was a trained professional conservator and diver who had worked on many underwater archaeological projects, dating back to 1969 with Fischer on the excavation of the steamboat *Bertrand* in Nebraska and again in the early 1970s with Fischer at Fort Jefferson National Monument in the Dry Tortugas. Mike Pomeroy was an older returning student. A psychologist by training, he had worked on many underwater scientific field projects. Here he played the important role of dive master and technician.

Investigation of the Legare Anchorage Shipwreck site was going to be largely nondestructive in nature. Unlike treasure salvage, the goal was not simply the discovery and recovery of objects per se but understanding the horizontal and vertical juxtaposition of artifacts and their relationship, not only to each other but to the wreck site itself. Understanding an artifact's horizontal and vertical provenience or its place in time and space—known as "context"—gives meaning to that artifact when it is related to other artifacts. Without that meaning or context, the objects are simply curios. We might envision context as a form of "value added" or "extrinsic" value. For instance, whereas raw gold may sell for $700 an ounce, and that is its intrinsic value, a one-ounce gold coin may have an extrinsic value of, let's say, $900. It is not because the gold in coin form is inherently more valuable. Rather, it may be because it is of a rare mintage or perhaps because it came from a known source such as a shipwreck. That (as anyone who watches *Antiques Roadshow* will know) is provenance or, in the more common use in archaeology, provenience. Context is the place in time and space for a specific coin or other item that gives it inherent value. At this site, for example, hundreds of shards of bottle-glass were observed on the sea floor. That information tells us only that a lot of glass bottles were being utilized. But when the glass shards are mapped, we can then recognize patterns that might reveal where they were used and perhaps what function a certain area of the ship had—whether they were in storage as cargo or stashed in the officer's quarters.

On the basis of the photo-mosaic and partial map made in 1980, the site's approximate center had been tentatively established while still in the pre-project planning stage. Once in the field, the project directors verified that the longitudinal axis of the vessel correlated with that identified in the 1980 research. A project-permanent rope grid, corresponding with this axis and covering 810 square meters of ocean floor, was then laboriously established (figure 7.2). Each investigative unit within this grid was 3 × 3 meters square or roughly 10 feet to a side. The resulting central ninety units incorporated

Figure 7.2. Russell Skowronek and Richard Vernon establishing part of the rope grid. (Courtesy of the National Park Service/Southeast Archeological Center.)

the intact, in situ structural remains of the vessel. Later the grid was extended east, west, and north to incorporate other loose and structurally unassociated artifactual data (figure 7.3).

In the early stages it was determined that due to lack of relief and the nature of the data collection no special measures would need to be taken for vertical control. During excavation, however, vertical measurements of excavation depth were made from the unit's surface.

At the conclusion of the project the center line was left in place, later to serve as datum and reference points for monitoring seabed and biological changes to the site. Additionally, two PVC (polyvinyl chloride) pipes set in cement were placed on the line adjacent to the grid stakes to act as backup datum points in the event of vandalism.

After the grid was in place and before the bottom was altered in any way, overlapping black-and-white 35 mm photographs were made, showing the surface condition of each unit. Made with a Nikonos IV camera, each photograph included a photo-board with the date, unit number, north arrow, and scale inscribed on it. These photographs form a companion photo-mosaic to the 1980 photo-mosaic of the site core, which could be used for documenting any changes in the seabed, whether natural or due to human intervention.

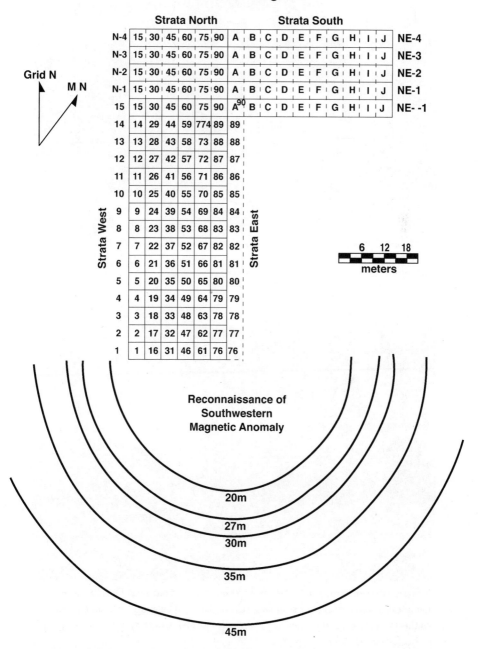

Figure 7.3. The 1983 project studied a large area of Legare Anchorage. (Courtesy of the National Park Service/Southeast Archeological Center.)

Figure 7.4. Russell Skowronek hand-fanning one of the units. (Courtesy of the National Park Service/Southeast Archeological Center.)

Figure 7.5. Russell Skowronek flagging a bayonet for later retrieval. During conservation it was discovered that its scabbard was still intact. It currently is housed at the Southeast Archeological Center in Tallahassee, Florida. (Courtesy of the National Park Service/Southeast Archeological Center.)

Figure 7.6. Richard Vernon drawing a detailed plan map of one of the 3 × 3 meter units (Courtesy of the National Park Service/Southeast Archeological Center.)

Next a controlled surface collection was made of each unit. All surface collections were by the fan and grab technique. Each unit was systematically hand-fanned by a staff archaeologist and partner (figure 7.4). Artifacts deemed diagnostic or of museum quality by the archaeologist were collected or, if fragile or large, were flagged for later specialized lifting and and/or collection (figure 7.5). Other nondiagnostic artifacts (including hull fittings, bricks, timbers, barrel hoops, shot, guns, and ballast) were left in situ and were mapped in the data books kept for each unit throughout the project. In addition to surface collections, the archaeologist recorded in the unit data books observations on the relative amounts of ballast pebbles present. Similarly, information on natural bottom conditions such as "loose, unconsolidated sand, turtle grass, sea fans" was recorded. This again was designed to provide the maximum amount of information regarding marine life and bottom conditions that could be used to monitor and protect the site.

Before mapping, the units were again lightly hand-fanned to remove loose sand from the structural elements and other artifacts in situ. After clearing, the units were mapped on underwater graph paper using a 1.5-square-meter mapping frame, divided into 10-centimeter units (figure 7.6). The sand was then fanned back onto the extant structural elements to protect them from attack by marine organisms. Maps included structural elements, in situ artifacts, plant life, metal-detector readings, and general notes relating to bottom conditions. The unit maps were compiled daily into a master field map incorporating structural members and larger objects, including immovable in situ artifacts such as guns and ballast. Clear plastic overlays indicating patterns of classes of surface-collected materials and metal-detector readings were prepared. These were keyed to the master field map for use in deciding the location of test excavation units in the later phases of the project.

One of the goals of the project was to locate presumed subsurface structural remains and thus more precisely delimit the site boundaries. Probing with a long metal rod was therefore utilized to accomplish this goal rapidly without major alteration of the site surface and disruption of underlying remains. In turn, the results of the probing could then be verified in the following test excavation portion of the project. Probing was limited to the ninety core units of the site. Every unit was systematically probed to a depth of one meter with a quarter-inch T-bar (figure 7.7). Probes were made every meter, for a total of 1,104 tests. The results were recorded in the unit data books by depth and assumed composition of the materials encountered, based on the sound and texture of the probe limit—for instance, a "ting" was generally considered metal, a "thunk" wood, and a "tank" possibly coralline, whereas sand was simply penetrated. Again, we hoped that this information could be used over time in monitoring physical changes to the site that would in turn be correlated with the series of data points embedded in the sea floor.

A hand-held White's-PI 1000 metal detector was passed over each core unit to locate buried iron concentrations and to determine the composition of other concreted objects during the mapping process. In this way, most unrecovered, undiagnostic artifacts could be identified as being of ferrous or nonferrous composition. Buried iron objects were located and identified by the magnitude of the reading. All metal-detector results were reported on the individual unit maps, which were then compiled on the base map for the overall site.

To determine the magnetic stability and equilibrium of the site and to ascertain the presence or absence of detached components of the vessel in adjacent areas, a Geometrics G-866 Proton Precession Magnetometer (a new, simpler, and better instrument than the by then antique G-806 that had been used to find the site) and marine sensor were operated over the

Figure 7.7. J. P. Montegut using a T-bar probe. More than 1,100 probes were completed to record buried parts of the wreck during the 1983 project. (Courtesy of the National Park Service/Southeast Archeological Center.)

site and the surrounding area. Three six-meter-wide lanes running from grid north to south provided coverage of the site core. Magnetometer readings indicated that the site could be considered in relative magnetic equilibrium before the lifting of the guns. The work also showed that the extent of the structural components of the site was almost completely confined to the identified and gridded area. One magnetic anomaly, however, was encountered forty meters to the southeast of the southeast corner of the site. A circle sweep swimmer survey covered 6,360.5 square meters of the suspect area but located no detached components of the vessel. The anomaly was never identified.

According to the research design, testing of the Legare Anchorage Shipwreck site was going to be limited to a 3 percent sample of the 810 square meters of the site core. Twelve 1 × 1 meter units, representing a 1½ percent

BISC - UW - 20

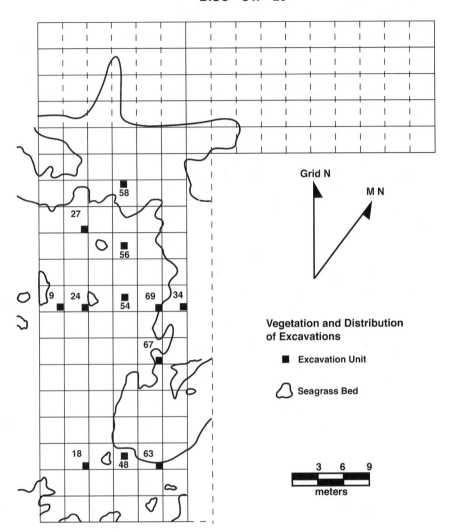

Figure 7.8. Plan showing the twelve 1 × 1 meter units that were excavated over the main part of the site. (Courtesy of the National Park Service/Southeast Archeological Center.)

sample, were actually excavated to culturally sterile zones (figure 7.8). Excavations were aimed at providing latitudinal and longitudinal subsurface views of the site, where expected surface features were not visible. Placement of the units was determined by examining trends in surface-collected material culture, metal-detector readings, probing results, vegetation pat-

Figure 7.9. An airlift team was composed of four divers: two controlled the airlift, and the others wrote notes and collected artifacts. (Courtesy of the National Park Service/ Southeast Archeological Center.)

terns, and the interpolation of extant structural remains on the basis of trends in naval architecture. Generally covering the known limits of the site, yet testing of only a portion, might be referred to as a "stratified sampling strategy."

Excavations into the soft sand of the bottom were conducted within a one-square-meter caisson of sheet metal construction. This caisson not only delimited the immediate area to be excavated but also inhibited slumping, while at the same time providing a convenient rest for the airlift apparatus (figure 7.9). Actual excavation utilized a four-inch PVC airlift, powered by a 1½–horsepower engine and 14-cfm (cubic feet per minute) compressor. Sediments were hand-fanned into the airlift. All observable artifacts were collected from the unit by the archaeologist before they went up the airlift. The archaeologist not only collected the artifacts but kept detailed notes regarding the unit's features and made the final decision to suspend excavation (figure 7.10). Effluence from the airlift was piped to the surface and then screened through ¼-inch hardware cloth to recover any smaller, unnoticed artifacts. Particulate spoil from the floating screen was in turn directed back to the bottom via a large plastic-sheet-tube that came to be referred to as "the whale condom" (figure 7.11). This careful return of sediments to

Figure 7.10. An airlift team takes a moment to write notes and collect an artifact. The item held by the third diver from the left was later identified as a linchpin. It was marked with a Broad Arrow. (Courtesy of the National Park Service/Southeast Archeological Center.)

Figure 7.11. A 1 × 1 meter sheet metal caisson and a floating screen with sediment pipe were important in the excavation and preservation of the site. *Left to right*, Ken Wild, David Brewer, Diana Barrera, Ken Hoeck, and Richard Vernon. (Courtesy of the National Park Service/Southeast Archeological Center.)

Figure 7.12. Yes, you can shovel underwater: Diana Barrera backfilling units. (Courtesy of the National Park Service/Southeast Archeological Center.)

particular spots on the ocean floor not only protected surrounding reef life from particulate fallout but additionally maintained good bottom working conditions (i.e., good visibility) and provided discrete "backdirt" piles for the refilling of the excavation units. Screens were constantly monitored and were emptied between units.

We recognized that hydrological research would have to be done at some time in the future, focusing on factors such as current, surge, and corresponding sand transport regimes around the wreck. Without the seagrass to stabilize the substrate, any sand overburden could be put in motion during rough weather or exceptional tides. This would also undercut the sand that was supporting the remains of the wreck and expose additional areas to the ravages of marine organisms and other biological and mechanical changes.

With those concerns at the forefront of our minds, all excavation units were backfilled to original bottom level with spoil from the floating screen. The venting of these sediments back to the ocean floor via the whale condom resulted in conveniently located sand piles, which were finally hand-shoveled back into the excavation units (figure 7.12). To camouflage the site and inhibit attacks by *Teredo navalis* (shipworms) and other marine borers on exposed hull members, a thin layer of sand was fanned over the wood.

This project also saw the implementation of an initial experimental attempt at passive burial. The National Park Service had been presented with fifty units of Seascape, an artificial seagrass used to inhibit shoreline erosion in shallow high-energy areas elsewhere in the country. Used with reported success at Cape Hatteras National Seashore, the Seascape consisted of inert fiberglass cloth tubes with floating, Styrofoam-supported fronds. The tubes were filled with sand and sealed onshore. Once on the site, they were placed in various aspects, generally counter to the normal winter erosional tidal flow over the wreck site. As in the case of a snow-fence, the object of the Seascape was to waft in the passing particulate-laden currents, "catching" waterborne sediments and causing the sediments to drop (figure 7.13). If it worked correctly, over time an accretion of sand would result in the passive burial of the site. This "experiment," which in fact is what it was, has been criticized repeatedly as a failure because the "fronds" of the Seascape were no longer floating when the site was visited a year later. The fronds had been buoyed with a thin piece of Styrofoam. At thirty feet of depth the Styrofoam had compressed, thus lessening the buoyancy of the fronds. When they grew heavy with algae they sank. Nonetheless, the site was also noted to have an overall accretion of sand atop it at that time. An experiment? Yes. A failure? Well, what experiment is ever a failure?—even those that do not yield the expected outcome teach us something. The Seascape minimally served like sandbags impeding the movement of sediments and thus protecting a small portion of the site, and the collapsed fronds provided further cover for the site surface.

While active and passive burial of the ship's remains was undertaken by the project's participants, the park oceanographer carried out his own experiment by planting seagrass over the site in an attempt at vegetating the entire site core. The results of these transplanting activities were mixed. First, the shoots of turtle grass (which had been collected from shallow waters, to which they were acclimated) were unable to survive at thirty feet of depth. Perhaps the twelve-penny steel nail "spikes" to which they were attached and pinned to the ground also began an electrolytic process that simply killed the grass shoots (duh). In any case, the archaeologists were skeptical of this process from the beginning, and now the site is littered with some 1,200 modern steel nails, all emitting an electrochemical "aura" that will undoubtedly confuse and contaminate any future archaeological and/or remote-sensing investigations. It might be further noted, though,

Figure 7.13. Diver inspecting Seascape units in place around a gun at the Legare Anchorage site. (Courtesy of the National Park Service/Southeast Archeological Center.)

that when transplanted by hand, without the nails, the seagrass adjacent to the site appeared to thrive.

Most of the artifacts were collected using the aforementioned techniques. Some items, however, required specialized retrieval. Fragile artifacts such as pewter plates, cutlasses (figure 7.14), bayonets, and copper pots or large, heavy artifacts like cannonballs, ballast, guns, eyebolts, bricks, or barrel hoops required specialized field handling. While all of these "special items" were considered part of the given lot and provenience, they were flagged for separate lifting.

The small, fragile or delicate artifacts such as bayonets or cutlasses were supported and sometimes tied onto a rigid support board or container before being lifted from the bottom and out of the water (figures 7.15, 7.16, 7.17). More robust artifacts like cannonballs were separately carried to the surface by divers. Heavy materials such as an iron ballast block and a deadeye and strap were floated to the surface with lift bags and physically lifted to the deck of the research vessel.

Near the end of the project, it was decided that a single cast-iron gun was to be removed. Weighing more than 3,000 pounds, it presented its own set of recovery problems. To effect this lift, National Park Service divers

Figure 7.14. Iron-hilted cutlass in situ on the sea floor. We were painfully aware that it would take special handling to bring it to the surface after more than two centuries of submersion. When it was conserved, an intact scabbard was discovered. (Courtesy of the National Park Service/Southeast Archeological Center.)

Figure 7.15. Conservator Carl Semczak and master diver Michael Pomeroy preparing to lift a cutlass in a rigid container. (Courtesy of the National Park Service/Southeast Archeological Center.)

Figure 7.16. Snuggled into its tube, the cutlass is ready to be carried to the surface. (Courtesy of the National Park Service/Southeast Archeological Center.)

Figure 7.17. Mike Pomeroy and Carl Semczak carrying the cutlass to the surface. As underwater archaeologists will attest, the water/air interface puts fragile items in great jeopardy of breaking. The rigid tube was easy to pass to willing hands on board the boat. (Courtesy of the National Park Service/Southeast Archeological Center.)

were aided by the late Herbert Bump (1932–2007), historic conservator for the Florida Department of State's Bureau of Archaeological Research. His methodology included the use of two modified military aircraft fuel wing tanks, which were sunk on either side of the gun (figure 7.18). Then they were linked to the iron tube with chain (figure 7.19). Slowly filled with air, the tanks acted as rigid lift bags, and the gun gently rose to the surface. Finally, it was towed by open boat through Caesar's Creek to the park head-quarters at Convoy Point (figure 7.20). There, in the fading light of the day, the gun was lifted by a mechanical winch onto a waiting truck (figure 7.21) and then driven to Tallahassee to undergo a year-long conservation process at the State of Florida's laboratory facilities in the Bureau of Archaeological Research. As the gun emerged from the water, a crowd formed on the dock. Most of the people, locals preparing for a weekend on the waters of Biscayne Bay, were thrilled to see a "piece of history"—but not everyone. One unidentified individual spoke out: "By all rights, that belongs to us." The weary but still altruistic and very naïve field director, Russ Skowronek, replied: "No, sir, it belongs to everyone." Was he ever wrong!

Figure 7.18. Pete Steuer, Herbert Bump, and ranger Randy Bidwell passing modified jet fuel tanks over the stern of the 45-foot work boat while Ken Wild looks on from the chase boat. (Courtesy of the National Park Service/Southeast Archeological Center.)

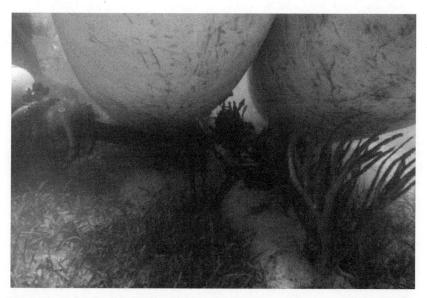

Figure 7.19. After the fuel tanks sank they were chained on either side of the gun and filled with air. (Courtesy of the National Park Service/Southeast Archeological Center.)

Figure 7.20. Richard Curry towing the jet fuel tanks and attached (submerged) gun to Convoy Point. Gregg Stanton "rode" the tanks in case the gun worked itself loose, but it didn't. (Courtesy of the National Park Service/Southeast Archeological Center.)

Figure 7.21. Herbert Bump (*left*) guides the gun onto a truck for the 700-mile drive back to Tallahassee for conservation. (Courtesy of the National Park Service/Southeast Archeological Center.)

On returning to the site a few days later, after the long weekend, crew chief David Brewer went over the side of the 45-foot work boat to retrieve the anchor mooring line. Time was growing short for the project. There was work to be done, and it appeared that Dave was taking his own sweet time. Finally, ten minutes later, he surfaced far from the boat. His regulator came out of the water, sputtering and bubbling. Dave tipped his mask back onto his head.

Skowronek could see Dave's face. He looked upset, as if he was about to cry, or perhaps it was—yes, anger!

"Dave! What's wrong? . . . Where's the line?"

"Goddamn it! Those jerks!" he shouted. "Gone, all gone! They got it all. You better see this."

Skowronek put on his tanks and stepped off into the cool water. Dave paddled over and said, "Follow me." As the air bubbled out of the buoyancy compensator, Skowronek sank past the ten-foot thermo-cline and equalized the pressure in his ears. The overcast skies that morning now made the site look darker and somewhat sinister. Two decades later Brewer recalled that the site, once alive with fish, was seemingly bereft of all sea life. Particulate matter floating in the water added to the mystery . . . and then he

Figure 7.22. Part of the site in 1984 after destruction by parties unknown. (Courtesy of the National Park Service/Southeast Archeological Center.)

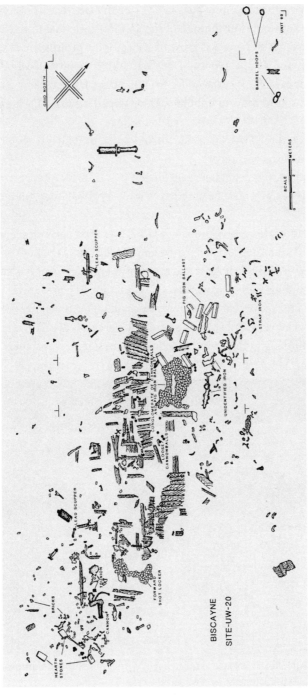

Figure 7.23. Plan view of the discoveries made during the 1983 field project. (Courtesy of the National Park Service/Southeast Archeological Center.)

saw it. The site looked like a plow had been dragged through it. There were furrows in the seabed where an anchor obviously had been dragged. Planks were torn up, and the rope grid floated in a tangled, broken mass (figure 7.22). Persons unknown had made certain that if they could not have the wreck no one could. They had really shown the eggheads.

The pair silently surfaced and returned to the boat. The crew stood at the stern and heard what had happened and then radioed Park Headquarters with the news. No one knew what to do. It was as though a family member had died. Then Skowronek said: "Drop the anchor. We have a site to close up and put to bed. Let's get to work, guys" (figure 7.23).

Skowronek learned two things that day. Not everyone understands what is right and, yes, you can cry underwater.

8

Reconstructing the Legare Anchorage Ship

Peter Pan could do it, and now so could he: fly. Is there any person who has not dreamed of flying? Whether you have read *Peter Pan*, seen it on the stage or on the screen, or only ridden the attraction at Disneyland, you have sensed what it is like to look down and observe, at your own speed and with complete freedom, to get as close or as far away as needed. Those of you who have been fortunate enough to work on archaeological projects will understand the frustration of not having the "big picture." At best, we get only a window or series of small windows to peek into the inner workings of a complex site. Often it is also because we get so enmeshed in the minutiae that we don't take the time to see the whole. But even with the best site maps, it sometimes helps to get an overall perspective. On terrestrial sites, "cherry picker" lifts, small planes, and even balloons have helped researchers see the big picture. From midwestern cornfields, where subtle soil changes mark thousand-year-old Mississippian Period temple towns, to the Nazca region of southern Peru, some sites can only be fully appreciated from nearby hills or from the air. That same reality certainly applies to underwater sites, and the Legare Anchorage wreck in the clear water of the Keys was no different.

Four weeks of eighteen-hour days had pushed the crew and its directors to their limit. Each dive was minutely planned and focused on either a single or handful of 3 × 3 meter units. As the field aspect of the work began to wind down, Skowronek was already looking forward to the "interpretation" of the site, the part of archaeology where art meets science. He realized that he had just not looked around enough to let the thoughts sink in and coalesce.

Anyone who has been in charge of a project will attest that there are a million things that constantly need attention. You know them: telephones ringing, logistics, money, crew members complaining about one another or about the conditions or just to complain for the sake of complaining. Machinery breaks. Someone is sick, hung-over, petulant, crying, or depressed. It is too hot, too cold, or too rough. And everyone is asking for attention. On terrestrial sites there is no less respite, but on an underwater project it can be different.

With his friend Richard Vernon, Skowronek suited up for just such a tour. It felt ostentatious simply to dive without a job per se. They hit the water and began to descend. The quiet of the underwater world was calming: no throbbing engines, no radios or other distractions. The water was cool after the heat of the boat. For the first time they stopped about twenty feet above the sea floor and began to cruise around the two working dive teams and the wreck.

All too often we are drawn into the excitement of shipwrecks by fantastic images from novels, movies, or Disneyland: largely intact ships lying on the sea floor. A skeleton is tied to a wheel, and tattered sails hang from the spars, while a shark circles and a giant clam opens and closes . . . Sure, the Legare Anchorage wreck had moray eels, sting rays, anemones, and octopi; but to the untrained eye there was nothing that could be recognized as a ship there, only the coral-encrusted detritus of a long-forgotten accident. Scientists know, however, that things rarely happen in random ways. The living or systemic world is patterned. From technology to ideology, we do things as part of a culture, in patterned ways. When the living cultural system succumbs to the natural and passes into the archaeological context, that context will also have a pattern. The pattern reflects the patterns of the living context, scrambled by the patterns of the natural. That is, things like gravity and prevailing winds, waves, and water currents will transform a ship into the wreck site we see. The ship had a patterned "living" context that reflected its cultural origins and its function. Once it passed from that context into the archaeological context, nature created its own patterns. If we as archaeologists can discern those archaeological patterns, we can in turn reconstruct the living patterns and thus understand past lifeways.

Pattern recognition had become part of their professional lives as archaeologists. Skowronek and Vernon swam over the site, and details of the wreck stood out in bold relief relative to the surrounding sand and turtle grass. They "flew down" to investigate and then rose again to continue their tour. Flying was possible in this circumstance and produced the desired result: the recognition of those disarticulated patterns. It was making sense to them. Now it was time to put it back together.

At the end of June 1983 the team returned to Tallahassee and began the analysis. Skowronek made certain that the field notes, photographs, and maps were delivered to the National Park Service repository at the Southeast Archeological Center. Armed with copies of the same, he packed up his office and home. He was moving to Michigan, where he would continue his education at Michigan State University in the Ph.D. program in anthropology. Skowronek already had master's degrees in anthropology and history. He knew his strengths in material culture and historical archaeology and also what he didn't know well enough—naval architecture. In the eight weeks before the commencement of classes in East Lansing he would drive to Nova Scotia and crawl through every wooden sailing vessel he could find, to help him better understand the scattered skeleton of timbers that once was a ship and then interpret it.

This was not a new endeavor for Russ. In the fall of 1981, when he had begun his research in England on the *Fowey*, he had visited HMS *Unicorn* at Victoria Dock in Dundee, Scotland, and HMS *Victory* in Portsmouth when he was not poring over old manuscripts in the British Library in London, the National Maritime Museum, Greenwich, and the Public Records Office in Kew, near the London suburb of Richmond.

The 1983 trip north to Nova Scotia took him to visit John Broadwater and Harding Polk, who were working on the American Revolutionary War wrecks in Yorktown, Virginia. From there he went to St. Mary's City, Maryland, home port for the *Dove*. The next stop was Baltimore and the USF *Constellation*. At that time the *Constellation* was still thought to date to the turn of the nineteenth century.

Then it was on to New England and the replicas of HMS *Rose* in Croton, Connecticut, and the *Beaver* in Boston. In the Charlestown Navy Yard he visited the USS *Constitution*. The last stop was in Erie, Pennsylvania, to see the *Niagara*. Along the way, other vital information was collected at a series of locations, including Independence National Historic Park and the Maritime Museum in Philadelphia; the Peabody Museum and Salem Maritime National Historic Site in Salem, Massachusetts; the National Museum of American History, Smithsonian Institution, Washington, D.C.; and the Mystic Seaport Museum in Connecticut.

Significantly, the research did not end there but continued into Canada. In Halifax, Nova Scotia, the Citadel, the Maritime Museum of the Atlantic, and the Nova Scotia Public Archives provided extremely useful information on British naval operations in the region during the 1740s. But the most important stop was farther north, at Cape Breton Island at the Fortress of Louisbourg. This French-colonial fortified port had been captured twice by Anglo-American forces in the first half of the eighteenth century. For more than forty years the staff members of Parks Canada have excavated and restored the citadel. They have created a grand repository for eighteenth-century French-colonial material culture and rich documentary archives to complement it.

With his Florida tan fading and the days growing shorter, Skowronek pointed his overworked '74 Toyota Corona westward. Rod Stewart's *Maggie May* blared. It was late September, and he "really should be back at school." As he headed to Michigan, he knew the Legare Anchorage site was about to give up its secrets.

No project is conducted in a vacuum, and this one was no different. Interpreting the site would require drawing on information provided by the original salvor, Gerald Klein, both the 1980 and 1983 National Park Service projects, and other material analyses and documentary research. The task of sorting and evaluating the thousands of artifacts and pulling together the supporting evidence is a meticulous and difficult undertaking. It is also what makes archaeology worthwhile and fun. This project, however, also had the serious mission of objectively evaluating the site. That included not only determining its physical condition but the pressing need for positive identification. The first goal had to be reconstructing the ship.

Architecture and Aspect

The 1983 project revealed that the remains of the Legare Anchorage ship are oriented from east (stern) to west (bow). People tend to remember only when things go right. Mistakes are never trumpeted and rarely even recognized, because people don't like to have their shortcomings revealed. Nonetheless, it is fair to say that we were wrong in our original analysis of the evidence compiled from 1980 to early 1983, before the field project (Fischer and Johnson 1981; Skowronek 1984a). From earlier misguided observations, we had projected the vessel turned ninety degrees. Fortunately, that was eventually corrected. Unfortunately, the corrections came after we already had finished a number of reports and publications. This book should help set the record straight.

In 1986 the late J. Richard Steffy (1924–2007), an internationally known expert on the construction of wooden sailing vessels at the Institute of Nautical Archaeology at Texas A&M University, interpreted these remains as representing a hull that had opened athwartships, just abaft or behind the foremast (Steffy 1986). Steffy felt that the evidence found in the kitchen area indicated that the vessel listed to port on sinking. This interpretation was later confirmed in 1993. The Submerged Cultural Resources Unit (now the Submerged Resources Center) of the National Park Service, with support from the University of Maryland and the Maritime Archaeological and Historical Society, was sent to document the condition of the site following Hurricane Andrew (figure 8.1). According to an entry in the *British Museum Encyclopedia of Underwater and Maritime Archaeology* (Delgado 1997: 445), this work identified gun and sweep ports, which supported Steffy's 1983 identification of the remains as representing a side of the vessel.

This project also supplied other information that we hope will one day be of great interest to nautical engineering historians as well as dispel other troubling hearsay about what has been found. For example, Eric Adams (1996: 34) reported that the 1993 project found that a knee or brace that served to support a gun deck was described as a composite of wood and iron. If the identification of this particular architectural element is accurate, it poses a troubling dilemma. Most naval historians date this construction practice to the nineteenth century. In fact, the oldest British-built warship still afloat is HMS *Unicorn*. When launched at Chatham in 1824, this 1,080-ton frigate with forty-six guns claimed to be one of the first ships to have iron knees and diagonal riders in an otherwise completely wooden constructed vessel. Could this practice have been developed at an earlier date in the eighteenth century? Well, as early as the 1730s the use of iron knees in at least one British ship was noted by Blaise Ollivier, the chief constructor of the Brest dockyard (1739 [1992]), so it is possible.

Sometimes what is most informative is what is not found on a site: negative evidence can be just as informative as positive evidence. In the case of the Legare Anchorage wreck, neither anchors nor a rudder assembly were found. These features are of course critical in the control of large vessels. Their absence may tell us something about the demise of the ship. Another absent architectural element that could be useful in dating the wreck was copper sheathing.

HMS Fowey Main Site

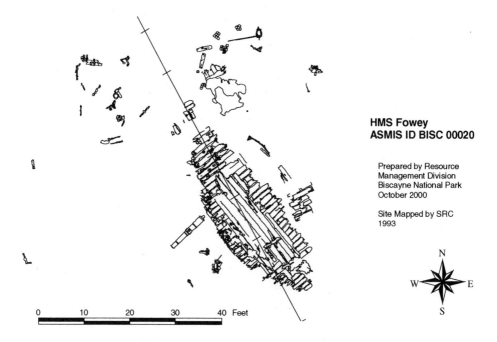

HMS Fowey
ASMIS ID BISC 00020

Prepared by Resource
Management Division
Biscayne National Park
October 2000

Site Mapped by SRC
1993

0   10   20   30   40 Feet

Figure 8.1. In 1993, following Hurricane Andrew, the Submerged Cultural Resources Unit of the National Park Service, with support from the University of Maryland and the Maritime Archaeological and Historical Society, made this detailed map of the exposed remains of the wreck. (Courtesy of the National Park Service/Southeast Archeological Center.)

Copper sheathing was rarely used on British vessels before 1750 and was unknown on Spanish ships before 1800. Before that time the bottoms were either covered with a combination of sulphur, horsehair, and soft woods or given a thin lead sheathing. When the bottoms began to rot on the unsheathed vessel, small lead patches were often tacked over the bad areas (Mansir 1981: 46). A perforated lead sheet or patch was found on the site by Gerald Klein, but otherwise no other indication of sheathing was present.

Ballast: The Hold

Ballasting of the ship, although not an integral part of the structural architecture, served largely in that capacity. The vessel represented at BISC-UW-20 carried a small amount of loose stone and many large pigs of iron ballast. Initially identified in the 1980 project (Lenihan 2002: 101), the ballast pile covers six square meters of ocean floor and rises one and a half meters above wooden architectural remains (Unit 53). This stack represents about 26,880 pounds or 13.44 tons of deadweight. The pigs are three feet long with a six-inch square cross section and weigh 320 pounds each. Holes diagonally pierce each end of the bars emerging on one plane of the pig. The holes are one inch in diameter and three inches long and probably represent a convenient means of attaching hooks for the placement of the pigs in the hold. One interesting yet heretofore unmentioned attribute of the bars is the mark of the British Crown—the Broad Arrow (Peterson 1973: 6). A Broad Arrow or pheon is a type of arrow with a typically flat barbed head. It is also a symbol used traditionally in heraldry. Cast in relief in a cartouche on the side opposite the hole-pierced plane is a five-inch-long Broad Arrow (figure 8.2). While iron ballast of this size has been reported on other vessels—such as HMS *Charon* and the "Cornwallis Cave" wreck at Yorktown, Virginia (Steffy et al. 1981); HMS *Unicorn* in Dundee, Scotland (Skowronek 1981); USF *Constellation* in Baltimore, Maryland (personal observation, September 1981, September 1983); HMS *Bounty* (Marden 1957: 761); HMS *Looe* (Peterson 1973: 6); and HMS *Victory* (personal observation, June 2006)—no previous reports of such a mark have been made.

The exact date for the introduction of specifically cast pig iron ballast blocks is unknown. As early as 1703 British merchant and warships were ballasted with stone and scrap iron (Perkins 1979; Peterson 1973: 129). Beginning in the second quarter of the eighteenth century, British warships began carrying this block form of permanent ballast. Only much later in the Industrial Revolution, when costs fell, did British merchant ships start carrying iron ballast. Spanish ships of the sixteenth through eighteenth centuries, both military and merchant, were exclusively ballasted with large river cobbles (Peterson 1973: 129; Skowronek 1984b).

When iron block ballast was used, it required specialized placement. A science of stowage developed so that the extreme weight of the bars would not affect the fabric of the ship. Richard Hall Gower (1808: 155) wrote that "the easiness of a round-bottomed vessel depends upon the situation of her center of gravity; thus should the cargo be heavy and its center of gravity low, the stability will be so great as to return the vessel to her erect position with such violence as to endanger the masts." In the placement of "a vessel's cargo, if she is to be deeply laden, the cargo should be . . . halfway between

X-ray view of pig iron ballast showing channels utilized as lifting aids for permanent placement between the frames of the hull.

Typical British pig iron ballast
Dimensions: 6" x 6" x 3'

Figure 8.2. This six-inch-square by three-foot-long block of iron tipped the scale at 320 pounds. The incuse-cast Broad Arrow marked ownership by the British Crown. (Courtesy of the National Park Service/Southeast Archeological Center.)

the keelson and the center of motion, or . . . a quarter of her beam up the hold. Otherwise keep low to minimize pitching."

Further, Gower stated that "the extremities of a vessel may not be loaded beyond their capacity to bear, that the weight be collected toward the center of the vessel between the main mast and the fore-hatchway and that the extremities be loaded with the lightest articles."

Gower accounts for the loading of a ship with cargo, but Robert White Stevens (1867) deals more intimately with the shipping of ballast. On stowage he says:

To avoid the shifting of ballast, or even of coal, especially in sharp-built ships, when bad weather is expected, the hold is sometimes fitted with ballast stanchions and boards. The lower ends of the stanchions are set in at the keelson, and the upper lashed to the beam, a few feet from the side; five or six on each side, with planks lashed or nailed fore and aft to the stanchions, 12 to 18 inches apart; the ballast is thus divided into three portions, which prevents the possibility of shifting. (Stevens 1867: 59)

Stevens adds that:

... when using pig iron ballast masters should use sufficient dunnage, so that the bars shall not . . . come direct on the skin [of the ship], where they are rather prone to place it. To save extra pressure in the bilges, one experienced owner recommends iron to be kept as much as possible fore and aft on the flat of the floor, and that when chequering, the chequers should be closer over the keelson and amidships than toward the sides.

Therefore:

. . . when stowed close in the bilges, and the ship heaves over, the pressure must be excessive. The keels and keelsons of iron-laden ships have been sometimes injured when they have taken the ground, in consequence of all of the weight being placed on the frame of the ship and none on the keelson. (Stevens 1867:270)

The Legare Anchorage site preserves such a chequered or carefully stacked pile, and it appears to be largely in situ. This may suggest that when the vessel settled it was more or less upright; later, as the vessel was weakened due to the ravages of marine organisms and wave action, it would have split and fallen into the sandy bottom. Perhaps if and when the Submerged Resources Center report on the 1993 project is published we will learn how accurate Steffy's interpretation really was.

Storage: The Hold

Water, victuals, powder, and mercantile cargos all require special containers. Wooden crates were and are still used extensively in this way. Until well into the twentieth century they were augmented with barrels and casks. In the Spanish world, large ceramic storage vessels or *tinajas*, commonly known as olive jars, were ubiquitous and were used until the turn of the twentieth century (Goggin 1960). Olive jars as storage vessels in shipping are largely a phenomenon associated with the maritime trade of southern Europe (Spain, Portugal, Italy) and may be considered a Mediterranean-associated artifact rather than strictly Spanish in origin. Contrary to earlier field identifications made during the 1980 project (Lenihan 2002: 101), there are no sherds of Spanish olive jar storage containers in either the Klein collection or the National Park Service collections for 1980 and 1983. If some were found in 1993 they have not been reported. Every collection from the 1733 *flota* contained olive jar sherds (Skowronek 1984b).

The prominence of wooden casks as common shipping containers in northern Europe might well be seen as a function of those countries' proximity to a cheap, available, and more practical (i.e., with less tendency for breakage) source of materials: the trees from their forests (Fairbanks 1973: 143).

A partially intact wooden cask from Unit 18 (figure 8.3), barrel hoops, and other strap fragments litter the east center of the Legare Anchorage

Figure 8.3. Our limited excavations revealed how well preserved the wreck was. This partially preserved wooden cask was left in situ and reburied because our limited budget could only cover the conservation of diagnostic artifacts. We assume that the cask was destroyed by Hurricane Andrew or in subsequent recovery projects. (Courtesy of the National Park Service/Southeast Archeological Center.)

Shipwreck and can be found in lesser quantities both north and south in the core grid (figure 8.4). Most were made of iron (8 cm or about 3 inches in width) and were up to 62 cm (about 24 inches) in diameter. Three examples of copper barrel hoops and numerous fragments were found. These average 2.5 cm (1 inch) in width and were 40 cm (16 inches) in diameter

BISC - UW - 20

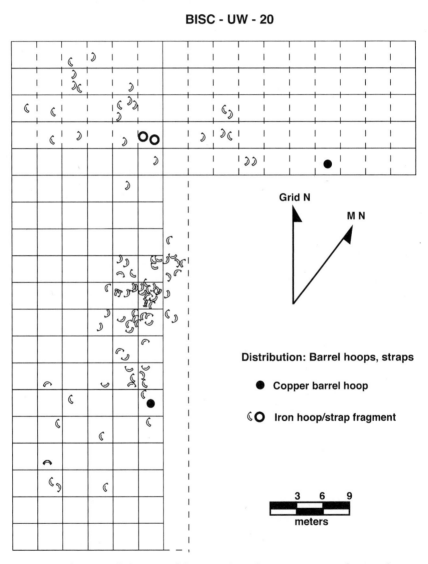

Figure 8.4. The controlled survey of the site indicated a concentration of iron and copper barrel hoops and thus the lower reaches of the ship, as shown in this plan. (Courtesy of the National Park Service/Southeast Archeological Center.)

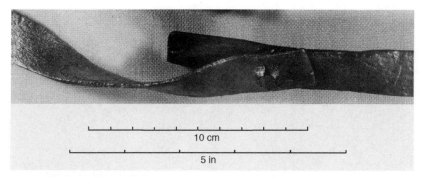

Figure 8.5. Copper barrel hoops were used on gunpowder kegs because sparks cannot be struck from copper. This one is marked with Broad Arrows, indicating ownership by the Crown of England. (Courtesy National Park Service/Southeast Archeological Center)

and match one recovered earlier by Gerald Klein from the site. The ends of both iron and copper hoops overlap and are secured by a rivet of the same metal. Copper hoops have a Broad Arrow incised into the band adjacent to the rivet (figure 8.5). Similar copper-bound barrels have been found at Fort Ligonier, a British outpost used during the French and Indian War (Grimm 1970: 79, 98–99). There they are associated with storage of the highly combustible black powder. Copper hoops, unlike iron, cannot strike sparks, therefore making them the preferred choice for powder storage (Neumann and Kravic 1975: 28).

The location of both iron and copper hoops appears consistent with other stowage practices of the eighteenth century. HMS *Victory*, built in 1759 (Naish 1975: 14–15), and the Dutch East Indian *Amsterdam*, lost in 1748 (Marsden 1974: 121), had their ships' stores centered around the mainmast. Their powder stores were in the stern (the warship *Victory* had an additional magazine forward).

Other heavy items that would have been stowed low in the hull were cannonballs. Four sizes of solid, cast-iron shot were collected and/or noted on the site. They were of two-, six-, nine-, and eighteen-pound sizes (figure 8.6) for use in a swivel gun and the larger ones in corresponding 3.67-, 4.22-, and 5.3-inch caliber guns (Peterson 1973: 115). While the presence of nationally marked shot, including the Broad Arrow (English), "A" (Dutch, Amsterdam), and fleur-de-lis (France), has been noted at other sites (e.g., HMS *Looe*, 1743; the 1733 *flota*) (Skowronek 1984b: 94–95), those from the Legare Anchorage site do not bear such markings. Location of the shot in

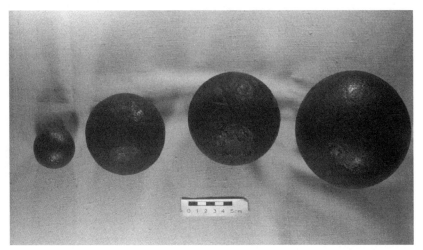

Figure 8.6. Two-, six-, nine-, and eighteen-pound cast-iron round shot found at the site. (Courtesy of the National Park Service/Southeast Archeological Center.)

two discrete locations probably represents (1) the main shot locker amidship, and (2) garlanded shot (stored in shot racks or "garlands") from an upper deck that got trapped in a single location during hull dispersion (Steffy 1986). A trail of shot leading away from the site may mark the remains of the trail of the ship as it headed to its final resting place. The shot would have spilled through a hole in the bottom after hitting a nearby reef.

The Kitchen: Forward

If it is assumed that the Legare Anchorage ship is a representative sailing vessel (and all indications point to that), generally built in accepted ways, then the bow should exhibit a kitchen area and the stern should be reserved for the captain and his officers (Muckelroy 1978: 188). The results of our work, from both surface collections and excavation in the grid south areas of the site core, supported the premise that the ship is oriented toward the southeast. We would have expected to find the anchors in this area. Nonetheless, centered in Units 3 and 18 (figure 8.7) are a concentration of granitic stone slabs (50 × 80 cm), ceramic tiles (½ inch × 6 × 10 inches), and bricks (2.2 × 8.75 × 3.75 inches). These represent the kitchen area of the vessel. Beginning in the 1750s, iron stoves began to be used in the Royal Navy (Rodger 1986: 142). Prior to this, ovens and stoves of bricks-and-stone were constructed on ships. On the Legare Anchorage wreck the stone slabs were what might be considered heat-shielding hearths for a three-vaulted brick-

and-tile oven/stove similar to one seen on the reconstructed HMS *Bounty* that is berthed in St. Petersburg, Florida (personal observation, December 1981). Bricks and tiles from the wreck site match statute English sizes (Noël Hume 1968: 124) and similar finds on the Yorktown wreck sites of 1781 (Site 44Y012, Harding Polk, personal communication, August 10, 1983). Contrary to earlier speculations, they do not dimensionally match bricks from

BISC - UW - 20

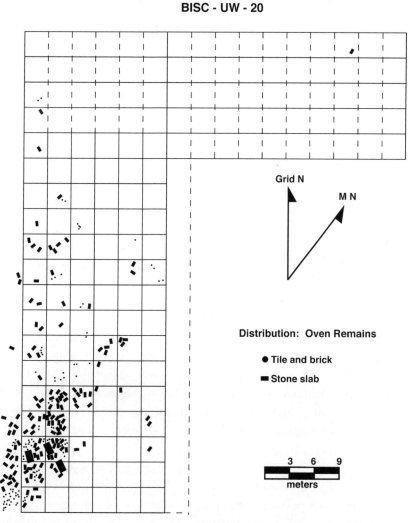

Figure 8.7. Plan showing a concentration of granite stone slabs and ceramic tiles and bricks, which may represent the ship's stove and kitchen area. (Courtesy of the National Park Service/Southeast Archeological Center.)

the 1733 *flota* (Logan 1977: 41; Skowronek 1982: 75), known as *ladrillos*. The two most common sizes on those wrecks were 11 inches × 4.5 inches × 1.5 inches and 7 inches × 3.5 × 2 inches.

Test excavations in the presumed kitchen area (Unit 18) recovered the intact remains of a barrel and indications of in situ hull members some 50 cm below that. Work along the western margin of Unit 18 further revealed what was interpreted as the wooden support frame for the foundation of the stove/oven. Testing in Unit 48 located loose unarticulated wood fragments overlying intact in situ ship's timbers, contiguous with those present on the surface in the central and northern sections of the core grid, which argues for their destruction through the forces of various natural agencies or site-formation processes. These would include loss at the time of wrecking; exposure to *Teredo navalis* during natural erosive periods; and/or outright destruction or exposure by treasure salvors. Once intact on the sea floor for some time, the remains were eventually and repeatedly disrupted; the lighter fraction was moved about and the heavier items remained in situ, with most of the lighter-fraction wooden remains gradually disintegrating. Steffy (1986) observed that the distribution of the hearth supports the idea that the ship listed to port as it settled to the bottom.

From Pattern to Reconstruction

The architectural remains identified at the Legare Anchorage site are rich in information regarding the function, age, and cultural affiliation of the ship it represents.

The vessel undoubtedly functioned as a small warship rather than a merchantman. This interpretation is based on the presence of multiple sizes of shot (two-, six-, nine-, and eighteen-pounders) and fixed permanent ballast. Larger warships would have carried larger ordnance that would have fired twenty-four- and even thirty-two-pound shot and would also have had even more ballast. Merchant ships, while frequently armed, though lightly, might only mount a single caliber of gun and not one as large as an eighteen-pounder. This was because the larger guns weighed more and required a larger crew and thus more victuals. That meant less room for cargo. The presence of fixed permanent ballast and a corresponding absence of concentrations of identifiable trade goods or containers for cargo items show that the ship had a more constant function, such as a naval vessel, wherein small fluctuations in dunnage would relate to the consumption of victuals, shot, and powder rather than the carriage of mercantile cargos.

The age of the ship is placed in the second quarter of the eighteenth century. One indication of this time frame is the presence of the 320-pound, 3 inch × 6 inch × 6 inch pig iron ballast blocks, a rare commodity in the late seventeenth and early eighteenth century (Peterson 1973: 128). Another indicator of an early-eighteenth-century date is the absence of copper sheathing, with only limited amounts of lead patching (Peterson 1973: 123).

A British or British-colonial cultural affiliation is suggested by the presence and absence of a number of factors. The kitchen bricks and tiles fall in the range of statute sizes of English bricks for the period (Noël Hume 1968: 124). Ballast blocks and several copper barrel hoops bear the mark of the British crown—the Broad Arrow. Absent from the wreck are any Spanish-made ceramic storage vessels.

What emerges from these patterns is a reconstructed small British warship from the second quarter of the eighteenth century. From the surviving remains we can ascertain that it may have listed to port at the time it was lost but probably still had some of its rigging and masts standing clear of the water. This interpretation is based on a number of charred pulley sheaves recovered by Gerald Klein. When ships were historically salvaged, they were often burnt to the water line in order to retrieve certain metal fittings more easily. This suggests that some salvage probably took place shortly after the ship was lost, which may also explain the absence of anchors and guns, if they had not been tossed overboard or otherwise lost during the time adrift. Parts of the sides of the vessel are still preserved at the site in the form of two lead scuppers or drains, one on each side. We may also infer that this was not a gentle sinking from evidence preserved in a piece of the standing rigging—an iron-bound deadeye and strap. Deadeyes were large wooden (generally *Lignum vitae*) fasteners that held the tarred lines that in turn supported the masts of the ship. Encircled with a strap fitting made of wrought iron, this particular one shows evidence of twisting and breaking from the fastener or chain-plate that attached it to the hull (figure 8.8), and it was not burnt. Finally, the absence of anchors and a rudder assembly may be significant in the identification of the wreck, vis-à-vis the condition of the deadeye. Their absence might just as easily be the result of later salvage, however, or simple bias in our recovery work.

Figure 8.8. The standing rigging tied the masts to the hull. This rigging passed through the wooden deadeyes (usually made of *Lignum vitae,* a very hard wood). They were held in an iron loop that was then attached to the hull. The example from the Legare Anchorage wreck showed evidence of being wrenched from its attachment to the hull. (Courtesy of the National Park Service/Southeast Archeological Center.)

Is this evidence conclusive? No. The documentary record may have thrown us a curve ball. Our earlier research had shown that during the second quarter of the eighteenth century the 1733 plate fleet (*flota*) had also been lost in this part of Florida (Marx 1969: 47; Meylach 1971: 24). In a deposition taken from a British chief mate in Havana in 1733, it is stated that at least eleven of the ships in the *flota* were of English origin and a significant number of the others were of foreign construction (deposition of Edward MacIver; Calendar of State Papers, America and the West Indies 1733: no. 338ii). Peter Copeland (1969), in his paper on the small arms from the wreck of the *San José,* one of the so-called "ill-fated" ships of the 1733 fleet, references a letter from an English ship's captain who saw the fleet at anchor and attested that the majority of the ships were of non-Spanish origin and that several were of English construction. Copeland proposes that ships purchased by the Spanish might also have all the necessary gear already aboard, including armament; and indeed the English Broad Arrow was located on at least one artifact from the *San José* (Copeland 1969). The Broad Arrow–bearing iron ballast blocks found on the Legare wreck might also support those historic observations.

Could the Legare Anchorage wreck be the remains of a British ship purchased by the Spanish? Were Mendel Peterson and Gerald Klein right? Could it in fact be the site of *Nuestra Señora del Pópulo*? To answer that question, the other artifacts would have to be evaluated.

9

Identification of the *Fowey*

Documents and hunches would be insufficient. The architecture alone could not be relied upon for accurate identification of the wreck. We needed to evaluate everything. To do that, the artifacts needed to be analyzed, identified, and compared to other collections of known age and cultural affiliation. As we had already discovered, short of finding a nameplate, that would be the only way to build a case for a specific identification. This meant using information not only from other shipwrecks but also from terrestrial sites.

When we explain how sites are interpreted to our students we often use the analogy of a book where most of the pages are missing, including the title page, and those that remain are mixed up. Books are made up of individual stories, all tied together, usually with a theme or plot. When many of the pages are missing, it is up to the reader to connect them into specific story lines, themes, or plots. Seeing the story line in part depends on the reader's intelligence and education and in part on cultural perspectives, but in every circumstance we need to look closely at the existing information, look at similar cases, and then fill in the story line based on our best evaluation.

The 1983 work on the Legare Anchorage site revealed the remains of a ship that had listed to port when it settled on the sea floor. How this particular ship exactly sank is unknown. If it rolled or heeled to one side, loose items would have shifted and probably collected on that side of the vessel. As the ship disintegrated, these dislocated items were deposited in discrete locations, reflecting their original clustering on a specific deck. In a relatively low-energy area such as Legare Anchorage, we would expect that this site formation process would leave discernible evidence of activity areas on the ship if the artifacts remained undisturbed. Undocumented or—more to the point—illicit and sloppy retrieval of artifacts destroys the context and thus destroys the necessary information that could reveal discrete activity areas. The artifacts collected by Gerald Klein are an example of lost information. Although they can certainly be considered information from the wreck in a general way, we cannot associate them with a specific area or with any specific actors and activities on the ship. Uncontrolled collecting by anyone results in this same tragic loss of potential information. Similarly, if this collecting is done in conjunction with inappropriate or slovenly excavation techniques (such as the use of a blower, for instance), some artifacts will be displaced from their original provenience and in turn will lose their contextual information. Nonetheless, the range and breadth of the types of artifacts from the Legare Anchorage site told us an interesting story about this ship and its travels.

Weapons

Our initial thought that this was a naval vessel was borne out in the armaments found at the site. In 1980 four guns were observed on the site. Three were capable of firing nine-pound shot, and the fourth could fire eighteen-pound balls. Unit 20 contained the eighteen-pounder gun, while those in Units 19 and 43 are nine-pounders (or 4.22 caliber).

These were muzzle-loading weapons. Cast in iron, the bore would receive a charge of black powder and then an iron ball. A small vent at the breech served as the point of ignition or "touch hole" for the gun. These tubes were supported by protrusions, commonly known as trunnions, on a carriage. The trunnions served as a pivot point for elevating the weapon, while the carriage meant that it could be fired across an arc of nearly 180 degrees. Together they could be used to aim a gun at the enemy. From 1600 to 1850 there was little change in these weapons except in the relative placement of the trunnions. Before 1750 most were positioned below the midline of the tube. Trunnions on the guns found in Legare Anchorage are all placed below the midline.

The first gun, which was retrieved in 1983, bears a significant number of markings and thus much information (figure 9.1). Cast onto the left and right trunnions, respectively, are a "G" and an "H"—probably the makers' marks (figure 9.2a) (Peterson 1973: 154; Peterson 1969: 42). Engraved onto the top of the tube in the first reinforce is the Broad Arrow (figure 9.3), marking ownership by the British Crown, and the numbers "26-0-23," representing the weight of the gun in hundred-weights and fractions thereof. A hundred-weight is 112 pounds. Thus this gun weighs 2,935 pounds and

Figure 9.1. Russell Skowronek in 1987 next to the nine-pounder recovered during the 1983 project. Note the "H" on the right trunnion. The gun's improper display on the lawn led to new deterioration. (Courtesy of the National Park Service/Southeast Archeological Center.)

therefore is the proper size for a nine-pounder. It was always important to know the weight of the gun, in order to be able to set the trim of the ship quickly by balancing the deadweight of the guns.

On the second reinforce is cast a Crowned Tudor Rose, which was used through the reign of Queen Anne (1702–1714) (Gooding 1980: 22; Peterson 1969: 38). Also on the second reinforce, immediately adjacent to the right trunnion, is an incised number "18," representing a date of testing and acceptance by the Board of Ordinance or simply a piece number (Peterson 1973: 110). After initial conservation treatment, this tube was returned to the park, where a staff member reported observing that an original number "49" seemed to have been scratched out and the number "18" stamped over it.

A second tube was the subject of an unauthorized recovery later in 1983 by park staff, under direction of the superintendent at the time. This gun, the nine-pounder that was located in grid Unit 43, was recovered without any archaeological controls. This piece was also transported to the Florida Bureau of Archaeological Research laboratories in Tallahassee, where it was cleaned and underwent conservation treatment. The tube of this second

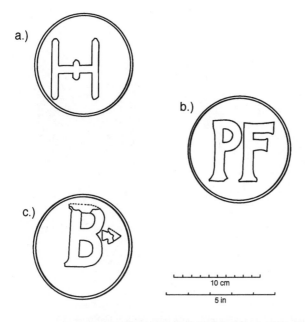

Figure 9.2. A number of distinct founder's marks were discovered on the trunnions of the guns found at the Legare Anchorage site. These include (*a*) a modified letter "H"; (*b*) the letters "PF"; and (*c*) the letter "B" followed by a Broad Arrow. The foundries have not yet been identified. (Courtesy of the National Park Service/Southeast Archeological Center.)

Figure 9.3. Many of the guns carried the Broad Arrow on their tubes. (Courtesy of the National Park Service/Southeast Archeological Center.)

Figure 9.4. Detail of a Crowned Tudor Rose cast onto the second reinforce of each gun. (Courtesy of the National Park Service/Southeast Archeological Center.)

gun bore markings similar to those of the first: the royal Broad Arrow and the Crowned Tudor Rose. The weight marks were 25-3-18, indicating a gun weighing 2,902 pounds. There was also an incised number "19" adjacent to the right trunnion (figure 9.4). The left trunnion of this tube bore no marks. The right trunnion was also marked with the letters "PF" (figure 9.2b).

The third nine-pounder was left at the site. It was marked on the right trunnion with the letter "B" followed by a Broad Arrow (figure 9.2c). Nothing else is known about the eighteen-pounder that was observed but left at the site.

One artifact that should be associated with these large guns is a wrought-iron linchpin 26 cm (10.2 inches) in length. Used to hold the wheels on gun carriages, this cotter-like pin is marked with the Broad Arrow (figure 9.5). Similarly marked linchpins have been reported at Lake George, New York, and in the Citadel in Halifax, Nova Scotia (Calver and Bolton 1950: 217; personal observation, August 15, 1983).

Flintlock mechanisms were used to fire pistols and muskets (Stewart 1980: 6), and a lead-wrapped gun flint was found in Unit 54 adjacent to the shot locker. Similar lead-wrapped flints have been found at West Point (Calver and Bolton 1950: 217). The lead wrap was used to cushion and hold

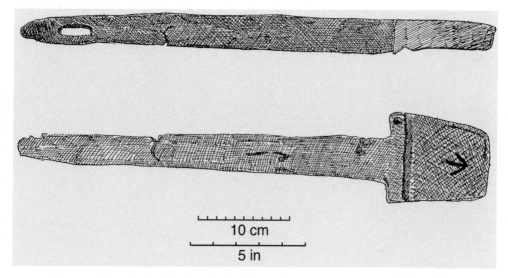

Figure 9.5. Wrought-iron linchpin bearing a Broad Arrow. (Courtesy National Park Service/Southeast Archeological Center)

the flint in the jaws of the cock. No muskets or pistols to go with the flint were recovered, although one .75 caliber lead ball was found in Unit 56. The Gerald Klein collection from the site included twenty-seven pieces of lead shot, varying from .52 to .75 caliber. Eighteenth-century French Charleville muskets fired .69 caliber and smaller shot, whereas British Brown Bess muskets could handle balls as large as .75 caliber. No muskets or pistols (or parts thereof) were found on the site in 1983.

A number of bladed weapons were found on the site. Gerald Klein had recovered two cutlasses, which were permitted to dry without conservation treatment and subsequently disintegrated into fragments. During the 1983 SEAC-sponsored project, two cutlasses, three bayonets, and a boarding axe (figure 9.6a, b, c) were found north and northeast of the site core. The location of these items so far from the site core suggests extensive alteration of the stern area of the ship, where small arms were stored under the watch of the officers and away from the men.

The bladed weapons and spike-headed iron boarding axe are somewhat similar to types found on the 1733 *flota* (Skowronek 1982: 160). Both cutlasses are straight-bladed (29-inch blade, 33.5 inches overall), with an elliptically shaped iron knucklebow fastened flush to the iron grip. One was found still encased in a plain leather scabbard, while the other still had bits

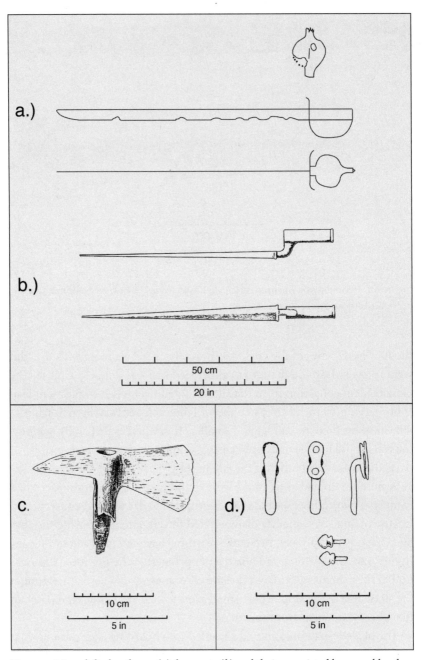

Figure 9.6. Iron hilted cutlasses (*a*), bayonets (*b*) and their associated brass scabbard suspension clips and decorative tips (*d*), and an iron boarding axe (*c*) are some of the weapons found at the Legare Anchorage site. (Drawings by Teresa Paglione and Elwood Mills.)

of leather adhering to the blade. Neumann (Neumann and Kravic 1967: 264) calls these "English cutlasses of standard design." An intact cutlass (albeit unsheathed) of this type is on display at the Salem Maritime National Historic Site (personal observation, August 20, 1983). The three bayonets are all of one style and are all still in their scabbards. Each has a 4-inch socket and an 18-inch blade. In size and socket treatment they match British bayonets used with the Brown Bess musket after 1720 (Neumann and Kravic 1967: 48, 1973: 26, 37). The scabbards are decorated with brass tips and cross-belt clips, which correspond to types found in known English contexts (Grimm 1970: 127, 128, 115; Stone 1974: 197; Hanson and Hsu 1975: 71) (figure 9.6d).

The western margin of the core of the site was littered with a mixture of iron, glass, ceramic, pewter, and brass artifacts that represent a cross section of personal items and objects associated with the officers, marines, tradesmen, or crew of the ship. When these are combined with the artifacts without provenience collected by Gerald Klein and those recovered in the 1980 survey, we can gain a better appreciation for life at sea.

The Crew

Berthed on the gun deck, most common sailors had very few personal belongings. All of what they used on a regular basis would be rolled up in their hammocks during the day. Their best clothes and other more personal items might be stored either on the orlop deck (the lowest deck, used primarily for storage) or in the hold in a sea chest. Those other items often included silver shoe buckles and bright brass-buttoned clothing (Rodger 1986: 64). All used the communal toilets or "heads" (at the head of the ship) and ate communally. A sailor would be part of a mess, a group scheduled to eat together. One of the messmates would bring their food to the others in a communal wooden trencher. Dining would take place at a table suspended between the guns, with each sailor using his own utensils.

The few items owned by sailors on the ship were highly portable but would have been stored with other personal items when not in regular use. Most of these personal items lack precise provenience information. For example twenty-nine pewter spoons may be found in both the Klein and 1980 NPS collections. Some were decorated with initials ("DW," "DMB") or graffiti (figure 9.7).

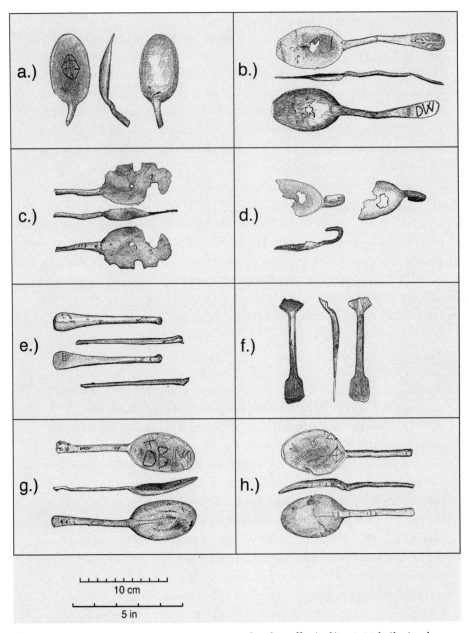

Figure 9.7. Pewter spoons were sometimes engraved with graffiti (*a, h*) or initials (*b, g*); others were left unaltered (*c, d, e, f*). Perhaps "personalized" items were the private property of individual sailors, while unmarked spoons were part of the officers' mess. We will never know because these spoons were found by Klein and hence are without provenience. (Drawings by Teresa Paglione and Elwood Mills.)

One of the problems that emerges in archaeology is the self-fulfilling prophecy. People often only see what they want to see and then argue vociferously for their own personal point of view. When the Legare Anchorage wreck appeared, there was a burgeoning degree of conviction among all the concerned parties that it was a Spanish ship. After the artifacts were examined by Mendel Peterson in 1980, for instance, he suggested that many were similar to those found on a number of Spanish ships lost in the second quarter of the eighteenth century. Was he wrong? No. Perhaps he was asked: "Is there any chance these could be Spanish?" Then the questioners may have heard the various possibilities on how the artifacts might in fact be Spanish—what they wanted to hear. In fact, more complete analysis showed that some of the many artifacts were not really indicative markers of cultural origin. Skowronek's (1984b: 50) study of the 1733 *flota*, for instance, noted that some of the spoons from those obviously Spanish wrecks matched other finds made at French- and English-occupied Fort Michilimackinac in Michigan, Fort Ligonier in Pennsylvania, and Williamsburg, Virginia (Grimm 1970: 148; Noël Hume 1969b: 183; Stone 1974: 185). The Dutch East India ship *Amsterdam* also had spoons in these same forms (Marsden 1974: 177–179). Those spoons also bore graffiti and in some cases the owner's initials. Thus spoons, as a category of artifacts, reveal little that can help us identify a particular ship. Had there been better provenience information, however, we might have gained considerable insight into how they were stored when not in use, which would have been interesting in its own right.

Twenty brass, pewter, and silver buckles were found by Klein and again during the initial 1980 project (figure 9.8). Those recovered would have been used to secure shoes, belts, and other leather goods. Once again, they are similar in form to those found on other foreign vessels, such as the ships of the 1733 *flota* and the *Amsterdam* (Marsden 1974: 170–171; Skowronek 1984b: 117–127) and therefore have little value in identifying the particular ship.

The maintenance of the ship and crew fell to the warrant officers and their mates. These included gunners, armorers, coopers and carpenters, sailmakers, and surgeons. The Legare Anchorage wreck contained artifacts that can be associated with these specialists.

The gunner was charged with caring for the guns and shot. One of his tools was a flat, circular bronze cannonball gauge. Found in Unit 69, adjacent to the presumed shot locker, it is 13 cm in diameter and is similar

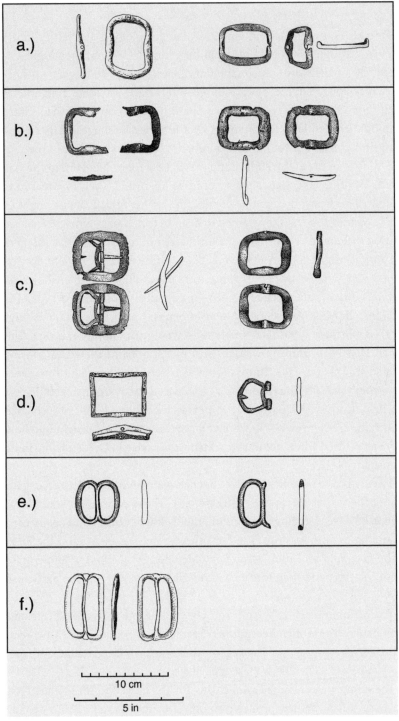

Figure 9.8. Brass, pewter, and silver shoe buckles (*a, b, c, d*) and brass cross-belt buckles (*e, f*) were found by Klein and during the 1983 project. (Drawings by Teresa Paglione and Elwood Mills.)

to ones found in the *Amsterdam*, lost in 1748. Armorers would have been responsible for small arms, repairing muskets and pistols and sharpening cutlasses. Two of the recovered objects were hones or whetstones used for sharpening edged tools or weapons. Sailmakers made and repaired sails and the lines that composed the running rigging of the ship. A metal "thimble" or sailor's palm, for pushing needles through the heavy canvas of the sails, was found (figure 9.9a). Coopers and carpenters would have made repairs to the vessel and ensured that barrels and other wooden containers were sound. An adze blade for thinning and trimming lumber was recovered by Gerald Klein (figure 9.9b). Another specialized tool was an iron hammer with a fid-shaped handle (9.9c). A fid is used when splicing rope together.

Physician/surgeons were an important part of a naval ship's crew. Broken limbs, ruptures, wounds, and a variety of illnesses killed on the average 6 percent of Royal Navy crews in the 1740s (Marcus 1975: 128–142; Rodger 1986: 99, 103–104). The Legare Anchorage ship most likely had one of these specialists or someone who served in that capacity on board. Compelling evidence from the Klein collection includes a brass double-headed pestle for powdering herbs and medicines and a combination pewter bedpan/urinal (figure 9.10). Mendel Peterson noted during his evaluation of the bedpan that a similar one was found on the *Tolosa*, a Spanish ship lost in 1724.

Pharmaceutical glass is an all-encompassing category of artifacts that embraces everything from small vials (or phials) to flasks and bottles, which once held any special liquid such as perfumes, patent medicines, or drugs (Noël Hume 1969b: 72–76). Glassware classed in this category is usually distinguished by its range of color (e.g., light green, aqua, amber), thin walls, and flattened lip or flaring mouth. Within this category, one item recovered was a small pale green bottle base, with a pronounced conical kick-up (depression in the base), found during the 1980 NPS project. Many authoritative works on the subject of pharmaceuticals have been written (Noël Hume 1969b; Brown 1971; Smith 1981), based on collections that have survived in a relatively intact condition. The collection from the Legare Anchorage site was extremely small and very fragmentary. For these reasons, the sample was subjectively classified based on the qualitative categories of color and thickness. Rim and base shapes, when identified, appear similar in color and style to a bottle dated to 1730 by Ivor Noël Hume (1969b: 7) and to other fragments in the Klein collection. Similar pale green pharmaceutical bottles with everted lips were recovered at Fort Frederica, Georgia,

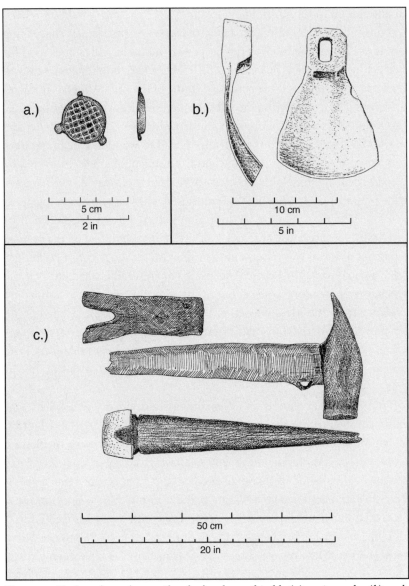

Figure 9.9. Tools such as a brass sail maker's palm or thimble (*a*), an iron adze (*b*), and a combination iron claw hammer/fid (*c*) were found at the site. (Drawings by Teresa Paglione and Elwood Mills.)

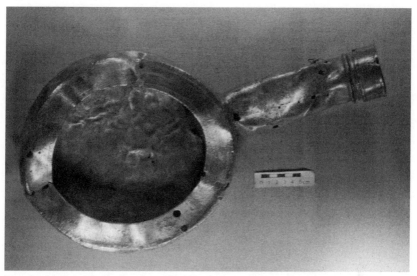

Figure 9.10. A pewter bedpan must have been part of the surgeon's stores. (Courtesy of the National Park Service/Southeast Archeological Center.)

a British site dating from the second third of the eighteenth century. Associated with these fragments are two green ground-glass bottle stoppers (4 cm × 1.7 cm) from both the Klein and 1983 collections that match one recovered at Fort Ligonier (Grimm 1970: 153, 169). Whatever the original functions of the glass vials and stoppers were at the site, it is assumed that the very delicate nature of the vials made them more likely to have been in the possession of either an officer or a specialist such as a physician, who knew and appreciated the value of the small quantity of liquid therein, and not in the gnarly hands of a common seaman.

The Officers

On naval vessels officers supervised shipboard activities and oversaw the navigation of the ship. A number of the artifacts found by Gerald Klein or during the 1980 and 1983 projects were navigational tools. Two pairs of iron dividers (10 and 12 cm long, one possibly brass-plated) were recovered from the site core (figure 9.11a). They are similar to dividers reported from Fort Michilimackinac (Stone 1974: 298, 310). A brass-bound wooden folding ruler (3.8 cm wide) may be just that or may possibly be an artillerist's brass gauge and angle finder (Neumann and Kravic 1975: 18).

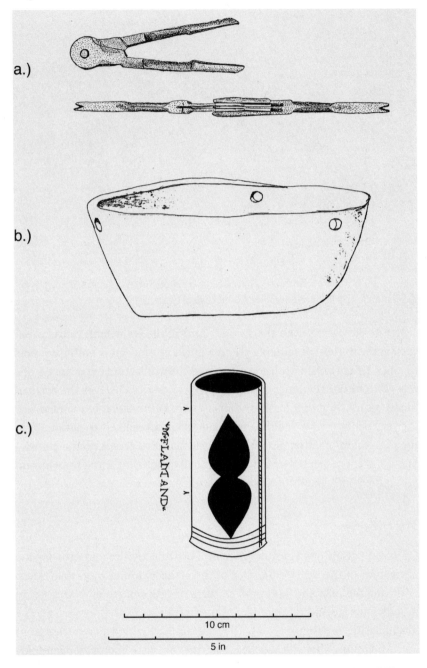

Figure 9.11. Navigational tools included brass dividers (*a*), a lead compass bowl (*b*), and a brass mercury timing glass (*c*). The timing glass bears the maker's name "M. Flamand." (Drawings by Teresa Paglione and Elwood Mills.)

The Klein collection contained a lead compass-bowl (figure 9.11b) and other compass-related artifacts. Mendel Peterson noted that "similar" compasses had been found on the 1733 fleet. Another item, found in 1980, is the brass case for a mercury timing glass. Used by the navigator to time the log line, the case is engraved with the name "M. Flamand" (figure 9.11c) and is thought to be French-made. Peterson noted in his examination that "similar" items had been found on Spanish shipwreck sites in Bermuda.

Life among the officers of a naval vessel was considerably better than the life experienced by their crew. The captain's cabin was located in the stern of the ship. Forward of that the commissioned officers berthed in the after end of the main deck, in the area known as the wardroom, and the remaining warrant and inferior officers occupied the aftermost part of the gun deck, away from the crew. Officers were somewhat limited in what they could take to sea but nonetheless enjoyed a far more genteel lifestyle than did the crew. Most had small private cabins and washroom. They took their meals together, but they enjoyed eating their repast from individual pewter and ceramic plates. Officers also had access to wine and other spirits.

Officers' "country" was identifiable in the collections from the Legare Anchorage site. This included a fragment of "bull's-eye" window glass. This variety of window glass is discussed by Noël Hume (1969b: 234). Panes were 16.5 cm–square and were light green in color, with the bull's-eye resulting from the spinning of the glass on a "pontil" while in molten form, much like the spinning of pizza dough, to create a large flattened piece, which was then cut to size to fit the stern window frames. Evidence for a washroom was inadvertently discovered by Gerald Klein during his amateur treasure salvage recoveries. A section of lead pipe with a copper petcock was recovered (figure 9.12). It is a superb example of shipboard plumbing. Before visiting their washroom, the denizens of the wardroom had the opportunity to enjoy the bounty of their larder in either their candle-lit cabins or the wardroom. The washroom was undoubtedly for the exclusive use of the officers, since the crew was "washed" often enough by the weather.

Fragments of two brass candlestick holders were found during the 1980 and 1983 projects. According to conservators at the Florida Bureau of Archaeological Research, they look "remarkably similar" to one found on the *San José*, based on the way it was made (Skowronek 1984b: 150, 152). Noël Hume (1969b: 94) believes that this form dates to the early eighteenth century and may originally have been Dutch or Flemish in origin. The *Amsterdam* also contained similar candlesticks (Marsden 1974: 170–171). Thus

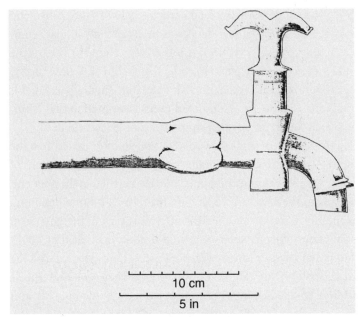

Figure 9.12. Lead and copper plumbing fixtures were one of the "perks" of being an officer. (Drawing by Teresa Paglione and Elwood Mills.)

the candlesticks, although handsome and functional, did not help in the identification of the wreck's age or cultural affiliation.

Artifacts made of fragile materials such as glass and ceramics are sometimes the best objects to use for identifying the age and cultural affiliation of a site. That is because these items have a relatively short use-life and are generally inexpensive to produce, thus quickly changing style over time.

BISC-UW-20 was strewn with fragments of dark-green bottle glass from both case (gin, rum, and other spirits) and round (wine) bottles. The few neck-and-mouth fragments that were recovered all had well-applied string rims. By far the most intact parts of all bottles observed and/or recovered were their bases. In 1983 forty-two bottle bases were recovered. They had an average basal diameter of 10.79 cm, with a kick-up height of 5.117 cm. The five intact bottles from the Klein collection and the neck and rim fragments found in 1980 mirrored these finds (figure 9.13). These measures and bottle styles match examples identified as being English in origin by Noël Hume (1969b: 65) and dated to 1740.

The contents of these bottles may well have been sampled in what are known as stemmed tavern glasses. Examples of two of these heavy glasses

Figure 9.13. Dark-green glass bottles match those associated with English-made forms made circa 1740. (Courtesy of the National Park Service/Southeast Archeological Center.)

were found by Klein and NPS-1980. Because of their weight, it is thought that they are English in origin and were made prior to 1745, when the Glass Excise Tax was passed (Noël Hume 1969b: 192). Another solid drawn wine glass stem is identical to a collection from Port Royal and dated to the period 1725–1745 (Noël Hume 1968: 15, 31). The glass artifacts point to a date in the second quarter of the eighteenth century and English manufacture.

In addition to glass artifacts, officers had access to pewter tablewares. Three pewter plates (figure 9.14), all 23 cm in diameter, were found and recovered in 1983. Touch marks indicate that they and an accompanying pewter cup (figure 9.15) were made in London. Stylistically, the Legare Anchorage site pewter plates match similar pewter (Neumann and Kravic 1975: 111) and silver (Skowronek 1982: 53) plate specimens elsewhere from the eighteenth century. The Klein collection also had other pewter tablewares. One, a small basin, had identifiable hallmarks associated with the Tidmarsh family of London (figure 9.16). Their pewter was manufactured from 1691 through 1752 (Masse 1921 [2004]: 211–212). The other was a dou-

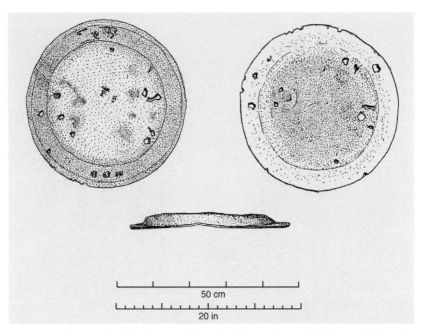

Figure 9.14. Pewter plate found on the site. (Drawings by Teresa Paglione and Elwood Mills.)

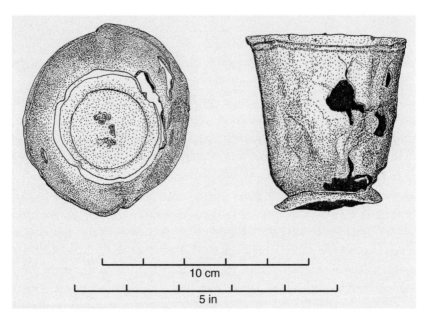

Figure 9.15. Pewter cup found on the site. (Drawings by Teresa Paglione and Elwood Mills.)

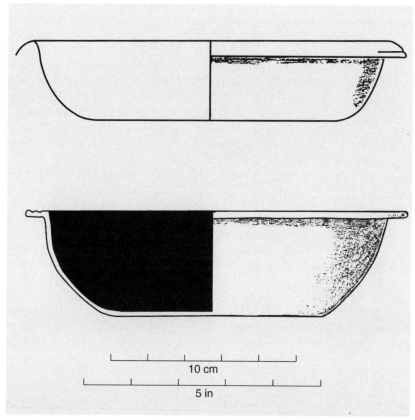

Figure 9.16. Pewter basin found on the site. (Drawings by Teresa Paglione and Elwood Mills.)

ble-handled pewter porringer (figure 9.17). These durable English-made artifacts again point to the first half of the eighteenth century.

Salt cellars were also used on the mess-room table. Two salt cellars were found in 1983 (figure 9.18). Molded in clear common glass, they were wheel-engraved: one with a daisy motif (6.9 cm × 8.2 cm) and the other with a herring-bone pattern (7.3 cm × 6.4 cm) (McNally 1982: 146). The Klein collection contains a fragment of a third salt cellar. Mendel Peterson felt that it was "probably" of English origin although it was "possibly" Spanish. A similar one has also been found at Fort Frederica in Georgia. Once again, it is an artifact that does not provide any further definitive insight into the cultural affiliation of the wreck.

The Legare Anchorage site contained both tablewares and utilitarian ceramic wares, of which tablewares were the majority (85 percent). Ceramics

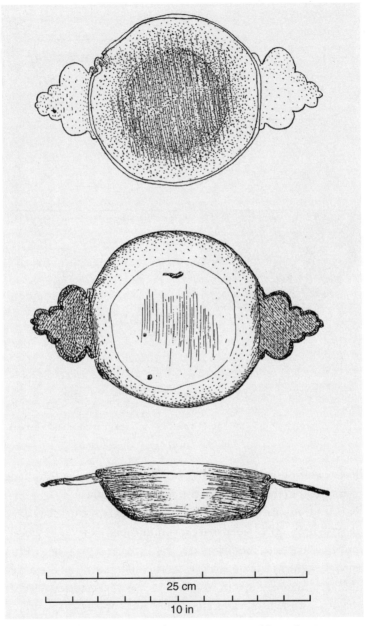

Figure 9.17. Pewter double-handled porringer recovered from the site.
(Drawings by Teresa Paglione and Elwood Mills.)

Figure 9.18. "Place setting" of pewter tablewares, a glass salt cellar, wine bottles, and a French faience pitcher. (Courtesy of the National Park Service/Southeast Archeological Center.)

are important to archaeologists because their decoration and construction technique are sensitive indicators of the date and place of fabrication. Furthermore, their inherent fragility, especially in shipboard contexts, makes them especially useful in understanding the ship and its travels. Unlike the 1733 *flota*, which was filled with thousands of sherds of tin-glazed ceramics from Puebla and some Chinese-made porcelains, no Mexican-made or Mexican-trade ceramics were found on the Legare Anchorage site (Skowronek 1984b).

Ceramics recovered from the Legare Anchorage Shipwreck included French-made tin-glazed ceramic known as faience, some Chinese-made porcelain, and a variety of English-made stone wares, tin-glazed ceramics known as delftware, and various glazed and unglazed coarse earthenwares.

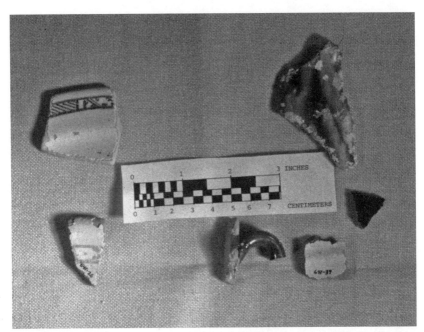

Figure 9.19. Fragments of French-made plain white, blue-on-white, and brown faience were recovered on the site. (Courtesy of the National Park Service/Southeast Archeological Center.)

Fragments of French-made faience included plain white, blue-on-white, and exterior brown (figure 9.19). The brown faience had a robin's-egg blue tin-glazed interior and a brown lead-glazed exterior. The Gerald Klein collection includes two nearly intact ceramic pitchers decorated in this way (figure 9.18). Nicholas Honerkamp of the University of Tennessee and Kathleen Deagan of the University of Florida examined these ceramic vessels and dated them between 1730 and 1760, based on their respective studies at Fort Frederica, Georgia, and St. Augustine, Florida. Two fragments of Chinese-made underglazed blue-on-white porcelain were also found at the site during the 1980 and 1983 projects. As a major trade item, porcelain had been exported from China for more than two centuries by the mid-eighteenth century, through the Philippines to Mexico and then on to Europe. As a result, it occurs widely in colonial America and is not especially datable or attributable to a specific ethnic group.

In 1980 a fragment of a Rhenish gray-stoneware mug was found bearing the cipher "GR" (for George Rex), standing for the English monarch George I (1714–1727) or his son George II (1727–1760). The mold was used over the entire forty-six-year period and thus does not represent a specific date for fabrication or use (Noël Hume 1969b).

Plain, blue-on-white, and polychrome English delftwares were recovered (figure 9.20). One blue-on-white sherd is of the Mimosa pattern, which dates from 1690 to 1740 (Garner 1948: 22, 32–33). Interestingly, both were decorated with parrots.

One sherd of coarse earthenware with red paste and an interior brown slip is similar to sherds described from Fort Michilimackinac as possibly of American colonial origin (Miller and Stone 1970: 51).

The small number of sherds and their great variety support the notion that this was a warship. The quality and quantity of these ceramics, unlike those cargo items associated with the 1733 *flota*, do not indicate anything other than personal use.

Dating this ceramic assemblage accurately, however, presents some problems. Most of the types represented, including delftware, faience, and Rhenish stoneware, were manufactured throughout the seventeenth and eighteenth centuries. The TPQ or *terminus post quem* (Latin for "date after

Figure 9.20. Plain white, blue-on-white, and polychrome English-made delftwares as well as fragments of agatewares were found. (Courtesy of the National Park Service/ Southeast Archeological Center.)

which," meaning the date after which an event could occur: the earliest possible date) for the formation of the archaeological site was provided by one sherd of agateware. Archaeologists look for artifacts with well-known dates of production. If a coin is found that is dated 2000 in a "closed context" then that context was not formed until 2000 or later. The ceramic type known as agateware was first produced in 1740, seven years after the demise of the 1733 *flota*. Thus the Legare Anchorage wreck had to have occurred after the date of 1740, thus eliminating any possible connection to the Spanish catastrophe. How convenient! Yet the convenience was short-lived . . .

Scientists are obliged to interpret everything they find. They cannot ignore artifacts that fail to fit and must find a way to explain how the objects arrived on the site. Also found on the Legare Anchorage site was one errant sherd of hand-painted blue-on-white pearlware, which caused great consternation. Some discussion is necessary to explain why it does not belong in this assemblage. It is well known that lead-glazed refined earthenwares and white salt-glazed stonewares became popular very quickly after being introduced in the 1750s. Many of the tin-glazed coarse earthenwares represented in our collection rapidly declined in popularity as a result. An assemblage containing pearlware would very likely be dominated by creamware, pearlware, and white salt-glazed stoneware. Since this assemblage is not so dominated, we must assume that the pearlware sherd discovered in 1983 arrived there by accident at a later date. In 1993 the Submerged Cultural Resources Unit found two other ceramic sherds that were similarly troubling (Adams 1996: 34). The lack of a report detailing the finds of that project is problematic, because it is not clear whether they might be from the same ceramic vessel found a decade earlier (possible, although unlikely). Pearlware has a TPQ of 1780, which would rule out the wreck site as the *Fowey*. At the same time, this also forces us to look for a possible source of contamination.

Legare Anchorage is named for the USS *Legare*. This vessel anchored here in 1855 while making detailed nautical charts of the area. Pearlware ceramics were still very much a part of the material culture in 1855. The errant sherd found in 1983, as well as those found in 1993, could well have been deposited during the visit of the *Legare*. Others will need to study the reports associated with its cruise to ascertain if they encountered the wreck; otherwise, it seems implausible that the *Legare* would anchor directly atop the earlier wreck site and inadvertently contaminate the site by tossing a broken teacup or two over the side.

Notwithstanding these considerations, the overwhelming bulk of the evidence indicates that the ship can be dated to post-1740 and pre-1750s. The latter date is derived from the absence of white salt-glazed stoneware and creamware on the site. This is also known as the TAQ or *terminus ante quem* ("date before which" an event can only occur). Some inventions are immediate successes. They are so popular that they seem to appear everywhere at once. The absence of such items, known as "horizon markers" to archaeologists, can provide a TAQ for an archaeological site. The absence of white salt-glazed stoneware and creamware, two ceramic types ubiquitous on English colonial sites in the 1750s onward, supports the idea that the ship sank before the middle of the eighteenth century.

We can say with 99 percent certainty that, based on the makeup of the ceramic assemblage, this was not a Spanish vessel. The absence of Mexican-made majolicas and olive jar storage containers, which are ubiquitous on Spanish vessels of the era, precludes that affiliation. The ceramic assemblage does not, however, point unanimously to a British origin for this ship. A quarter of the assemblage is unquestionably English in origin, while another 9 percent is possibly English. In contrast, 15 percent of the sherds are French in origin. The remaining ceramics consist of stonewares, porcelain, and coarse earthenwares of various or indeterminable origins. Stoneware and porcelain were imported by both France and Great Britain from Spanish sources, as well as being captured and pillaged. So, although it is definitely not Spanish, the ceramic assemblage cannot be positively considered either English or French (Vernon 1984: 2–4).

Interpretation of the vessel's age, function, and cultural affiliation flows from the identification of the complete collection of artifactual materials and structural remains.

Interpretation of the ceramic and glass assemblages suggests a date between 1740 and 1750. Similarly, the presence of iron ballast blocks and a lack of copper sheathing imply the second quarter of the eighteenth century. Evidence from the guns, including the presence of the crowned Tudor Rose motif and the placement of the trunnions below the midline of the tube, suggests that it dates to the first half of the eighteenth century.

The ship functioned as a warship and not as a cargo vessel. This interpretation is based on the multiple sizes of the guns. Additionally, there were small arms, including cutlasses and axes. We can infer that there were muskets, because we have found bayonets for exclusive use on the Brown Bess musket (Neumann and Kravic 1967, 1975). Those found at the Legare

Anchorage site were lying in scabbards decorated with brass fittings that match those used by the British Army and Royal Marines. This suggests that a contingent of marines was on board. Marines were a part of the company of all British warships.

Finally, the cultural affiliation of the vessel is somewhat more difficult to ascertain. Nonceramic artifacts suggest a British or British-colonial origin. The guns, ballast, and a gun carriage linchpin were marked with the Broad Arrow, the mark denoting ownership by the British Crown. The wine bottles morphologically appear English in origin (Noël Hume 1969b: 65), as do the pewter and glass tablewares. Recovered iron-hilted cutlasses match known English types in size and style (Neumann and Kravic 1967: 264), as do the scabbarded bayonets with brass clips and tips (Neumann and Kravic 1975: 30, 36, 37, 39). Further, the guns are cast with a Crowned Tudor Rose, an English mark indicative of the royal family until 1714 (Peterson 1969: 28), but which continued in use until later in the century (David Lyon, personal communication, October 2, 1986).

It is the ceramics that are problematic, because they contain both French- and English-made materials. Certainly, these materials were widely exchanged: they are broadly found in sites in the English, French, and Spanish New World colonies. Does it make sense to find a mixture of this kind on a naval vessel?

The picture comes into clear focus when the documentary evidence is added to the evidence of the material. The archaeological picture painted from the data presented shows a warship dating from the second quarter of the eighteenth century. Artifacts from the site exhibit a general English affiliation, with some predilection for certain French items. There are no indications of Spanish materials.

Given the remains, an identity from the historic record is fairly simple. Only four relevant wrecks consistent with interpretations of the recovered material culture are documented as being lost in the vicinity of what is now Biscayne National Park: two ships of the 1733 *flota*, *Fowey*'s prize the *Judah*, and HMS *Fowey*, lost in 1748. Supporting a 1733 *flota* identification is historical documentation that described the fleet's pre-Hispanic multi-national construction and ownership (Marx 1979). This corresponds with the mixed picture presented by the archaeologically collected data. Data from salvaged wrecks of the same fleet, however, indicate that these ships should have been ballasted exclusively with stone and that the site should have been littered with Spanish or Spanish-colonial ceramics, including the ubiquitous olive jar. The presence of olive jar storage containers would correspond with a lack of barrel hoops, bottles, and other European ceramics (Skowronek 1984b).

The Legare Anchorage site fails to meet these criteria for those Spanish ships or for the *Judah* (*St. Judea*). A better candidate for the vessel's identity is HMS *Fowey*. Classed as a fifth-rate Royal Navy vessel, 127 feet in length and 36 feet in beam (Colledge 1969: 218) and mounting a total of forty-four six-, nine-, and eighteen-pound guns, the *Fowey* matched the guidelines established by the Admiralty for the armament of vessels of that size (ADM 1/5292; Peterson 1973: 111). Movements of the vessel are known from its construction in Hull, England, in 1744 to its loss on "the Cape of Florida" in 1748. During 1744 and 1745 the *Fowey* was active in the English Channel and in the waters off Gibraltar (Nova Scotia Archives MG100, vol. 178, no. 12 and RG1, vol. 19). In the spring of 1746 *Fowey* escorted troop transports to the recently captured fortress of Louisbourg, Nova Scotia (where possibly they helped themselves to certain French-made goods) and was then reassigned to a split duty station off the Virginia coast in the summer and the Caribbean in the winter. At one point it was the only British naval vessel patrolling the coastal waters south of Boston to the coast of South Carolina. The following May (1747) HMS *Fowey* returned for a three-week stay at Louisbourg (ADM 7/571/171). During January 1748 *Fowey* captured a French prize and participated in the attack on the French island of Guadeloupe. In June a Spanish ship, the *Judah* or *St. Judea*, was taken while *Fowey* was stationed in the Caribbean (ADM 36/1187). It was while escorting the *Judah* and two New England merchant ships north to Virginia that the unsheathed *Fowey* was lost on the Florida coast (ADM 1/234, p. 157). The court-martial proceedings (ADM 1/5292) make it clear that following the initial grounding of the ship at 25 degrees 25 minutes north, on the morning of June 27, 1748, Captain Francis William Drake disabled and hove overboard his six-pounders, two nine-pounders, and one eighteen-pounder in a vain attempt to lighten and free the *Fowey*. Then one anchor was lost in an attempt to pull *Fowey* free. At five in the afternoon, after thirteen to fourteen hours on the reef, *Fowey* floated free. This freedom was short-lived, however, because the ship immediately grounded again. This time the *Fowey* was bilged or stove in, and the water began to rise in the hold as the ship floated free a second time and drifted north with the Gulf Stream (May 1958).

By four in the morning of June, 28, 1748, the water in the hold was over two feet deep. Captain Drake and his officers decided that the now-anchored *Fowey* was lost. They determined that it would be better to drive the ship aground onto the reef rather than allow it to sink in four fathoms of water, where lives might be lost. Having made the decision, they cut their second anchor line. *Fowey*'s sturdy construction must have awed its officers, for it broke over the reef, lost its rudder, and continued to drift. Drake set small sails and put out sweeps by which to steer the now rudderless vessel. At 4:30 he let go his sheet anchor, the last one. He ordered all guns to be spiked and the small arms (with the exception of thirty-three muskets) thrown overboard. The launch, cutter, and long-boat transported the crew to the accompanying merchantmen, while the carpenter cut away the foremast and bowsprit and scuttled the ship by opening the sea stopcocks in the hold.

Archaeological research has provided the Legare Anchorage site with form, age, function, and cultural affiliation. A British warship from the 1740s is known in shadow form. The data show that the Legare Anchorage wreck matches the historic *Fowey* in age, function, and cultural affiliation. It also matches the location given by *Fowey*'s pilot, Robert Bishop, when quoted in a later survey of the Florida coast (Romans 1775 [1962], 1775 [1999]). This correlation is based on the presence and absence of key known items from the ship and reference to historical documents. These matches include an unsheathed bottom; sweep ports; six-, nine-, and eighteen- pound shot; nine- and eighteen-pounder guns; and bladed weapons. Absent from both the *Fowey* and the Legare wreck at the time of sinking and/or archaeological recovery were anchors, six-pounder guns, small arms, rudder assemblies, and large quantities of personal items. Coincidental is the presence of faience ceramic wares matching types known to be present in 1745–1747 contexts at Louisbourg, a port visited twice by this particular historic *Fowey*. There are discrepancies, however. If the Legare Anchorage wreck is the *Fowey*, where are the missing thirty-seven guns, and why do the recovered guns bear no signs of spiking? Is this a case of reading between the lines: the difference between an action and an order? We may see human nature at work, with the ship's officers not acknowledging their own failure to comply with standing orders.

Or perhaps the vessel was salvaged by the Spanish. The crew of the *St. Judea* sailed to Havana. Did they lead a salvage team to the wreck site, where the surviving superstructure was burnt for ship fittings and many of the guns were salvaged? Or were many of the guns salvaged by treasure hunters in the 1950s and 1960s?

No identification can be absolutely certain; but until a new, better, and even incontrovertible argument becomes available that can discount this mountain of historic, archaeological, and circumstantial evidence, the Legare Anchorage Shipwreck site of Biscayne National Park must be considered the resting place of His Majesty's Ship *Fowey*.

Fowey found!

10

The Final Legal Salvo

Setting an Important Legal Precedent

From *Perry Mason* to *Law and Order*, we have come to believe that the wheels of justice turn quickly and that justice can and will be meted out in roughly sixty minutes, less commercials. Reality is far from this. While the assessment of the research was underway, the continuing legal battles were slowly being ground out in the courtroom. The following account can be reconstructed from court records and information from those who were present. We provide this account to try to untangle its complicated web and to clarify how the case shook out through time.

Following the success of the summer 1980 search, in October 1980 attorneys for Gerald Klein requested detailed information on the results of that initial archaeological project. This request included a list of the participants, the discoveries, and the number of dives made. About this same time the Southeast Archeological Center learned that at Klein's restaurant, Joan's Galley, a "Treasure Hunt Special" was being offered with dinner after 5 p.m. With that purchase, the diner would receive a "Free treasure map of authentic sunken galleon with cannons, artifacts etc." (figure 10.1) in the form of a place mat that precisely recorded the location of the Legare Anchorage wreck. Since it had been taken from him by the court, Klein decided to publish its location for the world. From the perspective of the court, that was not a wise move, because it undermined the plaintiff's sincerity in doing right by the site.

A month later, on November 19, attorney Rebecca Donnellan provided the requested information regarding the activities of that summer's project. Included in the "interrogatories" was a list of finds, one of which noted that five fragments of Spanish ceramics were recovered. In fact, none were of Spanish or Spanish-colonial origin.

Figure 10.1. Place mat from Joan's Galley. (Courtesy of the National Park Service, Southeast Archeological Center.)

On December 15, a year after Klein's lawyers had submitted a "Memorandum of Law" arguing for "the predominance of Admiralty and Maritime law over the regulations of the NPS," a hearing was held in Key West to determine if the Southern District Court had admiralty jurisdiction that would include wrecks within the national park. No decision was made at that time, but the presiding judge took it under advisement.

Seven months later, on July 7, 1981, the U.S. District Court ordered an end to "any and all salvage operations" by Gerald Klein. This was followed a month later, on August 10, by a hearing in Key West regarding the interrogatories and the information contained therein. On October 24 attorneys for Gerald Klein filed a motion to produce the artifacts collected in the NPS 1980 Project in court. Fischer and the National Park Service said that was impossible, given the fact that they were undergoing conservation treatment.

Gerald Joseph Klein was murdered in Miami on January 1, 1982, during an armed robbery of Joan's Galley, adding a tragic but bizarre dimension to the case. His family decided to continue in the quest for title to the wreck.

His ashes were later scattered on the site, which seemed fitting, because the shipwreck had meant so much to him. The court noted, however, that it was in violation of the restraining order for Klein's associates to be on the site. The archaeologists felt that this did not represent any adverse impact on the site and in fact was probably minimally useful in reburying it.

Nothing happened for the rest of 1982 until December 12, when the case was transferred from Judge James Lawrence King, whose docket was filled, back to Judge Alcee Hastings. It was felt at the time that Hastings was more sympathetic to the case presented by the federal government because Judge King had ruled in favor of Mel Fisher against the State of Florida in 1981, regarding the ownership of a Spanish wreck dating from 1715. Unfortunately for the government, Judge Hastings was not hearing cases because of a number of bribery accusations against him.

Almost a year had passed when Judge Hastings resigned on February 4, 1983, and moved on to other things. At that time more information was revealed that would further prejudice the case against Klein, when seven witnesses came forward saying that they dove with Gerald Klein on the wreck. In earlier depositions he had said there were only five.

At the end of February the photo-mosaic of the site and color slides of the Legare Anchorage wreck taken in July 1980 were provided for the legal proceedings by the Southeast Archeological Center.

About this time, Fischer recalls:

I personally asked our assistant regional director where we stood in terms of jurisdiction. He said it had been cleared with the Justice Department that we were to treat the salvor's collection as if it was our own, in matters of conservation and curation, and were free to collect further materials from the site as was appropriate within constraints of NPS policy, an approved research design, and a Section 106 Statement (historic preservation compliance statement, to the uninitiated). Both these documents were required by the NPS anyway for any research involving possible disturbance of archaeological resources. As depredations and looting of the wreck were continuing, despite the court's order, which arrested and gave judicial protection to the site, the court granted the NPS permission to conduct limited testing and evaluation of the wreck in order to determine more definitely the historical parameters, and possible identity of the site, and to initiate means for its short- and long-term conservation and protection.

Plans were formulated at the Southeast Archeological Center in Tallahassee for a testing and evaluation project to determine the "age, function, and cultural affiliation" of the Legare Anchorage wreck. This work could only proceed with the permission of the court, because the July 7, 1981, order had ended "any and all salvage operations."

On May 4, 1983, Rebecca Donnellan asked the U.S. District Court to modify the restraining order to allow for archaeological testing and evaluation of the site. Nine days later, on May 13, Judge C. Clyde Atkins ordered that the United States could conduct "salvage [*sic*]" on the Legare Anchorage Shipwreck.

Within a few weeks the joint National Park Service–Florida State University project was fielded that successfully tested and evaluated the wreck site.

After nearly four years of litigation, the case finally went to trial in the spring of 1983. George Fischer remembers it as clearly as if it were yesterday: "I was the sole Government witness that very long afternoon and found that position, and the attention, very uncomfortable."

The case was ultimately decided in favor of the ship (and the United States). The judge noted that in terms of the salvage requirement of "marine peril," the site had apparently been snugly buried and relatively stable, and no peril appeared to exist until the salvor began work on the site (a critical element in the trial).

On July 28 Judge C. Clyde Atkins submitted his final opinion on the ownership of the Legare Anchorage wreck. In the Findings of Fact and Conclusions of Law, Judge Atkins rejected Gerald Klein's claim and found that the wreck was in fact the property of the United States. He noted that the wreck was embedded in the seabed (another critical element) and was within the confines of Biscayne National Park and that Klein had not applied for a permit for exploration as laid out in the Antiquities Act of 1906. He also rejected the claim for a liberal salvage award. Judge Atkins was already impressed with the precisely scaled photo-mosaic and the 30-minute videotape made in 1980. With those documents in hand, and the rest of the information collected subsequently, the judge understood that the members of the Park Service knew what they were doing and could protect the site. He commented on this in his decision, a third critical element in the trial: "Unfortunately, the plaintiff's unauthorized disturbance of one of the oldest shipwrecks in the park, and his unscientific removal of the artifacts, did more to create a marine peril than to prevent one" (*Orlando Sentinel*, July 29, 1983, p. B-5).

So the judge thought that the ship was more in need of rescue from the salvors than from the ravages of the sea and time, and the legal owner did not want it rescued anyway.

On Tuesday, August 2, 1983, the District Court for the Southern District of Florida at Miami upheld the claim of the United States to title to the ship. All this represented a reversal in the tide of treasure salvage litigation in the United States. This landmark decision formed the legal foundation that Congress followed in the Abandoned Shipwreck Act of 1987. Moreover, it was the precedent or basis for several subsequent legal actions protective of these irreplaceable cultural resources, including the *Craft* (CV 92 1769 [1992]) case (Channel Islands National Marine Sanctuary), *Lathrop* v. *The Unidentified, Wrecked & Abandoned Vessel* (817 F. Supp. 953 [M.D. Fla. 1993]) (Canaveral National Seashore), and *U.S.* v. *Fisher* (No. 92-10027 [S.D. Fla. 1997]) (Florida Keys National Marine Sanctuary).

In *Lathrop* v. *The Unidentified, Wrecked & Abandoned Vessel*, the United States successfully argued that Randy Lathrop, who was salvaging an alleged eighteenth-century Spanish galleon without a permit in Canaveral National Seashore, needed both an Antiquities Act permit and a Rivers and Harbors Act dredge and fill permit. Lathrop took the position that admiralty law exempted him from complying with any act of Congress such as the Antiquities Act or the Rivers and Harbors Act. The United States countered by arguing that several congressional enactments, including both of these acts, were enforceable against Lathrop, as the substantive law of admiralty can be modified and/or supplemented.

In August 1984 an appeal of the findings of Judge Atkins was argued at the U.S. Court of Appeals, Eleventh Circuit. Klein's lawyers appealed on January 4, 1985; but four months later, on April 29, 1985, the Court of Appeals affirmed the U.S. District Court decision in favor of the United States. Though it was upheld on appeal, there was one dissension. The dissenting judge felt that the Justice Department should also have pursued a case against the salvor, for violation of the Antiquities Act of 1906.

As indicated above, the precedent had now been set for the government to prevent looting and unwanted salvage of historic shipwrecks that are owned or controlled in federal marine protected areas. This test case meant the supremacy of federal ownership or control over the law of finds in the United States. Ole Varmer (personnel communication, February 2008), attorney for the National Oceanic and Atmospheric Administration (NOAA), observed:

> I agree that Antiquities Act is part of the decision; however, the court primarily relied on a property law concept—an exception to the law of finds. In the subsequent NOAA cases we convinced federal admiralty court judges of the Supremacy of the National Marine Sanctuary Act, but it was also important in our arguments to note how the application of the NMSA was also consistent with the Klein case where under the exception to the law of finds where NOAA as trustee for historic sanctuary resources under the NMSA also had constructive possession of the wreck and thus it fell within the exception to the law of finds. The constructive possession or ownership is also important under the law of salvage as the owner or agency with constructive possession has right to deny salvage under salvage law.

The National Park Service was relieved, and we could also breathe a sigh of relief. The site was saved from commercial salvage. Now there was a need to put the site to bed, preserve it from further depredation, and ultimately protect it from the elements.

Courtroom drama had been in short supply, but Fischer recalled what little there was:

> Witnessing a trial such as this provides insights not only into the process but into the individuals involved themselves. Over a period of four years we had several judges presiding over different portions of the legal actions. The judge who presided over the trial and issued the judgment, Clyde Atkins, was the one I thought best, probably because he seemed to agree with our position. During the trial, when plaintiff's counsel addressed some comment to the judge, his reply of "Well, it *is* a National Park" gave me some confidence that he was going to be all right, and he was.

Early in the process the case was assigned to a judge who did not seem as sympathetic and who in several similar cases had decided in favor of the plaintiffs. As we were preparing for one of the aborted trials, during a hearing he suggested to Rebecca Donnellan that she give the plaintiff immunity from prosecution for violations of the Antiquities Act of 1906 in exchange for his testimony on what exactly they had done on the site during their recovery activities. She responded that only an assistant attorney general had the authority to give immunity, and we did not have the time to negotiate that. Although that seemed straightforward enough, the judge kept revisiting that subject anyway, which frustrated Donnellan considerably.

One other aspect of that situation was that it revealed something interesting about Donnellan. As the judge seemed to be jerking her around with this subject and the proceedings progressed, she seemed to become increasingly frustrated. She would become quite red-faced and almost looked as if she was going to start sputtering. At a later stage she did not become incensed but rather, despite appearances, became more cold, calculating, and incisive. When she got red-faced, it was time for those giving her a bad time to run for cover.

At that point in the trial, while plaintiff's counsel was addressing the bench, he leaned a little forward and clasped his hands behind his back in a theatrical lawyerly pose. Those seated behind him could see that he was simultaneously flipping Donnellan the bird. That was a mistake. She became red-faced.

A third judge, Alcee Hastings, who presided early in the case, issued several orders that seemed highly supportive of our position, and he was an early favorite. He got into some trouble later though. He was impeached by the U.S. House of Representatives for corruption and perjury and convicted by the Senate. He became only the sixth judge in the history of impeachment in the United States to be removed from office by the U.S. Senate. That certainly had a negative impact on his legal career. Ironically, he was subsequently elected as a member of the U.S. House of Representatives.

In the years since the court case George Fischer has repeatedly been contacted regarding the case and the project. He responded to a number of those on the Internet Underwater Archaeology message board SubArch who had questions regarding the case:

> Questions have been raised over why the court audaciously awarded custody to the U.S., and where we came off collecting materials from a site which is now felt may be claimed by the United Kingdom [in the early parts of our work on the site, we did not know the identity and nationality]. . . .

At that time no precedents existed. The State of Florida had for years been permitting salvage of the 1715 and 1733 Spanish fleets, and other wrecks, and Spain said nary a word. HMS *Looe* and HMS *Winchester* were openly salvaged, and information on them was disseminated in both public and professional publications, and the British raised no question as to rights to the sites, or ownership.

In each case, including HMS *Fowey*, neither Spain nor the United Kingdom was notified by the U.S. Department of State about the salvage efforts. Neither nation broached the subject with the United States on its own accord either, probably because their foreign offices and navy departments were unaware of the salvage activity. Of course, the identification of the site was not confirmed until after the 1983 investigations. If we had known that it was the *Fowey* and the UK had become involved in the case, however, it appears that this would not have altered the court's decision and reasoning. It would still have been a landmark case. The Department of Interior now consults with the UK, which fully supports the in situ preservation. Thus it is apparent that the UK, as owner, would not have consented to the salvage or recovery of HMS *Fowey*. As indicated above, this was the first prong of the court's rationale under the exception to the law of finds.

In addition, regardless whether the vessel was owned by the United States or by the UK, because HMS *Fowey* was identified as a park resource in the management plan, the Department of the Interior/NPS would still have "constructive possession" sufficient to come within the exception of the law of finds. This "constructive possession" is also sufficient to deny salvage, as was found by other courts in subsequent cases such as *Craft*, *Lathrop*, and *U.S.* v. *Fisher*. The United States and UK take the same approach to respecting the ownership and sovereign immunity of sunken warships and also respect the regulatory authority and jurisdiction of the territorial waters of coastal nations in which the sunken warships came to rest. Other maritime powers, like France, Spain, Germany, and Japan, take the same approach as the UK and the United States do.

For example, the French navy located the site of the Confederate raider CSS *Alabama* off the coast of Cherbourg in 1984 and issued a permit in 1987 for initial survey and eventual recovery work. Although the U.S. Department of State notified France in 1987 that the CSS *Alabama* and its artifacts were the property of the United States, and bills were introduced in 1988 and 1989 in the House and Senate of the U.S. Congress reaffirming this, it was not until 1989 that France and the United States signed an agreement confirming ownership by the United States and cooperating on research and management of the wreck site.

As Fischer's SubArch post noted:

> In regard to remarks made concerning an NPS policy of "secrecy" regarding this shipwreck, we must point out that the opposite was the case in the 1980s. In addition to being front-page news in various newspapers, our activities were well reported in several professional and public forums. These include periodic news notes in the Society for Historical Archaeology's *Newsletter* and the *International Journal of Nautical Archaeology and Underwater Exploration*. Several papers were presented at the Society for Historical Archaeology meetings and published in the *Proceedings* of those meetings. A summary article was published by our 1983 Field Director Dr. Russell Skowronek in *Archaeology Magazine* (22-7 1985). The cover article in the October 1983 issue of *Smithsonian Magazine* also discussed our work on the site. A definitive article was published by Dr. Skowronek, R. Johnson, R. Vernon, and myself in 1987 in that august British based *Journal of Nautical Archaeology and Underwater Exploration*. (16-4 pp. 313–324). In fact, we were the centerfold of that issue. A number of manuscript reports were also produced, which SEAC made available to the public free upon request during my tenure there, or in the case of the more extensive manuscripts and limited distribution publications, including Dr. Skowronek's extensive report on our 1983 investigations, for the cost of copying. Of course, none of these provided the precise location of the wreck.
>
> SEAC's multi-million item archaeological collections, for which I also happened to have management responsibility, were open to any reasonable and legitimate request for access. The *Fowey* collection and associated data were examined by many researchers in this country, and from elsewhere. An FSU press release on this subject was carried by the Associated Press in 1986, with a picture of me fondling *Fowey* artifacts.
>
> Documentary research was undertaken by Dr. Skowronek, beginning in 1981 in the British Library, Public Records Office, and National Maritime Museum, with full knowledge and cooperation of their staff. At this point I would assume the British Government was

well aware of our activities, and could have intervened, but did not. As this was a very high profile case, the research design for our 1983 investigations was reviewed at multiple levels within the NPS, Department of Interior Solicitor's Office, and the Justice Department [not to mention Florida State University's Department of Anthropology and the Academic Diving Program], and received outside peer review. I suppose I could have sent a copy to the Queen, just to be on the safe side, but that seemed beyond the bounds of my authority.

Archaeologists, salvors, and government agencies had not paid much attention to the possible ownership rights of nations to sunken historic warships until the topic was raised repeatedly beginning in the mid-1980s. It started with discovery of the Confederate raider CSS *Alabama* and enactment of the Abandoned Shipwreck Act of 1987, followed by development and issuance of the Abandoned Shipwreck Act Guidelines. Although the Abandoned Shipwreck Act applies only to abandoned shipwrecks, its guidelines provide the first written guidance for archeologists and federal and state agencies concerning historic shipwrecks entitled to sovereign immunity. The guidance seems to have been ignored, however, with regard to the French ship *La Belle*, discovered in Galveston Bay, Texas, and the Spanish ships *Juno* and *La Galga*, said to be in the waters of Virginia off Assateague Island. In the case of *La Belle*, the United States and France signed an agreement saying that the Texas Historical Commission would preserve, study, and exhibit the recovered remains on behalf of France, the sovereign owner. In the case of *Juno* and *La Galga*, the government of Spain, the Commonwealth of Virginia, and a salvor ended up in litigation (Michele Aubry, personal communication, 2007).

In July 2000 the U.S. District Court of Appeals for the Fourth Circuit ruled in favor of Spain in the case of *La Galga* and *Juno*, lost off the coast of Virginia, stating that Spain had not in fact abandoned the vessels and that commercial interests could not conduct salvage on them. Had this legal precedent been available in 1979, the situation regarding HMS *Fowey* might have been considerably simpler for us, but the landmark outcome would have been the same.

The United Kingdom would have been more than welcome to join the litigation in the same category, as any help would have been appreciated. Initially we were uncertain as to the national identity of the site, however. It is appropriate, of course, to address the interests of the British in this site and others like it. In 1979 that interest was unknown, because we did not ask them and they did not tell us. Since then the United Kingdom has officially advised the United States of its policies on sunken warships and other vessels entitled to sovereign immunity, and the two nations have communicated about HMS *Fowey* in particular. We wish this had been done when we needed help during the litigation.

The bottom line of all this is that the United States won the case and won it decisively. In the course of the legal actions several very significant legal precedents were established. They have been used in litigation regarding shipwrecks since that time and have provided them very significant protection. With those precedents in place, a case such as the Legare Anchorage Shipwreck will never occur in the future, and HMS *Fowey* is about as well protected legally as it can be.

11

Epilogue

They Didn't Listen

" . . . to conserve the scenery and the natural and historic objects and the wildlife therein and to provide for the enjoyment of the same in such manner and by such means as will leave them unimpaired for the enjoyment of future generations."

National Park Service Organic Act of 1916

"As custodian of the national park system, the National Park Service is steward of many of America's most important natural and cultural resources. It is charged to preserve them unimpaired for the enjoyment of present and future generations. If they are degraded or lost, so is the park's reason for being."

NPS-28

There was always a certain symmetry to it. Captain Drake had been exonerated for the loss of HMS *Fowey* 235 years earlier, and now George Fischer, the National Park Service, and the people of the United States concerned with historic preservation had won in court.

The SEAC crew believed at the time and still do that—according to the law of diminishing returns—this limited investigation, the 1983 NPS-SEAC/FSU Field Project, supplemented by considerable historical documentation, provided us with perhaps 80 percent of the qualitative information from the site, and further work would tend to be redundant. In the coming months and years the team members met their professional responsibilities by completing reports and delivering and publishing their findings in both popular and professional venues (e.g., Fischer 1988; Skowronek 1984a, 1985, 1988; Skowronek et al. 1987; Vernon 1984, 1988; Wild 1988). To some degree we had a reason to feel good. In a letter dated July 21, 1986, chief anthropologist Scovill and chief historian Bearss commended us for providing a report that "more than meets standards, as well as the canons of their professions. The interdisciplinary approach followed, and methodology employed, enhance the value of this undertaking" (Jerry L. Rogers, July 21, 1986).

But winning in court and "doing the right thing" for your colleagues was not enough: the ultimate preservation of the site was still a concern. In the report written on the 1983 project (Skowronek 1984a), both archaeological and preservation recommendations were made. It was noted then that the site had been a management problem for the better part of a decade, because of the depredations of treasure hunters. Other than continued Park Service surveillance, a proposal was also made to involve the U.S. Navy and use a satellite-linked monitoring system that they could assist the NPS in acquiring and installing, with active camera and warning devices. A program of increased public education regarding the site, its significance as a submerged archaeological resource, and its relationship with the park was also proposed. At the same time a number of actions were undertaken to consider protecting the site by burying it.

These included an experimental transplanting of turtle grass at the west end of the site. It was hoped that revegetating the areas disturbed by illicit salvage activities would lead to the accumulation of a protective covering of sand. The seedlings were "pinned" to the sea floor with ten-penny nails. Unfortunately, the marine biologists associated with this project failed to take into account two important issues. First, seagrass (*Thalassia* sp.) is sensitive to depth changes. The smaller shoots came from shallow water and were quickly moved to a depth of thirty feet. Then there was the issue of electrolytic reactions caused by the large steel nails to which the grass was attached. Not only did the grass not survive, but now the experimental area was contaminated by large modern nails.

During the 1983 project the research team placed dozens of units of Seascape across the site (figure 7.13). These fiberglass sandbags, with their floating sea fronds, had been developed for use in high-energy areas as a sort of "snow fence" for sediment-accumulation. In those areas where they have proven effective, sand-laden currents are slowed by the fronds, and the particulate matter falls to the sea floor, slowly building up overtime. At the Legare Anchorage site this experiment failed as well, because—in this low-energy area, and with the availability of ambient sunlight—sea life began to grow on the fronds. They then grew heavy and sank, thus eliminating any accumulating beneficial effects (figure 7.22). Finally, the park's marine biologists planned to monitor the accumulation or loss of sediments in the area with a number of stakes later placed across site. The monitoring, however, was sporadic, inconsistent, and relatively unscientific in its approach. As a result, when the site was affected in 1992 by Hurricane Andrew, there was no data set with which to compare the effects of the storm.

Barring the success of any of these techniques, George Fischer suggested that the site be buried under a blanket of sandbags or a hopper dredge load of sand or gravel. Because of cost, neither was ever seriously considered or implemented. In hindsight, sandbags would have been the best and cheapest solution and would at the very least have provided some temporary site stabilization, as they have in similar applications on other shipwreck sites.

Nonetheless, the archaeological recommendations were more specific. Park managers just wanted the "problem" to go away or be taken away, to be solved by someone else. In their monomaniacal minds complete excavation was almost always the answer. It was not, since 80 percent of the information that the site might yield had already been revealed through the 1983 project (Skowronek 1984a):

> The remedy for BISC-UW-20, or any other archeological site, is not total excavation to eliminate the problem. Total excavation of any site is not only lengthy and very costly, but may be detrimental to the recovered data, and results in destruction of nonrenewable cultural resources. Our current methodologies are light years ahead of archeological work conducted only twenty years ago. With time, more and more information can be wrested from sites that are left *in situ* and relatively intact. In underwater sites, this is especially true. Knowledge of the effects of submersion and subsequent alteration of wreck sites is only being studied at its most basic levels. Suggestions that the removal of guns and other ferrous materials might upset the delicate electrical equilibrium of an ancient wreck, thus renewing its deterioration, have been made. Such things could be given consideration. For these reasons, testing of archeological sites should continue at the level of the Legare Anchorage Shipwreck Project of 1983. That is, largely non-destructive, with a maximization of minimal information, thus preserving the bulk of these resources for future, more sophisticated, investigations. Therefore, it is this archeologist's opinion that unless mortally endangered, the site should be *left alone*; protected from the ravages of nature and man.

The report went on to say:

Toward protection and preservation of the site, professional archeological monitoring should continue. On a regular basis, magnetometer runs over BISC-UW-20 should be made to determine the
stability of the site environs. Should there be high dipolar readings,
immediate actions should be taken either through the installation
of sacrificial anodes on larger iron concentrations, or renewed excavation. *The Park should be discouraged from making collections from
the site* [emphasis added]. Not only may the removal of large iron
artifacts endanger the rest of the site, but smaller unprovenienced
artifacts do neither archeology nor site preservation much good. *The
lost information represented by the Klein collection should not be inadvertently replicated piecemeal by National Park Service personnel*
[emphasis added].

It is worthy of note that complete excavation of a historic shipwreck
is very, very rare. The major reason—other than that it entails complete
destruction of the site—is that it is extremely expensive. Our project expenses in 1983 were about $30,000; and the NPS got a bargain basement
deal on that, with all equipment provided without cost by Florida State
University (since it was a field school) and many other gratis and in-kind
contributions—with only 3 percent of the site disturbed.

Another consideration, often overlooked by those not thoroughly familiar with archaeology, is the cost of conservation/preservation, analysis,
cataloguing, and curation of the materials recovered. As a rule of thumb,
depending on the circumstances, this can be expected to cost from four
to ten times the cost of recovery. The combined facilities of the Southeast
Archeological Center and the Florida Bureau of Archaeological Research
would be inadequate to undertake preservation of materials from such a
total-excavation project. Further, there would be a continuing responsibility and expenses for curation, storage, and conservation work on the collections for both the foreseeable and unforeseeable future.

The recommendations for site protection and stabilization made above
seem to have been ignored by those with management responsibilities. In
fact, subsequent activities may have exacerbated the problems of site preservation.

Less than a year after the conclusion of the 1983 project the Southeast
Archeological Center received a telephone call from Herbert Bump of the

Florida Bureau of Archaeological Research Conservation Lab "informing" the center that its "other cannon" was ready. "Other cannon"? We had only recovered one. There was no "other cannon." It quickly developed that, after the departure of our field crew in 1983, the park's superintendent had acted independently and had ordered park staff to recover a second gun and then had it sent to Tallahassee for conservation (but billed to SEAC). They did all this without consulting the National Park Service's own Southeast Archeological Center or, apparently, even notifying the Regional Office (and with no archaeological control). But why? What was the overriding cultural resource management issue that required the recovery of the second cannon? The superintendent wanted one to match the one SEAC had already recovered in 1983 (and would ultimately return to the park after analyses and year-long conservation). He felt that the cannons would look good as a matched pair fronting the two sides of the park entrance. When confronted with this, the park's resource manager stated a new consideration: the fear that the cannon would be stolen because it was exposed. At a weight of 3,000 pounds, and with a very distinct appearance, it was not at all portable, and the SEAC team did not believe it was ever in any jeopardy.

The first gun was never placed on display and ultimately ended up on the ground in the back of the park's maintenance storage area, where, not surprisingly, it suffered considerably more deterioration. It was later sent to Texas A&M University's Institute for Nautical Archaeology for retreatment. The authors viewed this artifact where it is now stored at the Southeast Archeological Center. At the time of the initial conservation treatment after recovery, the Florida Bureau of Archaeological Research's Conservation Laboratory staff described it as one of the best-preserved tubes they had seen recovered from a shipwreck site, "like it had just come from the foundry." When seen in 2006 it was heavily pitted and corroded, and its identifying markings were nearly obliterated (figure 11.1). There was no suggestion of the pristine state it had been in more than twenty years earlier.

About the same time, the site was marked on charts with a large triangle: "No Diving or Anchoring Area." Nonetheless, the site was revisited during David Brewer and Ken Wild's Southeast Archeological Center–sponsored 1984 underwater survey of Biscayne National Park as part of the site investigation and monitoring aspect of that project. They found that the site had been further disturbed and attributed it to illicit salvage activities. No incident reports had been made by the park in regard to these disturbances,

Figure 11.1. *Fowey*'s gun after the second round of conservation, currently housed at the Southeast Archeological Center in Tallahassee, Florida. It is no longer in "pristine" condition. Compare this view with figure 9.1 to see the changes. (Photograph by Russell Skowronek, 2006.)

although people had heard apocryphal stories of "sightings" by park staff of boats on the site working at night under lights.

Five years after the project, in 1988, Dr. Roger Smith, the Florida State underwater archaeologist, was surveying 1733 *flota* sites for inclusion as State Underwater Preserves. As part of that project he asked to examine those sites that lay within the boundaries of Biscayne National Park. While there, Smith and his students were asked by the park staff to help remove the 1983 Seascape sandbags with sunken fronds, because they were "unsightly." This was on a site that was ostensibly closed for public visitation, of course, and their removal eliminated whatever protective cover the sandbags and their collapsed fronds had afforded the site. At the same time, the monitoring stakes for measuring sedimentation were also removed. The rationale for this action was never explained. Perhaps it was because they were a reminder that no monitoring had been conducted. Again, these actions were taken without any consultation with or review by the Southeast Archeological Center, much less the regional archaeologist, who is responsible for all activities that might have an adverse effect on significant archaeological resources within the Southeast Region's parks.

The historic Coco Lobo Club building on Adams Key had been rehabilitated around this time, and the park wanted to display the recovered and conserved artifacts from the 1983 project on the island for boating visitors (the very limited number who had access to large enough boats to be able to go out and visit the offshore islands). The curatorial staffs of both the Southeast Archeological Center and the Southeast Regional Office, George Fischer for SEAC, and regional curator Dale Durham outspokenly recommended against this for a number of important reasons, including security, climate control for sensitive artifacts, lack of availability to the park's regular driving visitors, and, of course, the very real issue of hurricanes. This was contrary to the NPS policy of not locating exhibits below the hundred-year floodplain. Nevertheless, the exhibits were put in the club at the behest of the superintendent and with the acquiescence of NPS interpretive and museum planners. The SEAC team protested all this vociferously, but the chief of the Southeast Archeological Center preferred not to rock the boat. Fischer recalls that he "was not a strong supporter of NPS underwater archeology"; in fact, it sometimes appeared that he wished that this field did not exist at SEAC, and the record seems to bear this out (Binkley 2007: 124).

Figure 11.2. Maureen Mackenzie, Russell Skowronek, and Duncan Mackenzie at one of the fortifications protecting the town of Fowey in Cornwall. (Photograph by Margaret Graham, 1991.)

As the decade turned, Fischer and Skowronek entered new phases in their lives. After twenty-eight years with the U.S. Forest Service and National Park Service, Fischer retired and turned his attention to developing the underwater archaeology program at Florida State University, which became firmly established within the Department of Anthropology and developed into what was considered by many the third-ranked program in the United States. Meanwhile Skowronek completed his Ph.D. in Anthropology at Michigan State University and joined the faculty at Santa Clara University in California. There he pushed forward with documentary research on HMS *Fowey*. In 1991 he traveled to England and visited the town of Fowey in Cornwall. There he met with Duncan Mackenzie, Fowey's local historian, and gave him copies of the various publications that had been produced. Mackenzie hoped that someday an exhibit could be developed in Fowey about their namesake vessel (figures 11.2, 11.3). In fact, following the 1983 project, preliminary arrangements were made to contribute duplicate artifacts for exhibit in the UK, including an agreement with the U.S. Navy to transport the second preserved cannon for that purpose; however, there was no follow-up on this by the NPS. In 2006, during a *Fowey*-focused research trip to Kingston-on-Hull in Yorkshire, Skowronek met with Arthur Credland, maritime historian and keeper of maritime history at the Hull Maritime Museum. He too expressed great interest in this locally constructed ship and the possibilities it might afford for interpretation. Both Fischer and Skowronek continued to lecture on the *Fowey*, often referring to it as a highlight of their careers and generally considering it "their" site as researchers who have established a relationship with an archaeological site often do, especially in light of their published research.

On August 16, 1992, a tropical depression formed off the west coast of Africa. On the next day it became the first named tropical storm of the season. Over the next week Hurricane Andrew would grow to a Category 5 storm on the Saffir-Simpson Hurricane Scale. That meant wind gusts of more than 170 miles per hour and a storm surge that approached seventeen feet as it crossed the Bahamas. By the time it blew itself out ten days later over Louisiana, it had left twenty-three people dead and over $25 billion dollars in damage in South Florida alone. Until Katrina in 2005, it was the most costly hurricane on record.

At 4:30 a.m. on August 24, 1992, the ten-mile-wide eye passed directly over Biscayne National Park on its way to destroy 80 percent of the city of Homestead, Florida. Into the usually "gin-clear" waters of Biscayne Bay poured some 25,000 gallons of oil, detritus, and untold tons of flotsam.

Figure 11.3. Russell Skowronek at the Fowey Museum in Cornwall. (Photograph by Margaret Graham, 1991.)

Though blunted by the offshore reefs, the storm surge roiled the sands under the shallow nearshore waters. This fallout choked many of the coral polyps and killed huge sections of the living reef. In Biscayne National Park the restored Coco Lobo Club, housing exhibits relating to and artifacts from the Legare Anchorage wreck, was totally destroyed. Today a plaque commemorating the storm may be found at the park's headquarters at Convoy Point.

Within three weeks a "Cultural Resources Damage Assessment" of Big Cypress National Preserve, Everglades National Park, and Biscayne National Park was conducted. The Cultural Resources Case Incident Team considered both terrestrial and submerged sites and rapidly compiled a report on its findings (Smith et al. 1992).

On September 20, 1992, *Fowey* was visited for more than an hour by two archaeologists who were very familiar with the site. They were taken to the site by park ranger Bill Hudson. Larry Murphy of the Submerged Cultural Resources Unit had been part of the 1980 team that located the site, and David Brewer of the Southeast Archeological Center had been part of the 1983 team and had revisited the site in 1984. They found that much of the remaining hull structure was now exposed and that some smaller, portable artifacts had apparently been swept away. Nonetheless, the team identified and collected an intact glass bottle and a pewter plate and saw a heretofore unknown gun and fragments of a gun carriage. It is interesting to note that the team observed that the hull remains lay in a depression surrounded by turtle grass. They stated: "Intact turtle grass is apparently very resistant to erosion—little erosion was evident in the area surrounding this site, where the grass was intact" (Smith et al. 1992: 46, n. 47). Careful observations of a clean area below the coral growth on a gun revealed that some nine inches of sediment had recently been removed, probably as a result of the storm activity. The team felt that the remaining fabric of the ship and the site in general were now in imminent danger from looters, shipworms, and potential mechanical impacts from any subsequent storms. They requested daily patrols and a third round of intensive documentation, including photogrammetric mapping and some selective artifact recovery. One other odd object was found by Larry Murphy. The item, a valve assembly used for airlifts, may have dated from Klein's activities in the 1970s or perhaps could even be evidence for looting that may have occurred in the four years since the site was last "officially" visited by Roger Smith in 1988. We will never know: the park could neither confirm nor deny such activities, since there was no record of any site monitoring, systematic or otherwise, during that period. In fact two of the Seascape sandbags, which had been deemed "unsightly" by park personnel in 1988, had been overlooked and were still in place in 1992.

Subsequently the team was asked to produce an estimate for any further mitigation and projected that it would cost approximately $45,000 to cover the documentation project. This estimate included travel, logistics, some sample collections, and any additional special studies and was provided to the Case Incident Command System for Cultural Resources on this particular site.

Later that year meetings were held in Miami for Hurricane Andrew Damage Assessment funding distribution. At that time, based on the post-hurricane mitigation funds available, more than $100,000 was set aside for documentation and development of a stabilization plan for the Legare Anchorage Shipwreck site. Once the funds were transferred directly to the park, the park decided that this work was subsequently to be carried out under the auspices of SCRU in Santa Fe, New Mexico. In turn, SCRU subcontracted with the University of Miami and a group of avocational volunteers from the Maritime Archaeological and Historical Society, under the direction of Dr. John Seidel, then with the University of Maryland, who was also given a contract to act as project director to carry out the work during the summer of 1993. The Ocean Science Research Institute, a loosely organized private nonprofit "educational and research institution" focused on basic and applied marine sciences, out of La Jolla, California, was also contracted to develop a stabilization plan for the site (at the time of this writing the OSRI web site is nonfunctional and e-mail is returned). The research design for the project, which was formally requested by and tardily submitted to the Southeast Archaeological Center in July 1993, was entitled a "Documentation Plan" and stated that certain "Products" would be supplied by the end of the 1993 calendar year to the Southeast Archeological Center as a result. These included a "detailed site map in analog and digital format, feature maps, report of investigations that meets professional and federal standards, that includes historical context, past work, methodology, findings, conclusions, management recommendations, video and photo documentation and catalog."

During the SCRU-sponsored summer 1993 project, David Brewer was assigned by the chief of the Southeast Archeological Center to act as the representative of both SEAC and the Southeast Regional Office, considering his previous experiences on the site and his contribution to the Hurricane Damage Assessment fieldwork, the Cultural Resource Assessment report, and the resulting estimate. He was also the last remaining NPS-certified "blue-carded" diver left at SEAC, or the Regional Office for that matter, since responsibilities for conduct of underwater archaeology had been removed from the Southeast Region and transferred to SCRU in Santa Fe, New Mexico.

When Brewer finally saw the site again that summer, he later commented that he "was surprised at how much the site had been 're-covered' by sand" since the previous summer (personal communication, October 2006). In fact, there was so much sand on the site that it would now have to be dredged off to carry out the documentation mapping. According to Brewer, the team removed more sand than had been disturbed by the storm. He based that conclusion on photographs that he and Murphy had taken the year before in 1992, after Hurricane Andrew, which did not show an entirely exposed wreck. Nonetheless, the wreck was uncovered and successfully mapped, with some newly exposed details noted.

The park staff members apparently had less concern about dredged-up sand and silt landing on coral in 1993 than they had in 1983. Rather than using an airlift, the summer 1993 SCRU team used a Venturi-dredge, directing water through a pump, down a suction head-and-hose assembly that creates a strong suction current. The resulting "spoil" was shot into a dive bag at the end of the main suction hose to catch any loose artifacts, with the remaining sand and silt simply spewed outward. There was no requirement as in 1983 for a large plastic sheet tube (humorously referred to at the time as the whale condom) to collect backfill spoil and divert it to a central locale or several discrete locales to stockpile it for later use in reburying the site. In 1993, after the site was uncovered and mapped, the dredge was then used to dig a large deep pit off-site. After being mapped in, a large number of loose items were wrested from the site and deposited in a jumble in the bottom of the pit. These items included glass bottles, copper barrel hoops, and a variety of ship's fittings such as deadeyes and other components. The pit and the exposed structure were then covered with sand, sucked from the surrounding anchorage basin. Some of the details of this project were subsequently published (Adams 1996; Delgado 1997: 445), but a report has never been completed; nor have the supporting documents and/or "Products" promised in 1993 ever made their way to SEAC.

In the spring of 2007 an excellent administrative history of the Southeast Archeological Center was produced, which commented in some de-tail on these activities and the situation relating to the Legare Anchorage shipwreck. *Science, Politics, and the "Big Dig": A History of the Southeast Archeological Center and Development of Cultural Resource Management in the Southeast* by Cameron Binkley (2007), the regional historian, is a very through and interesting study. It traces SEAC's history back beyond the huge federal relief projects of the early 1930s to the genesis of what evolved into the Southeast Archeological Center, an organization that played a vital role in the development of archaeology in the Southeast and also played a significant national role.

The bureau historian made a significant comment on this history: "Bin-kley does not shrink from criticism where warranted—notably discussing the center's seminal role in launching a federal underwater archeology pro-gram and the mishandling of the promising initial efforts to the detriment of both effective underwater cultural resources management in the South-east Region and NPS-FSU relations" (Binkley 2007: ix).

There is a little dirty laundry that has to be dealt with now. Elements of the story we present that are critical of the organization we love and hold in such high esteem cannot be avoided in documenting the history of HMS *Fowey*.

In late 1983 a management decision was made to remove all responsibil-ity for NPS underwater archaeology and all related activities from SEAC and transfer it to the Southwest Regional Office in Santa Fe, headquarters of the Submerged Cultural Resources Unit (SCRU; later renamed the Sub-merged Resources Unit: SRU). We received this news in early 1984 with great confusion and disappointment but were told by the center chief that the decision had been made at the highest levels of the NPS and was "non-negotiable" (Binkley 2007: 124). At times it appeared that he would prefer that the field of underwater archaeology did not exist at SEAC, and thus it became so.

The profession in general and the NPS have long tended to hold a jaun-diced view of underwater archaeology and regard it as something less than fully professional; it was too new, too unconventional, looked like fun, had a romantic public image, and so forth. Because of these feelings, we often felt our accomplishments were made despite and not because of the leader-ship and support we received.

In early 1984 involvement with things related to *Fowey* terminated at SEAC, and interest in the site almost totally disappeared. Fischer's subsequent early exit from the Southeast Archeological Center and affiliation with Florida State University was in large part because of this decision.

Despite the recommendation of Chief Faust and other Southeast Region officials for SCRU to develop a protocol to ensure continued Park Service cooperation with Florida State, this never happened. Indeed, when Hurricane Andrew uncovered elements of HMS *Fowey* in 1993, SCRU chose not to draw on the site-specific experience of George Fischer or the diving facilities of Florida State through the NPS-FSU cooperative agreement to help it survey the shipwreck and do any hurricane-related mitigation work. Instead SCRU worked with the Department of Anthropology of the University of Maryland, which had no comparable experience. After SCRU failed to reference previous SEAC and FSU reports relating to HMS *Fowey* in new funding proposals, the FSU Anthropology Department voiced concerns to NPS management (Binkley 2007: 133–134). In the twenty years since the termination of the underwater archeology program at SEAC, the Santa Fe–based NPS underwater archaeological unit has never participated in a cooperative arrangement with Florida State to do underwater archaeology despite FSU's burgeoning capacity in the field and significant experience with submerged archaeology in Florida (Binkley 2007: 132–133).

Binkley (2007: 134 n. 234) notes:

Eventually SCRU received funding to conduct underwater archeological work to mitigate the effects of Hurricane Andrew upon HMS *Fowey*, but no NPS research reports have been published. A freelance writer with no NPS association did publish an article about SCRU's work on HMS *Fowey* (Adams 1996). Adams' article created a scandal, however, because allegations of plagiarism were made. Both George R. Fischer and Russell K. Skowronek, an Assistant Professor of Anthropology at Santa Clara University and a former FSU student who had worked with SEAC on HMS *Fowey*, wrote protest letters regarding the article. Skowronek stated, "when I finished reading it, the impression that I came away with was that John Seidel [University of Maryland] and Larry Murphy [SCRU] had made the first map of the wreck site and researched the vessel's background in the four years since Hurricane Andrew. Your readers will be interested to learn this is far from true." After listing various examples of the author's failure to cite previous work properly, Skowronek called the article "an abomination." (Skowronek 1997: 14; Fischer 1997: 3)

In 1995, using the remaining mitigation funding, a "Fowey Site Stabilization Seminar" was held at the Sheraton Key Resort on Key Largo to discuss the results of the contracted studies by the University of Miami and Ocean Sciences Research Institute and to solicit recommendations from various other outside sources. Among the presenters from the University of Miami's Rosenstiel School of Marine Sciences were coral soils specialists, submerged vegetation specialists, and water current specialists. One of the most outspoken was a chemical engineer, who was extremely verbal about "the pit problem," which he saw as an immediate overriding concern, even more pressing than the site stabilization. His opinion was that the conglomerate of different materials in the pit, besides having been removed from the wreck site and thereby destabilizing the electro-chemical balance of the overall site structure, was now brewing a electro-chemical stew in its own right. Thus it would require a great deal of time, effort, and money to remove and, ultimately, conserve the artifact conglomerate therein. Although strident in his opinions, he was largely ignored. A few months later at the Society for Historical Archaeology annual meeting in Cincinnati, Seidel and Murphy (1996: 3) reported: "Corrosion activity within the pit has been monitored through sampling of pore water and has been negligible," thus seemingly putting the matter to rest.

When a roundtable discussion was initiated at the Stabilization Seminar, David Brewer, as the representative from the Southeast Archeological Center, took the opportunity to voice his opinion on the site stabilization issue. He argued that sandbags were portable, cheap, removable, and environmentally neutral. They would protect the site and build up sediments and could be easily handled underwater with the use of lift bags if necessary. New types of bag material, such as Nalgene, were then available that would not deteriorate for centuries and could be ordered or made in various sizes. Stabilization experiments could be set up in which different bags of different weights and/or sizes could be placed in various configurations over the site, to be monitored over time and under different conditions. Mapped in place, any movement of bags of various size and weight would provide indications of storm surge strength and direction on-site. Finally, if the site warranted further work, the bags could easily be moved off-site with lift bags and compressors, to be placed back on-site once any necessary testing was finished. Meanwhile any surreptitious looting would involve an extended presence on-site to remove this sandbag overburden and thus could not be easily conducted in the dark of the night, much less during the day.

Another participant at the seminar, James Tucker, underwater archaeologist for Parks Canada, agreed and proceeded to give a slide presentation on the Red Bay Basque Whaling Station Wrecks Site in Labrador. There they used sandbags to preserve the site every year, before the ice set in. They removed them every year before they began to work again. These bags even protected the site from large ice floes whose extended subsurface "tails" would otherwise have scoured the site—the ice floes simply rode up and over the sandbags. Considering how well this stabilization technique had already worked in extreme conditions, it was his preferred recommendation as well.

According to David Brewer (personal communication, October 2006), who was present at the meeting, the use of sandbags was rejected out of hand when an NPS biologist loudly voiced the opinion that "they would have a serious impact on natural communities," although exactly how was not detailed. Discussions for the balance of the seminar turned to natural solutions, such as the use of seagrass to stabilize the sand over the site. This included the relocation and planting of turtle grass, which even the experts from Rosenstiel said was "iffy" at best. It is no wonder that they came to this conclusion, given past experience in the 1980s. The results of this seminar were to be written up and distributed.

More than fifteen years had elapsed since the 1983 project. Our recommendations for site protection and preservation had been ignored. Our pleas for monitoring the site's magnetic stability and not "picking apart" the wreck were discarded like dross. Now the site's integrity had been compromised, and there was no accountability, much less reporting, for what had transpired in the intervening decade and a half. In all fairness, even the Southeast Archeological Center seemed to have no concern over these developments, letting the 1993 work go unpublished without even a memo and never following up with the park on the Hurricane Andrew Cultural Resource Damage Assessment recommendations and funding. As Cameron Binkley (2007: 121–134) observes in his administrative history of SEAC, the center chief was not a strong supporter of NPS underwater archaeology, and this philosophy seemed to pervade the remaining staff.

Finally, in 2000, staff members at Biscayne National Park threw up their hands and said they were unable to protect the site from erosion and looting and therefore requested that it be totally excavated or removed. Of course, without a report from the 1993 project, it was impossible to know what new information had been revealed that had not been known in 1983. Furthermore, without the results of the 1995 seminar, with a list of stabilization alternatives, how could the park staff know that the site could not be preserved and protected? Without data-over-time monitoring of accretion and erosion of sand on the site, and without incident reports documenting vandalism, all that is left is hearsay and anecdotes. It is hard to justify the astronomical costs of a complete "rescue" (read "salvage") of the site, including recovery, analysis, conservation, and curation costs for this project, without this information. The decisionmakers realized there was just too much they did not know. Given subsequent developments, that may be just as well.

The decisionmakers also seemed to be unaware that on December 19, 1979, David F. McIntosh (an attorney with Corlett, Merritt, Killian & Sikes representing Gerald Klein) had submitted a "Memorandum of Law" to the U.S. District Court in Miami that stated: "The NPS is completely unable to preserve the wreck site [the Legare Anchorage Shipwreck site] from unauthorized salvors (pirates) who would not respect the Court's Order." He proposed that Klein be permitted to protect the site for the NPS by salvaging it. That suggestion was summarily rebuffed. Members of the treasure salvage community would probably have been delighted if the NPS had subsequently admitted that it could not protect the site and they ultimately had been granted permission to salvage and rescue it themselves.

At this point the last player in the story of the Legare Anchorage wreck entered: Major Denis B. Trelewicz (1932–2005) of Key Largo, Florida. Named an "Earth Day Hero for 2000" for his "tireless efforts to preserve and protect the natural environment," Trelewicz was a sixty-eight-year-old retiree from the U.S. Air Force Reserve. A graduate of the Massachusetts Institute of Technology and a Sloan scholar, he was a past president of the American Marketing Association. In 2000 Trelewicz was living in the Upper Keys. He was anything but retired and was not a treasure hunter. An avid diver, Trelewicz was a long-time volunteer with the Florida Keys National Marine Sanctuary's Maritime Heritage Resource Inventory Team and was on the board of the Historical Preservation Society of the Upper Keys. He was tenacious in his research and would develop a profound dislike of "big government."

Early in 2000 Major Trelewicz, in his role as a historian of the Upper Keys, asked his U.S. senator, Connie Mack, to help him obtain information relating to the Legare Anchorage wreck. His initial inquiries to the park had been rebuffed.

Angry at this outcome and without approaching SEAC, Trelewicz on September 9, 2000, made a request under the Freedom of Information Act (FOIA) "for reports including a listing of recovered objects along with permission to view and photograph them." According to Trelewicz (2001: 3) "ALL" of the reports were not provided because they were deemed "extremely sensitive" (by the park). On November 22, 2000, Trelewicz appealed the decision to the Department of the Interior. At about the same time he also took it upon himself to contact the Ministry of Defence of the United Kingdom, for its opinion regarding the ownership of the ship.

Before the U.S. Department of Interior replied to the appeal from Trelewicz, the British Ministry of Defence wrote on February 2, 2001: "The policy of the UK (United Kingdom) towards the sovereignty of shipwreck warships is that the UK retains sovereign rights and continuing ownership of its warships in accordance with the International Salvage Convention" (Trelewicz 2001: 3).

On March 12 Trelewicz received a negative reply from the Department of the Interior for a release of information, and on March 30, 2001, he filed suit in the U.S. District Court in Miami, Florida (Case No. 01-1311-Civ-Moore). Trelewicz would "lose" his FOIA request (Hitchcock 2006: 471), because some of the materials in the files contained information on the site's exact location. Of course, he always knew where the site was located through his own research and information readily available on the web and through other U.S. government venues, including NOAA. Major Trelewicz ultimately received the information he wanted and more: even internal memos regarding his request were included.

On April 5, 2002 Trelewicz received a final letter from Her Majesty's Naval Base in Portsmouth, England (MacDonald 2002). Its author, Peter MacDonald (Naval Personnel Secretariat of the Ministry of Defense), was housed in the Victory Building, not a hundred yards from HMS *Victory*. He wrote what may well be a fitting epitaph for HMS *Fowey*. In part it reads:

I have examined our files and can find no indication that we have ever asked the US National Park Service to follow any specific guidance in respect of the remains of HMS FOWEY. Indeed, I am not sure that any such guidance would be required in this case. As we believe that the wreck, lying as it does within the protective boundaries of the Biscayne National Park, has been responsibly protected and preserved by the United States authorities.

Importantly, MacDonald went on to add:

As you know, the United Kingdom applies the concept of "Sovereign Immunity" to its wrecked military vessels. As I understand it, the United States also accepts this principle. It follows from this that *we would expect to be consulted about any proposals for further recoveries from the wreck of HMS FOWEY or major preservation works thereon* [emphasis added].

After this period Major Trelewicz contacted us about the site. We provided him with copies of our publications. In turn he provided us with a copy of the materials given to him by the Department of the Interior, which had been otherwise unavailable to us. Denis B. Trelewicz died on November 19, 2005, at the age of seventy-three.

During this period when the requests from Trelewicz were gaining traction, colleagues began to ask us to write the definitive book on HMS *Fowey*. Although flattered, we ignored their requests because of the availability of our earlier popular and professional publications and our other ongoing work and research (e.g., Skowronek 2002). Finally, at the Society for Historical Archaeology annual meeting in Mobile, Alabama, in 2002, we were approached by Meredith Morris-Babb, director of the University Press of Florida. She felt that the story was not just a part of Florida history but would tell the larger story of underwater archaeology and the harsh realities of research. And with that this book was born. We realized that in addition to our own abiding and prejudiced interest in *Fowey* we had a very significant story to tell.

To paraphrase radio commentator Paul Harvey, "Now you know *most* of the rest of the story." Some might say, "Too much of the story"; but we would beg to differ. We promised in the preface to this book that we would tell how research is conducted through the twists and turns that life deals us. As we trust you have seen, it is never a straight line from problem formulation to conclusions. We may wish it were, but it never is. You were warned that this would be a cautionary tale and indeed it is; but do not dismay, for we also said it was a love story. And it was our love for this site that led to this book.

When this project started in 1979 there were no federal laws protecting shipwrecks and the concept of "Sovereign Immunity" rights to warships had never been applied to "historic" vessels lost before 1939. With the victory in the Klein case, which now stands as a landmark in historic shipwreck litigation and preservation, and the later passage of both the Archaeological Resources Protection Act and the Abandoned Shipwreck Act, "historic" wrecks gained protection under the law for illicit salvage. At the same time the door seemed to open for research on practically any vessel.

Now, at the dawn of a new century, we can see that the United Kingdom has an absolute legitimate claim on the remains of HMS *Fowey*. Perhaps the trail we have blazed to the cities of Hull and Fowey in England can, in addition to Biscayne National Park, provide venues for the interpretation of *Fowey*.

We have attempted to demonstrate that the post–World War II days of defending the notion of "finders keepers" and "seat of the pants" archaeology are long gone. As some say, the cowboy days of underwater archaeology have passed.

So just what have we learned from our involvement in this project?

1. Be passionate about your research.
2. Surround yourself with colleagues who understand the topic of research and then ask others to comment on what you have found.
3. Listen to everyone's suggestions.
4. Be prepared to be wrong and acknowledge it when it happens.
5. Keep precise notes and records, write your reports in a timely manner, and make the information readily available to your colleagues.

Finally we admonish you always to remember that scientists, archaeologists, and other researchers also have to be accountable for their actions, if for no other reason than simply because "they just don't make historic shipwrecks anymore."

Fowey has been found and will never be lost again. To us, this great ship and those events and people of the mid-eighteenth century have, however briefly, come alive again. His Majesty's Ship *Fowey* will always remain a high point of our professional and personal lives.

And thus ends the tale of our great adventure.

Appendix 1

Underwater Archaeology: Legislation and Regulation

George R. Fischer

"Mere notions or concepts of natural justice of a trial judge which are not in accord with established equitable rules and maxims may not be applied in rendering judgment."

Florida Supreme Court

The following notes were primarily produced for use in courses on underwater archaeology at Florida State University. They were informally compiled in the 1970s through the 1990s, are in some instances out of date, and have not been thoroughly reviewed by legal experts. They therefore can be expected to contain some errors and oversights. They do not consider some developments in legislation and case law in the past decade and more, particularly in terms of international treaties and agreements, and recent case law. This is one of those subjects where the more I learned about it, the less I knew. The purpose of presentation here is to provide a layperson with an appreciation of the nature and scope of legal issues relating to underwater archaeology. We are indebted to Michele Aubrey of the NPS Division of Archeology and Anthropology for her review and commentary, which provided the basis for some updating (I believe her main conclusion from review was that she would not want me as an attorney). Ole Varmer, attorney for NOAA, also very kindly provided information that is cited here as well as in chapter 10 and in appendix 2. We have tried to provide some updated information, but development of an accurate and comprehensive statement on this subject is beyond the scope of this book and would be outdated before it was published anyway. Suffice it to say, we hope the reader can learn enough from this to realize that in these matters you should find not just a good attorney but one who knows what she/he is doing in this subject area.

The legal issues that have swirled around the Legare Anchorage wreck and other archaeological sites are complex. The following compilation is provided as a starting point for a layperson's understanding of this complicated subject.

Historic Resources Legislation and Regulation

Underwater archaeology, although a fairly recently developed field of investigations, is affected by very ancient rules of law. Although essentially the same legislative principles apply as with terrestrial sites, underwater sites additionally are often affected by more complex legal principles relating to jurisdiction, ownership, admiralty law, and other subjects.

A key legal aspect of every shipwreck site (or almost all cultural resources for that matter) is ownership: they all belong to someone; the ship's owner, the insurance company, the landowner, and occasionally the discoverer. The main legal question often is who that owner is.

Shipwreck sites serve as classic cases, and in many instances as legal precedents, for legal principles that to a lesser and more subtle extent affect terrestrial sites. It is therefore to the advantage of the archaeologist wholly interested in land sites to have a basic familiarity with the legal situation relating to submerged sites. Among such examples are the principle of sovereign prerogative of Anglo-American law and the concepts of lost, misplaced, and abandoned property and treasure trove.

Antiquities Act

The Antiquities Act of June 6, 1906 (Public Law 59-209, 34 Stat. 225, 16 USC 431), and the Uniform Rules and Regulations prescribed by the secretaries of the interior, agriculture, and war to carry out the provisions of the act (12/28/1906; 36 CFR par. 2.20(a)(1) 1967; 46 CFR 3.1–3.17 1966), is the most basic legislation relating to archaeological resources. It makes it illegal to appropriate, excavate, injure, or destroy any prehistoric or historic ruin or monument or any object of antiquity situated on lands owned or controlled by the government of the United States without permission of the secretary of the department of the government having jurisdiction over the lands on which the antiquities are situated. It provides for issuance of permits to properly qualified institutions for investigation of antiquities, provided these are undertaken for the benefit of reputable and recognized scientific or educational institutions with the view toward increasing knowledge and the gatherings are preserved permanently in public museums. The punitive section provides for fines of $500 and imprisonment of three months.

This is the first and most basic piece of federal legislation dealing with antiquities. One factor that has been legally significant over the years is that courts have interpreted this act, and subsequent legislation, as indicating an *intent* on the part of Congress for a national policy of preservation of historic resources for public use and the public good.

National Park Service policy 9 (codified in 36 CFR) prohibits use of metal detectors or other subsurface locating devices for the search and recovery of metal objects of any kind, or other materials, as an archaeological activity subject to Antiquities Act control and regulation.

Archaeological Resources Protection Act

The Antiquities Act is essentially superseded by the Archaeological Resources Protection Act of 1979 as amended (P.L. 96–95 10/31/79) (As of this writing it has been amended four times.)

This legislation reinforces and carries further the intent of the Antiquities Act and says that "archaeological resources on public lands and Indian lands are an accessible and irreplaceable part of the Nation's heritage." In addition to Indian lands, it applies to lands owned and administered by the United States as part of the national park system, the national wildlife refuge system, the national forest system, and all other lands to which the United States holds the fee title other than lands on the outer continental shelf and lands under the jurisdiction of the Smithsonian Institution. It is quite specific in defining archaeological resources (a problem with the Antiquities Act) and the circumstances under which they should be protected or investigated, and further details and examples are provided in uniform regulations issued by the Tennessee Valley Authority (18 CFR 1312), the Department of Defense (32 CFR 229), the Department of Agriculture (35 CFR 296), and the Department of the Interior (43 CFR 7).

One of the most important things is that this law puts some teeth into antiquities protection. While the old law provided basically a slap on the wrist, the Archaeological Resources Protection Act has significant criminal penalties. Violation of the law may be prosecuted as a felony.

Criminal Penalties

First offense: $10,000 and 1 year imprisonment.

If the value of resources destroyed exceeds $5,000, the penalty may be $20,000 and 2 years.

Second and subsequent offenses: $100,000 and 5 years.

Civil Penalties

Violators may be forced to pay:

A. The archaeological or commercial value of the resources involved.

B. The cost of restoration and repair of the resource.

The Act provides for rewards to persons providing information leading to a conviction.

Forfeiture

All vehicles and equipment used in connection with the violation may be permanently confiscated (particularly significant in underwater archaeology resources, where expensive boats and other equipment may be involved).

As a practical matter, most convictions have been on misdemeanor charges, but civil penalties have a very serious impact on violators. As the colorful Carl Clausen, former Florida State underwater archaeologist, used to say, it provides the authority to confiscate everything but their jock strap and a thin coat of suntan oil.

Historic Sites Act

The Historic Sites Act of August 21, 1935 (P.L. 74-292; 49 Stat. 666; 16 USC 461–467) provides for the preservation of historic American sites, buildings and objects, and antiquities of national significance.

This law authorizes the Historic Sites Survey and Historic American Buildings Survey; provides for investigations and research, obtaining properties, contracting, and making investigations; establishes the National Park Service Advisory Board; and authorizes the secretary of the interior to seek and accept outside assistance in administering the act.

Specifically, the Historic Sites Survey and Historic American Buildings Survey identify sites of national significance, regardless of ownership, and grant recognition through the National Historic Landmark Program, which provides national recognition and some protection.

National Historic Preservation Act

The National Historic Preservation Act of 10/15/1966 (NHPA; P.L. 89-665; 80 Stat. 915 as Amended) provides for the expansion of the National Register of Historic Places, a listing of federal, state, and other properties of historic or cultural significance established by the Historic Sites Act of 1935. It also establishes a matching grant-in-aid program to states and the National Trust for Historic Preservation. The Advisory Council on Historic Preservation provides a review of federal undertakings that might affect register properties. Section 106 of the act requires federal agencies with jurisdiction over federal or federally assisted undertakings on register properties to afford the Advisory Council an opportunity to comment. This section provides considerable protection for historic sites and properties.

National Register Criteria

1. Association with significant historical events.
2. Association with significant historical persons.
3. Possessing distinctive characteristics representative of a style or period.
4. Has, or has the potential for yielding, information important in prehistory or history.

The last is of importance archaeologically, particularly considering "potential," which to an extent can be interpreted as making an archaeological site eligible until proven otherwise.

One of the more important aspects of this law is that by providing matching grants to the states it instituted a mechanism of state historic preservation programs and establishment of State Historic Preservation Officers (SHPOs).

Executive Order 11593

Executive Order 11593 (May 13, 1971, "Protection and Enhancement of the Cultural Environment") declares a policy, implied by Congress in the Historic Preservation Act, that every federal agency is responsible for protecting cultural properties under its jurisdiction. It requires agencies to survey and nominate to the National Register all qualified properties in their custody. The order provides interim precautions to avoid harming properties that may meet requirements but are not yet nominated. Working with the

Advisory Council on Historic Preservation, agencies are to make certain federal plans and programs contribute to preservation of nonfederal historic resources.

National Environmental Policy Act of 1969

All federal undertakings with significant environmental effect must be covered with an environmental impact statement. Cultural as well as natural values must be identified. Agencies must show compliance with both Section 106 of the Historic Preservation Act and the Executive Order on Environmental Protection and explain how they will mitigate the impact of their projects on the cultural values identified.

Department of Transportation Act

The Department of Transportation Act of 1966 spells out mitigation possibilities specifically for application to highway activities. This is significant for underwater archaeology in terms of bridge construction that could impact submerged resources.

Archeological and Historic Preservation Act of 1974

The Archeological and Historic Preservation Act of 1974 (P.L. 93-291) codifies procedures for salvage activities, extending the Reservoir Salvage Act of 6/27/1960 (P.L. 86-523). Most importantly, it provides for expenditure of up to 1 percent of the cost of a project on historic preservation activities to mitigate its impact.

Unique and Marine Sanctuaries

These sanctuaries were established under the authority of Title III of the Marine Protection, Research, and Sanctuaries Act of 1972, according to guidelines promulgated in the June 27, 1974, Federal Register.

The act provides for issuance of regulations to control activities. In the case of archaeology these can include prohibiting anchorage, requiring permits for research, prohibiting salvage or disturbing remains, prohibiting diving except for scientific purposes under permit, prohibiting dredging, grappling, or using explosives in the vicinity, trawling, and so forth.

Five sanctuaries were initially established, the USS *Monitor* being the first. Many others have since been established, including the Florida Keys National Marine Sanctuary, which encompasses areas running the length of the keys.

Problems may exist regarding protection of cultural resources, because some are included in submerged areas beyond U.S. territorial jurisdiction. Although NOAA has taken the position that they are fully protected by historic preservation law and regulation, there are conflicts with international agreements regarding offshore lands and other federal laws.

Abandoned Shipwreck Act of 1987

This law (P.L. 100-298 4/28/88; first introduced by Congressman Charles Bennett of Florida on January 22, 1979) is the most significant piece of legislation affecting historic shipwreck sites.

Its most essential point is that it removes shipwrecks from the purview of admiralty salvage. It declares the inapplicability of the laws of salvage and finds to historic shipwreck sites, declares federal ownership of three categories of abandoned shipwrecks in American waters, and returns title to the states when the sites are located within their jurisdiction unless the site is on lands owned by the United States or an Indian tribe.

The act also provides rights of access to the public, guarantees recreational exploration, encourages establishment of marine parks, and otherwise encourages the best nonexploitative use of historic shipwreck sites.

Sunken Military Craft Act

The Sunken Military Craft Act (P.L. 108-375, 10 USC 113 Note and 118 Stat 2094–2098, 10/28/04) is part of the Ronald W. Reagan National Defense Authorization Act for Fiscal Year 2005.

This is the most significant piece of legislation concerning sunken military craft (vessels) belonging to the United States. It says that the rights, title, and interest of the United States in regard to U.S. sunken military craft (1) shall not be extinguished except by an express divestiture of title by the United States and (2) shall not be extinguished by the passage of time, regardless of when the sunken military craft sank.

Marine Jurisdiction

The significant legal concepts in the classification of submerged lands discussed below are basically the *traditional* definitions of submerged lands categories—which is to say the older and simpler standards we learned (before the confusion caused by international treaties, arbitrary definitions

of individual states, and so forth). The zones are further defined by the 1982
United Nations Convention on the Law of the Sea:

1. Internal Waters (inside the coastal baseline)
    A. Navigable Waters (state owned): "susceptible to commerce" or,
       more practically, having been used for commerce historically.
    B. Non-navigable Waters (privately owned): When a water course
       is a boundary, the centerline delineates property ownership: ex-
       ceptions are the Potomac River and a few others.
2. Territorial Sea (3 miles from mean high tide): 1 league—the "Cannonball Limit" (the distance a cannon could historically be fired)
   jurisdiction—as if it were dry land. The UN Law of the Sea Conference extends the Territorial Sea to 12 miles, but the language of
   the presidential proclamation (December 27, 1988) establishing this
   limit in the United States exempts historic shipwrecks, so for our
   purposes the limit remains 3 miles.
3. Contiguous Zone: 3–12 miles (or up to 24 nautical miles from the
   coastal baseline): customs control, rights of passage, health and
   military regulation, and marine salvage under the Treaty of the
   Law of the Sea.
   Fishing Zone: usually the contiguous zone, until recently extended
   to 200 miles in the United States as the "Exclusive Economic Zone."
4. Continental Shelf: the seabed beyond the territorial sea to 100
   miles or 100 fathoms, whichever occurs first. Reserved for resource
   exploitation by the adjacent state (country). The formal definition
   of this is so convoluted and complex that it is next to impossible
   to explain. Just figure no more than 200 nautical miles from the
   coastal baseline.
5. High Seas: the open water beyond the other zones.

Non-navigable Waters: a private owner who owns the shoreline (the
   "riparian owner") owns the water and the subsurface land under it
   to the center of the water body.
Navigable Waters Defined: waters that were navigable by any vessel, even a canoe, on the date when the state involved entered the
   Union. Another, more reasonable, definition is that navigable waters are those that are presently, have been in the past, or may be
   in the future susceptible to use for purposes of interstate or foreign

commerce. The United States controls operations on and under the water (U.S. Coast Guard and U.S. Army Corps of Engineers), but the adjacent state owns the water and the submerged beds and will also have an interest in archaeological operations. Special laws deal with the Great Lakes, Florida, New York Harbor, and other areas. The Corps of Engineers should be checked regarding operations on navigable waters.

State Authorities—fresh waters: the states control the offshore lands. In the case of rivers adjoining federal property, the federal government controls to the center of the stream or river; if the rivers adjoin state property, the state controls to the midpoint (with the classic exception of the Potomac, which is controlled by the state of Maryland); and if the river is on private land, the owner controls to the midpoint. Under Anglo-American law the private landowner (called the littoral landowner) has title to the seashore as far as the low-tide mark and also has title to the shores of lakes to the low-water mark.

Submerged Lands Act

The Submerged Lands Act of May 22, 1953 (67 Stat. 29; 43 USC Sec. 1301 et seq.) relinquished to the states full control over all submerged lands to the extent of three miles offshore, except for Florida and Texas on the Gulf of Mexico, where the jurisdiction of the states has been extended to three marine leagues (a little over ten miles).

The three-mile limit is generally defined as beginning at the mean high-tide mark.

Outer Continental Shelf Lands Act

The Outer Continental Shelf Lands Act of 10/7/53 (P.L. 83-212; 67 Stat. 462; 43 USC Sec. 1331 et seq.) reserves submerged lands on the outer continental shelf (defined as to a distance of 100 miles or to a depth of 100 fathoms, whichever occurs first) to the federal government for jurisdiction, with the exception of those lands to which the Submerged Lands Act applies, and puts the regulation of these offshore lands under the control of the secretary of the interior.

The Antiquities Act states application to "lands owned or controlled" by the United States. In the light of the tidelands cases, in which it has been established that the United States controls the lands of the outer continental shelf, there is logic in an assertion that this act applies to the shelf. The Outer Continental Shelf Lands Act states: "The Constitution and laws and civil and political jurisdiction of the United States are hereby extended to the subsoil and seabed of the Outer Continental Shelf . . . to the same extent as if the Outer Continental Shelf were an area of exclusive Federal jurisdiction located within a State." Despite the argument that it was not conceived by Congress, much less being the intent of Congress, that historic preservation legislation would apply to the outer continental shelf, this act appears to specify that it can. The Archaeological Resources Protection Act of 1979, however, includes an explicit statement in the definition of "public lands" that it does not include lands on the outer continental shelf—so much for that idea.

The U.S. Supreme Court in 1975 established exclusive U.S. jurisdiction over the outer continental shelf. The Fifth Circuit Court of Appeals at the same time ruled that this jurisdiction did not extend to shipwrecks. The Outer Continental Shelf Lands Act language is incompatible with the Convention on the Continental Shelf, which became effective law in the United States eleven years after the act (1964) and therefore supersedes it, according to a Treasure Salvors, Inc., case. As state law is superseded by federal law, international law then supersedes all.

Marine Salvage

Maritime salvage, which is provided for in the U.S. Constitution, has evolved from some of the most ancient codes of law. It is, in fact, a subject in the Mesopotamian Code of Hammurabi (1728–1686 BCE), the earliest codification from which our modern Western systems of law are derived.

Salvage law applies to a ship, its cargo, or its other property; and the salvor does not recover but gets a cash award. Under the law, the property itself is liable. This means that an admiralty court (in our case a U.S. District Court sitting in admiralty) will fix the amount of salvage and then order the object sold to pay it. This applies to flotsam, jetsam, lagan, and other forms of lost or abandoned property in coastal areas beyond the low-tide mark.

Under the Admiralty Salvage Act of August 12, 1912 (P.L. 62-249) a salvage and wrecking license can be issued by a U.S. District Court under provisions of Title 46 USC Section 724. This applies both to navigable inland waters and to the open sea.

The salvor is supposed to rescue a ship and/or its cargo from "peril" with significant effort and personal risk. Salvage is a service voluntarily rendered that saves property: voluntary assistance is rendered to a vessel at sea or its cargo or both, thereby saving them in whole or in part from impending peril or recovery from actual peril or loss.

Three elements must be present: (1) marine peril, (2) a service voluntarily rendered when not required by an existing duty or special contract, and (3) success in whole or in part or a contribution to such success.

A finder may locate property with or without the permission or knowledge of the owner and claim just compensation for salvage by either sale of the property or suit against the owner following return.

Salvage Awards

The court decides the amount of salvage allowed and whether in kind or from proceeds of the sale of the property. If after a reasonable length of time no valid claim of ownership can be made, all proceeds go to the salvor.

Until 1988 historic shipwrecks could be "salvaged" under this law. Because of the supremacy of federal law, the states had no power to limit or control exploitation of shipwreck sites in their jurisdiction, regardless of whatever state legislation existed (that is an issue resolved by the Civil War). The Abandoned Shipwreck Act of 1987 changed that by superseding the Admiralty Salvage Act of 1912 (one of the main intentions of this legislation) and declaring its inapplicability.

Property

A second order of principles beyond those of submerged lands jurisdiction that are relevant to the underwater archaeologist lie in the area of property ownership and control.

The concept of property entails not the physical object but rights over it; essentially this means control. The definition of finding property is reduction of it to the possession of the finder.

Another example: real property is owned, but only in terms of a legal definition wherein the "owner" has certain rights over it, although the sovereign or assignees may have other rights (as in application of the sovereign's laws).

Mislaid Property: property meant to be left where it was placed but in a location later forgotten by the owner.

Lost Property: property that came to rest at a spot unknown to the owner and without the owner's knowledge.

Abandoned Property: property in a location of which the owner is or was aware but to which the owner has openly or by implication renounced all claims.

Decisions on property classification are often arbitrary and confusing: the classic English example is a case where a 99-year lessee discovered a prehistoric shipwreck that the courts awarded to the landowner, although under the lease the lessee could probably have kept the lessor off the premises. Another classic example is the CSS *Alabama*, a U.S. Civil War–period Confederate commerce raider wrecked off the coast of Cherbourg, France. It is property of the federal government of the United States but is imbedded in French sovereign bottomlands. So both governments have a valid claim for some rights over the site.

In offshore areas the English common law of finders need not apply, and maritime rules prevail: property belongs to the sovereign unless the true owner proves a claim, which includes shipwreck sites and cargo, including:

Flotsam: floating property wrecked, lost, or abandoned.

Jetsam: jettisoned property, lying on the bottom.

Lagan: property on the bottom but marked by a flag or float.

The states, as successors to the sovereign (United States), may assert this same claim under the principle of sovereign prerogative. A treasure trove often also falls under this doctrine of English law and belongs to the sovereign.

Treasure Trove

A treasure trove may be money or coin, gold, silver, plate, or bullion found hidden in the earth or in another private place, the owner thereof being unknown. Historically its status has changed from an original principle of ownership by the finder to ownership by the sovereign to the present concept of sovereign prerogative superseding, when appropriate, a salvage claim against the true owner or the finder.

On federal lands, treasure trove functions are the responsibility of the General Services Administration (GSA) (P.L. 89-30 6/2/55; 48 Stat. 75; 5 USC 297 and note 248a, 40 USC 310). This transfers responsibility for making contracts and other provisions for the preservation, sale, or collection of wrecked, abandoned, or derelict property from the Department of the Treasury to the General Services Administration.

Shipwreck Ownership

Generally speaking, the owner of the land owns abandoned property on it, including abandoned shipwrecks. A particular distinction is whether it is "buried," in which case the owner's case is particularly strong against a "finder." Beyond that, things can become very complicated. For instance, to make a claim the owner must exercise formal abandonment procedures. Another factor here is that, if lives were lost, the bodies are considered by naval tradition to be "entombed" and therefore not to be disturbed, which essentially makes many sites "off limits" to investigators for any purpose.

The Abandoned Property Act of 1870 claims for the U.S. "Property which ought to come to the Government." This was applied quite broadly in the past, but in a 1970s court case (concerning the *Bertrand*, an 1865 steamboat in the Missouri River), the judge determined that the intent of Congress was to confiscate all property of the Confederacy that might be reused for war, with jurisdiction delegated to the GSA.

> Under the principle of Sovereign Immunity of a warship (or ship leased for non-commercial purposes, such as transportation of weapons) if the state of ownership has not formally abandoned it, it remains in the ownership of that state, and that claim will be honored by the state of location under international law, which is superior to national law. Under the Abandoned Property Act of 1870 Civil War vessels, and blockade runners, are unquestionably United States Property. In the contiguous zone the adjacent state can control activities, including salvage, under the current treaty of the sea (which the U.S. did not ratify, but accepts), except for portions relating to ocean mining.

Under that application, all Confederate naval vessels, blockade runners, and chartered private vessels "ought to come to the Government" and fall under the authority of the GSA.

An example is CSS *Alabama* off the coast of France. It lies on sovereign lands of a foreign nation (and is essentially under the control of that nation—the term here is "constructive possession") but remains the property of the United States.

In the *Bertrand* case the judge cited a case that confirmed U.S. jurisdiction over sunken navel vessels, even though they lie in state waters, as property that "ought to come to the U.S." on the basis of previously exercised rights of ownership and confirmed the GSA disposition authority for abandoned vessels.

> The landmark case fully interpreting the provisions of 40 USC 310 and construing the English doctrine of sovereign prerogative is *Russell et al.* v. *Fort Bales of Cotton*, 21 Fed. Case No. 12,154 (S.D. Fla. 1872) (case affirmed on appeal), in which decision a study was made of the ancient Jewish law and Code of Justinian as well as the commentaries of Blackstone and Kent.

That does not really say anything of much value to us here, but I love the reference and so include it. There is probably not much more I can say on the subject to confuse the reader further, but I will continue.

The issue of treaties and passing of property from one nation to another is a further complicating factor. For instance, Spain has been taking the position that shipwrecks Spain owned should continue in its ownership. Some countries in South America and elsewhere are taking the position that the sites really belong to them, as successors to the Spanish Crown. That will form the basis of some complex litigation.

State Authorities

Many states with marine jurisdictions have passed specific laws dealing with antiquities underwater. Others, including some with only freshwater jurisdictions, apply antiquities legislation that was designed for terrestrial sites. Some states, notably Florida, have taken the position that they will permit salvage, under their control, and are entitled to a cut of the recovered treasure. They have been disappointed to discover that this has been much more of a burden than an asset, and they gradually seem to be getting out of the salvage business.

Texas has a law nearly identical to Florida's law that permits salvage. The state had to do that in order to get the law through its legislature but has chosen not to exercise that option. Instead it has established a viable program of scientific investigations under state auspices.

International Law

Various treaties, UN conventions, and individual agreements create a complicated situation regarding jurisdictions on the high seas and activities of individual countries. These often create conflicts between and within international jurisdictions. Governments have been increasingly laying claim to shipwreck sites outside their own jurisdiction on the basis that they have never relinquished title to ships that they owned and lost elsewhere. This has proven to be a very fertile ground for further ligation.

The UNESCO Convention on the Protection of the Underwater Cultural Heritage

The goal of this important treaty, ratified on November 2, 2001, is to thwart the activities of treasure hunters by prohibiting the sale of looted artifacts that are over a hundred years old. In essence it states that the UN and its member states are committed "to improving the effectiveness of measures at the international and national levels for the preservation in place of, if necessary for scientific or protective purposes, the careful removal of the heritage that may be found beyond the territorial sea." This has significant potential for controlling licit and illicit salvage and excavation only under state-of-the-art scientific control. It also raises interesting questions within the profession of policies of total excavation vs. nondestructive or minimally destructive investigations.

And where does HMS *Fowey* fit into this? The case accidentally became a legal landmark and watershed. Previously salvors and their attorneys were successfully contending that historic shipwrecks and their contents were just rolling around on the bottom rotting apart, waiting for someone to pick them up. Judge Atkins specifically pointed out that was not the case. The *Fowey* site was buried and therefore had acquired some protection; thus the materials had reached a relative stability in the more than two centuries during which it had been resting on and under the ocean floor. He pointed out that the main peril it faced was not from the elements but from being "rescued." An attempt was made to establish the point that the Admiralty Salvage Act of 1912 should supersede historic preservation legislation and regulation. The judge said that it did not.

The most significant development from the case was the issue of "constructive possession." As explained by Ole Varmer (an attorney for NOAA, who has successfully used the case as a precedent in several lawsuits), regardless of whether the wreck was owned by the United States (NPS), the queen of England, Gerald Klein, or anyone else, it was embedded in federal lands. The NPS had constructive possession of the wreck site because it was a park resource and was being protected and managed by the park. As such, even if it was subsequently determined to be owned by the UK or any other party, the NPS constructive possession was sufficient to deny unwanted salvage and prevent looting or disturbance (Ole Varmer, personal communication, February 24, 2008). So our humble little *Fowey* continues to exert an influence on events. The shipwreck was embedded in property of the United States, which had "constructive possession" and therefore was the first owner. Had the United States failed to exercise ownership, Great Britain, under international agreement, would retain ownership; failing that, because the site falls within the territorial jurisdiction of the State of Florida, it could exercise a third tier claim of ownership. And finally, "finders keepers," Gerald Klein would have a valid claim.

Appendix 2

Timeline of Events in the History of HMS *Fowey*:
The Legare Anchorage Shipwreck

1743 The keel is laid for a fifth-rate warship to be named *Fowey* in the Blaydes Shipyard in Kingston-on-Hull, Yorkshire, England.

1744 (September 6) HMS *Fowey* is commissioned in Hull, Yorkshire, England.

1748 (June 28) HMS *Fowey* is lost off the Cape of Florida.

1748 (December 5) The captain and crew are exonerated for the loss of HMS *Fowey* in Portsmouth, England.

1968 *Prospectus for Underwater Archeology* (in the National Park Service) is written by George Fischer and Marion Riggs: the program is initiated.

1968 (October 16) Biscayne National Monument is established.

1970 George Fischer and George Sites begin compiling a base map of underwater sites in Biscayne National Monument.

1973 (May 2) U.S. District Judge Charles B. Fulton condemns 95,064 acres of land in south Dade County and turns it over to the federal government for Biscayne National Monument (Case No. 70-477-Civ-CF).

1975 George Fischer writes an archaeological assessment and compiles a preliminary archaeological base map of Biscayne identifying forty-six known and potential shipwreck sites.

1975 George Fischer and Martin Meylach conduct a magnetometer survey to "ground-truth" many submerged sites in Biscayne National Monument.

1978 (October) Gerald Joseph Klein, while spear-fishing with his son south of Miami, finds a shipwreck in Legare Anchorage and begins collecting artifacts from the site.

1979 (October 4) Gerald Klein files a "Complaint in Admiralty" in the U.S. District Court for the Southern District of Florida, Miami Division, in admiralty claiming "The Unidentified, Wrecked and Abandoned Sailing Vessel (Believed to have sunk in 1740)" in Legare Anchorage.

1979 (October 22) The court of U.S. District Judge C. Clyde Atkins states that it will not issue a warrant appointing Klein the substitute custodian of "an ancient sailing vessel, sunk in 1715" until Klein contacts federal and state officials. He sets a hearing for October 26, 1979 (Case No. 79-4627-Civ-CA).

1979 (October 26) Judge Atkins orders that Gerald Klein be made the "Substitute Custodian" of the wreck, giving him the right to continue salvaging it. The court will decide later how the finds will be divided among Klein, the State of Florida, and the federal government. This is reported the next day in the *Miami Herald* and on October 29 in the *South Dade News Leader*. The wreck is described as an "almost intact Spanish treasure galleon."

1979 (October 26) Curtiss Peterson, conservator for the Florida Bureau of Historic Sites and Properties, informs George Fischer of the Southeast Archeological Center that the court has noted that both the state and federal governments might be interested in this case.

1979 (October 29) Gerald Klein turns in his salvaged collections to U.S. marshals and is required to catalogue and turn over all subsequent finds. George Fischer reports in an internal SEAC memo his suspicions that the wreck could be either the *Consulado* or the *Pópulo*, both members of the 1733 *flota*. He also notes that William J. Gladwin, Jr., will be the counsel representing the State of Florida.

1979 (November 1) The Regional Solicitor's Office for the U.S. Department of the Interior in Atlanta is informed by the Southeast Archeological Center of a "possible treasure salvage effort in Biscayne National Monument."

1979 (November 21) Rebecca A. Donnellan, attorney for the U.S. Department of Justice, Land and Natural Resources Division, asks Gerald Klein's counsel, David Paul Horan, if Klein has conducted any salvage on the wreck and has either "sought or obtained" permission from Biscayne National Park. Horan confirms that salvage has occurred and that only the court has given permission to conduct salvage.

1979 (November 27) Donnellan requests a temporary restraining order and preliminary injunction and asks that all artifacts be turned over to the National Park Service.

1979 (November 28) U.S. District Judge Alcee L. Hastings permits the United States to "intervene as defendant" for the wreck against Klein's claim. Donnellan requests a restraining order because the wreck lies "within the boundaries of Biscayne National Monument." She notes that the Antiquities Act of 1906 and the Archaeological Resources Protection Act of 1979 (October 31, 1979) are applicable and that Klein did not have a permit for any activities within the monument that were damaging the wreck and the ecosystem. Judge Hastings places a temporary restraining order on Klein and all salvage activities.

1979 (December 12) In the Miami Chamber of Chief U.S. District Judge C. Clyde Atkins, Bill Gladwin, attorney for the State of Florida, and David Paul Horan, counsel for Gerald Klein, agree that a representative of the State of Florida will be present during all salvage and that proper conservation methods will be followed (Case No. 79-4227-Civ-ALH).

1979 (December 19) David F. McIntosh, an attorney with Corlett, Merritt, Killian & Sikes representing Gerald Klein, submits a "Memorandum of Law" that states: "The NPS is completely unable to preserve the wreck site from unauthorized salvors (pirates) who would not respect the Court's Order." The memorandum further argues for "the predominance of Admiralty and Maritime law over the regulations of the NPS."

1979 (December) Russell Skowronek works with George Fischer and Bill Gladwin and prepares a paper on the protection of cultural resources on the outer continental shelf.

1980 (January 2) In a conversation with George Fischer, Dr. Barbara Purdy, archaeologist with the Florida State Museum, states that she has been asked to provide professional oversight of excavations by representatives of Gerald Klein.

1980 (January 8 and 10) Rebecca Donnellan argues the motion for a preliminary injunction. One of the witnesses for Gerald Klein is Mel Fisher. Nonetheless, the court grants the motion, names the secretary of the interior the substitute custodian, orders Klein to turn over all salvaged materials to the National Park Service, and directs the United States to locate and protect the wreck.

1980 (January 12) The *Tallahassee Democrat* prints an article titled "Federal Agency Is Proud Owner of Spanish Galleon It Can't Find."

1980 (January, February, March) Staff members of the Southeast Archeological Center try to clarify exactly what the court wants done and how they are supposed to do it and also have to find funding. On February 3 SEAC discovers that the staff members of Biscayne National Monument have been acting independently and were ready to begin their search before the judge issued his written opinion.

1980 (March 19) George Fischer of the Southeast Archeological Center travels to Miami and receives the collections from the site made by Gerald Klein.

1980 (April) The chief of SEAC asks the Mobile, Alabama, and Savannah, Georgia, offices of the U.S. Army Corps of Engineers for the loan of a magnetometer and requests that archaeologist Larry Murphy be temporarily assigned to the Southeast Region to operate the magnetometer.

1980 (June 26) Biscayne National Monument becomes Biscayne National Park.

1980 (June 26 through July 6) George Fischer directs an eleven-day project to find the "Unidentified, Wrecked and Abandoned Sailing Vessel" claimed by Gerald Klein.

1980 (July 4) The Legare Anchorage Wreck is located by the NPS. Twenty-one artifacts are collected.

1980 (September 29) A photomosaic of the Legare Anchorage wreck is provided to Rebecca Donnellan.

1980 (October 1) Attorneys for Gerald Klein request detailed information on the summer 1980 archaeological project, including the participants, the discoveries, and the number of dives made.

1980 (October) The Southeast Archeological Center learns that a "Treasure Hunt Special" is offered with dinner at Klein's restaurant Joan's Galley, including a "Free treasure map of authentic sunken galleon with cannons, artifacts etc."

1980 (Fall) Mendel Peterson of the Smithsonian visits Tallahassee and states that there is a 95 percent probability that the Legare Anchorage wreck is the *Pópulo*.

1980 (November 19) The United States provides the answers to the interrogatories requested on October 1. Five fragments of ceramic have been recovered, none of Spanish or Spanish-colonial origin.

1980 (December 12) Richard Johnson of SEAC writes a memo regarding the possibility that the Legare Anchorage wreck is British.

1980 (December 15) A hearing is held in Key West to determine if the Southern District Court has admiralty jurisdiction that would include wrecks within Biscayne National Park. No decision is made, but the presiding judge takes it under advisement.

1981 (January) Rich Johnson returns from the annual Society for Historical Archaeology and Conference on Underwater Archaeology meeting in New Orleans with information suggesting that the wreck could be HMS *Fowey*.

1981 George Fischer and Rich Johnson complete a draft of the 1980 survey report, which is rejected, basically because Fischer has not come up with an acceptable solution for the problem.

1981 (June 9) George Fischer reports to chief Richard Faust of the Southeast Archeological Center that research staff members from Biscayne National Park have recovered a shoe buckle and one fragment each of bone and wood from the Legare Anchorage site. He notes that Rebecca Donnellan reports that no actions are forthcoming.

1981 (July 7) The court restrains "any and all salvage operations."

1981 (August 10) A hearing is held in Key West regarding the interrogatories and the information contained therein.

1981 (October 24) Attorneys for Gerald Klein file a motion to produce the artifacts collected in 1980 in court.

1981 (October) Russell Skowronek travels to Great Britain to work in the National Archives (Public Records Office) and compiles a paper for the Southeast Archeological Center on historic resources pertaining to the Legare Anchorage site.

1982 (January 1) Gerald Klein is murdered in Miami.

1982 (December 12) The case (H2219) is transferred from Judge King back to Judge Hastings, who is considered more sympathetic to the NPS but is not hearing cases because of bribery accusations against him.

1983 (February 4) Judge Hastings resigns and moves on to senior judge status and only has to hear the cases he wants to hear. Seven witnesses come forward saying that they dove with Gerald Klein. He said that there were only five.

1983 (February 25) Color slides taken of the Legare Anchorage wreck are provided for the legal proceedings by SEAC.

1983 (Spring) Plans are formulated at SEAC for a testing and evaluation project to determine the "age, function, and cultural affiliation" of the Legare Anchorage wreck.

1983 (Spring) A trial is held in Miami, U.S. District Judge C. Clyde Atkins presiding.

1983 (May 4) Rebecca Donnellan asks the U.S. District Court to modify its restraining order of July 7, 1981, for archaeological testing and evaluation of the site.

1983 (May 13) Judge Atkins orders that the United States may conduct "salvage" on the Legare Anchorage wreck.

1983 (May–June) George Fischer of SEAC serves as the principal investigator for the testing and evaluation of the Legare Anchorage wreck. Russell Skowronek of SEAC is the field director.

1983 (July 28) Judge Atkins submits his opinion on the ownership of the Legare Anchorage wreck. In the Findings of Fact and Conclusions of Law he rejects Gerald Klein's claim and finds that the wreck is the property of the United States. He notes that the wreck is embedded in the seabed within the confines of Biscayne National Park and that Klein did not apply for a permit for exploration as laid out in the Antiquities Act of 1906. He also rejects the claim for a liberal salvage award. Atkins is reported to have said: "Unfortunately, the plaintiff's unauthorized disturbance of one of the oldest shipwrecks in the park and his unscientific removal of the artifacts did more to create a marine peril than to prevent one."

1984 (January 5–8) A symposium titled "Investigation of the Legare Anchorage Shipwreck Site Biscayne National Park" is held at the Society for Historical Archaeology and Conference on Underwater Archaeology annual meeting in Williamsburg, Virginia. George Fischer chairs the session, with papers delivered by Fischer, Rebecca Donnellan (in absentia), Richard Johnson, Russell Skowronek, Richard Vernon, and Kenneth Wild.

1984 (August) An appeal of the findings of Judge Atkins findings is argued at the U.S. Court of Appeals, Eleventh Circuit.

1984 The report on the findings of the 1983 Southeast Archeological Center project is completed (Skowronek 1984a).

1984 David Brewer and Kenneth Wild of SEAC visit the site as part of another project.

1985 (April 29) The U.S. Court of Appeals, Eleventh Circuit, affirms the U.S. District Court decision in favor of the United States.

1985 An article on the wreck by Russell Skowronek appears in *Archaeology Magazine*.

1986 Chief anthropologist Douglas Scovill and chief historian Edwin Bearss commend Skowronek and Fischer for the 1984 report on the 1983 SEAC project.

1987 An article on the wreck by Skowronek, Johnson, Vernon, and Fischer is published in the *International Journal of Nautical Archaeology*.

1988 (April 28) President Ronald Reagan signs the Abandoned Shipwreck

Act (Public Law 100-298). House Report 100-514 (parts I and II) notes that an affirmative act of abandonment is required of a sovereign to abandon sunken warships and that passage of time or lack of positive assertions of right is insufficient to establish such abandonment.

1988 The proceedings of the 1984 conference are published, with articles by Donnellan, Fischer, Johnson, Skowronek, Vernon, and Wild.

1988 Dr. Roger Smith, Florida state underwater archaeologist, visits the site.

1990 (December 4) The National Park Service issues the final *Abandoned Shipwreck Act Guidelines* (available through http://www.nps.gov/history/archeology/sites/subcul.htm) to assist state and federal agencies in carrying out their responsibilities under the act, including guidance concerning historic shipwrecks entitled to sovereign immunity, which are not subject to the act.

1992 (August 24) Hurricane Andrew strikes Florida.

1992 (September 20) David Brewer (SEAC) and Larry Murphy (Submerged Cultural Resources Unit) assess the site for storm damage.

1992 The Legare Anchorage wreck is cited in *Craft*, CV 92 1769 (1992). "In Klein, the Eleventh Circuit found that when the federal government creates a national park in navigable waters, possession of resources beneath those waters vests in the United States. Klein, 758 F.2d at 1514. Although that case involved a designation of a national park, the analysis is the same. In passing the [National Marine Sanctuary Act: NMSA] Congress asserted its possession in the [sanctuary]. As the Ninth Circuit has explained, under admiralty law principles, someone in possession may refuse services of would be salvors like the plaintiffs." *Craft*, 34 F.2d 918 (9th Cir. 1994).

1993 The Submerged Cultural Resources Unit, with support from the University of Maryland and the Maritime Archaeological and Historical Society, conducts a project on the Legare Anchorage wreck.

1995 The *Fowey* Site Stabilization Seminar is held at the Sheraton Key Resort on Key Largo.

1996 (January) John Seidel and Larry Murphy deliver a paper on the 1993 project and the 1995 conference at the Society for Historical Archaeology and Conference on Underwater Archaeology Annual meeting in Cincinnati, Ohio.

1996 (December) Eric Adams publishes an article on the 1993 project in *Naval History*.

1997 Fischer and Skowronek write to *Naval History* about the Adams article. Mention of the 1993 project is made in James Delgado's *British Museum Encyclopedia of Underwater and Maritime Archaeology*.

1997 The Legare Anchorage wreck is cited in *U.S. v. Salvors, Inc. (Fisher)*, No. 92-10027 (S.D. Fla. 1997) (NMSA precludes the application of the law of finds and salvage in the Florida Keys National Marine Sanctuary); *U.S. v. Salvors, Inc. (Fisher)*, 997 F. Supp. 1193 (S.D. Fla. 1997); *U.S. v. Fisher*, 34 F.3d 262 (11th Cir. 1994) (a preliminary injunction against salvage activities without a permit from the NOAA).

2000 (July 21) The U.S. Court of Appeals, Fourth Circuit, upholds the Kingdom of Spain's right as owner of its sunken navy frigates *Juno* and *La Galga* to prevent unauthorized disturbance or commercial salvage and orders the salvor to return to Spain's possession all artifacts it has removed from the sites.

2000 (September 9) Major Denis Trelewicz requests under the Freedom of Information Act documentation pertaining to the Legare Anchorage shipwreck.

2000 (November 8) The British naval attaché to the British Embassy in Washington, D.C., responds to an inquiry from Denis Trelewicz saying that the United Kingdom has not waived any rights to the HMS *Fowey* and that the U.S. Department of State is in discussions with the United Kingdom to gain permission to take steps to preserve the HMS *Fowey*, which has begun to erode and deteriorate since the passage of Hurricane Andrew.

2001 (January 19) President William J. Clinton issues a *Presidential Statement on United States Policy for the Protection of Sunken State Craft*, which includes sunken government vessels, aircraft, and spacecraft (state craft) of the United States and foreign nations (Weekly Compilation of Presidential Documents, vol. 37, no. 3, pp. 195–196, available through http://www.access.gpo.gov/nara/nara003.html). The statement reaffirms that title to sunken state craft is retained by a sovereign indefinitely unless title has been abandoned or transferred in accordance with the law of the sovereign and that such title is not extinguished, wherever located, by passage of time, regardless of when the sunken state craft was lost at sea.

2001 (February 2) The Ministry of Defence for the United Kingdom notes that the United Kingdom retains sovereign rights and continuing ownership of its warships in accordance with the International Salvage Convention.

2002 An entry on HMS *Fowey* written by Skowronek appears in the *Encyclopedia of Historical Archaeology*.

2003 (July 4) The Foreign and Commonwealth Office of the United Kingdom reaffirms to the U.S. Department of State its policies concerning ownership of sunken state vessels and aircraft, that such ownership rights are not lost by the passage of time, and that no action may be taken in relation to the United Kingdom's sovereign immune state vessels or aircraft without the express consent of the United Kingdom.

2004 (February 2) A book contract is finalized between Skowronek and Fischer and the University Press of Florida for *HMS* Fowey *Lost and Found*.

2004 (February 5) The U.S. Department of State issues Public Notice 4614 on *Protection of Sunken Warships, Military Aircraft and Other Sunken Government Property* (Federal Register vol. 69, no. 24, pp. 5647–5648, available through http://www.gpoaccess.gov/fr/index.html). The notice provides information concerning the policies of France, Germany, Japan, the Russian Federation, Spain, the United Kingdom, and the United States and includes contacts in the respective government offices for each nation as well as a contact for any other nation not listed above.

2004 (October 28) President George W. Bush signs the Sunken Military Craft Act, which is part of the Ronald W. Reagan National Defense Authorization Act for Fiscal Year 2005 (P.L. 108-375, Division A, Title XIV). It reaffirms that the right, title, and interest of the United States in and to any U.S. sunken military craft is not extinguished except by an express divestiture of title by the United States and is not extinguished by the passage of time, regardless of when the sunken military craft sank.

2007 (January) The National Park Service publishes *Science, Politics, and the "Big Dig": A History of the Southeast Archeological Center* by Cameron Binkley. It is distributed the following July.

2007 (July 31) Following anonymous review, *HMS* Fowey *Lost and Found* is accepted for publication by the University Press of Florida.

References Cited

Copies of many of the primary documents cited in this book may be found in the George R. Fischer Collection housed at the St. Augustine Lighthouse and Museum.

Primary or Unpublished References

British Library, London

1733 "Map of Florida Keys 1733" (call number 31357 NNN)
Lloyd's List, No. 1338, Tuesday, September 20, 1748
New York Weekly Journal, August 1, 1748, No. 763, page 2
South Carolina Gazette, June 27–July 9, 1748, No. 742, page 4

Legal Cases

Craft. 1992. CV 92 1769
Craft. 1994. 34 F.2d 918 (9th Cir.)
Sea Hunt, Inc. Plaintiff v. *Kingdom of Spain and Commonwealth of Virginia*. 2000. United States Court of Appeals for the Fourth Circuit, Eastern District of Virginia, at Norfolk (CA-98-281-2)
U.S. v. *Salvors, Inc. (Fisher)*. 1997. No. 92-10027 (S.D. Fla.)

National Archives (formerly the Public Records Office), Kew, Admiralty Records

ADM 1/234 Letters from Senior Officers, Jamaica 1746–1758
ADM 1/480 Letters from Commanders-in-Chief North America, 1745–1763
ADM 1/480 and 1/5292 *Boston Evening Post*, dateline Newport, R.I., July 22, 1748
ADM 1/5292 Courts-Martial, 1748–1749
ADM 6/17 Commission and Warrant Book, 1745–1751
ADM 7/571/171 Abstracts of the Proceedings
ADM 8/25 List Books
ADM 32/83 Pay Books
ADM 36/1187 Jaimaica Cheque [*sic*], Complement-Victuals-Muster Lists
ADM 36/1187 Muster Books, *Fowey*
ADM 51/340 Captains' Logs
ADM 51/3844 Captains' Logs

ADM 107/3 Lieutenants' Passing Certificates, 1712–1745
ADM 180/2 Progress and Dimension Books
ADM 180/3 Progress and Dimension Books, 5th Rates & Below, 1722–1775
ADM 354/141/17 Navy Board Out-letters, Correspondence 1749

National Maritime Museum, Greenwich: Draughts and Plans

Ranks and Titles of Naval Officers, 1983 (mimeograph no. 24487)
Reg. No. 1791, Box 33, Admiralty Whitehall
Reg. No. 1821, Box 33, Admiralty Whitehall

Nova Scotia Public Archives

MG100, Vol. 178, No. 12 or RG1, Vol. 19 (Extracts from Contemporary Correspondence
or Louisbourg Letters)

U.S. Government

Federal Register. 2004. Department of State [Public Notice 4614], Office of Ocean Affairs. Protection of Sunken Warships, Military Aircraft and Other Sunken Property, February 5, 69(24): 5647–5648.

Secondary References

Adams, Eric. 1996. Hurricane Uncovers 19th-Century Wreck. *Naval History* 10(5): 32–35.
Ansel, Willits. 1976. The Building of a Wooden Ship. Photocopy handout. Mystic Seaport Museum, Mystic, Conn.
Archibald, Edward H. H. 1968. *The Wooden Fighting Ship in the Royal Navy A.D. 897–1860.* Arco Publishing Co., Inc., New York.
Barton, Kenneth J. 1977. *The Western European Coarse Earthenwares from the Wreck of the* Machault. Occasional Papers in Archaeology and History, vol. 16. Parks Canada, Ottawa.
———. 1981. *Coarse Earthenwares from the Fortress of Louisbourg.* History and Archaeology Series 55. Parks Canada, Ottawa.
Bass, George F. 1979. The Men Who Stole the Stars. *Sea History* 12 (Fall): 30.
Bidwell, Randy. 1983. Preservation of Natural Resources-Elk Horn Reef, Case Incident Report #830240, July 14. Biscayne National Park and Southeast Archeological Center.
Binkley, Cameron. 2007. *Science, Politics, and the "Big Dig": A History of the Southeast Archeological Center and Development of Cultural Resource Management in the Southeast.* Cultural Resources Division, Southeast Regional Office, Atlanta, Ga.
Bishop, Robert. 1763. *Further Observations and Remarks Made in the Years 1761 and 1762 for the Safer Navigation of Divers Parts of the West Indies.* 1st edition. London. (Original in the John Carter Brown Library, Brown University, Providence, R.I.)

————. 1765. *Instructions and Observations Relative to the Navigation of the Windward and Gulph Passages, as Laid Down in Two Large Charts*. 2d edition. Dedicated, by Permission, to the Right Honourable the Lords Commissioners of the Admiralty. Printed by the author and sold, with the charts at the Jamaica Coffee-House, London. (Original in the John Carter Brown Library, Brown University, Providence, R.I.)

Blanchette, Jean-François. 1981. *The Role of Artifacts in the Study of Foodways in New France, 1720–60*. History and Archaeology Series 52. Parks Canada, Ottawa.

Broad, William J. 2000. Court Ruling on Spanish Frigates Foils Modern-Day Treasure Hunt. *New York Times,* July 31, pp. A1, A11.

Brown, Margaret K. 1971. Glass from Fort Michilimackinac: A Classification for Eighteenth-Century Glass. *Michigan Archaeologist* 17: 3–4.

Burgess, Robert F. 1980. *Man 12,000 Years under the Sea: A Story of Underwater Archaeology*. Dodd, Mead and Company, New York.

————. 1988. *Sunken Treasure: Six Who Found Fortunes*. Dodd, Mead and Company, New York.

————. 2000 [1977]. *They Found Treasure*. IUniverse.com, Lincoln.

Burgess, Robert F., and Carl J. Clausen. 1976. *Gold, Galleons, and Archaeology*. Bobbs-Merrill, Indianapolis.

————. 1982. *Florida's Golden Galleons: The Search for the 1715 Spanish Treasure Fleet*. Florida Classics Library, Port Salerno, Fla.

Calver, William L., and Reginald P. Bolton. 1950. *History Written with Pick and Shovel*. New York Historical Society, New York.

Charnock, John. 1797. *Biographia Navalis; or, Impartial Memoirs of the Lives and Characters of Officers of the Navy of Great Britain*. Vol. 5. R. Faulder, London. (Original in the Stanford University Library, Stanford, Calif.)

————. 1798. *Biographia Navalis; or, Impartial Memoirs of the Lives and Characters of Officers of the Navy of Great Britain*. Vol. 6. R. Faulder, London. (Original in the Stanford University Library, Stanford, Calif.)

Childs, R. G. 1983. Preservation of Natural Resources—Legare Anchorage, Case Incident Report #830317, September 1. Biscayne National Park and Southeast Archeological Center.

Clausen, Carl J., and J. Barto Arnold III. 1976. The Magnetometer and Underwater Archaeology. *International Journal of Nautical Archaeology and Underwater Exploration* 5(2): 158–165.

Colledge, J. J. 1969. *Ships of the Royal Navy, An Historical Index*. Vol. 1, *Major Ships*. David and Charles, Newton Abbot.

————. 1987. *Ships of the Royal Navy*. Naval Institute Press, Annapolis.

Copeland, Peter. 1969. Small Arms from Spanish 18th-Century Shipwreck Sites. *Military Collector and Historian* (Washington, D.C.) (Spring): 18.

Crankshaw, Joe, and Mary Voboril. 1979. Finders Keepers, Judge Lets Diver Keep Sunken Galleon, for Now. *Miami Herald*, October 27.

Culver, Henry B., and Gordon Grant. 1924. *The Book of Old Ships*. Garden City Publishing Co., Inc., New York.

Curry, Richard. 1983. Preservation of Resources—Legare Anchorage, Case Incident Report #830352, October 20. Biscayne National Park and Southeast Archeological Center.

Day, James. 1988. Seascape. *Philip Morris Magazine* 3(3): 40–43.

Deagan, Kathleen A. 1978. Ceramic Dates—St. Augustine Field School. MS on file, St. Augustine Historic Preservation Board.

Delgado, James P. (editor). 1997. *British Museum Encyclopedia of Underwater and Maritime Archaeology*. British Museum Press, London.

Donnellan, Rebecca A. 1988. Litigation regarding the Legare Anchorage Shipwreck. In *In Search of Our Maritime Past* (Proceedings of the Fifteenth Conference on Underwater Archaeology, Williamsburg, Va., 1984), ed. J. W. Bream, R. Folse-Elliot, C. V. Jackson, and G. P. Watts, pp. 147–148. Program in Maritime History and Underwater Research, East Carolina University, Greenville, N.C.

Elliot-Drake, Lady Elizabeth Fuller. 1911. *The Family and Heirs of Sir Francis Drake*. Smith, Elder and Co., London.

Fairbanks, Charles H. 1973. The Cultural Significance of Spanish Ceramics. In *Ceramics in America*, ed. I. M. G. Quimby, 141–174. University Press of Virginia, Charlottesville.

Federal Agency Is Proud Owner of Spanish Galleon It Can't Find. 1980. *Tallahassee Democrat*, January 12, p. 2B.

Fischer, George R. 1975. Preliminary Archeological Assessment, Biscayne National Monument, Fla. MS on file, Southeast Archeological Center, Tallahassee, Fla.

———. 1983. 106 Statement: Biscayne National Park Underwater Archeological Investigation Site BISC-UW-20. MS on file, Southeast Archeological Center, Tallahassee, Fla.

———. 1988. Investigation of the Legare Anchorage Shipwreck,, Biscayne National Park, Florida. In *In Search of Our Maritime Past* (Proceedings of the Fifteenth Conference on Underwater Archaeology, Williamsburg, Va., 1984), ed. J. W. Bream, R. Folse-Elliot, C. V. Jackson, and G. P. Watts, pp. 143–167. Program in Maritime History and Underwater Research, East Carolina University, Greenville, N.C.

———. 1997. Letters. *Naval History* 11: 3.

Fischer, George, and Richard E. Johnson. 1980. Interim Report: Underwater Archeological Survey of Legare Anchorage Biscayne National Park. MS on file, Southeast Archeological Center, Tallahassee, Fla.

———. 1981. (Draft) Legare Anchorage Wreck Survey, Testing and Historical Research. MS on file, Southeast Archeological Center, Tallahassee, Fla.

Fischer, George R., and Marion J. Riggs. 1968a. *Prospectus for Underwater Archeology*. Division of Archeology, National Park Service, Washington, D.C.

——— (compilers). 1968b. Legislative and Related Guidelines for Archeological Programs (mimeograph). Division of Archeology, National Park Service, Washington, D.C.

Garner, F. H. 1948. *English Delftware*. Faber and Faber, London.

Goggin, John M. 1960. Underwater Archaeology: Its Nature and Limitations. *American Antiquity* 23(3): 348–354.

Gooding, S. James. 1980. *An Introduction to British Artillery in North America*. Museum Restoration Service, Bloomfield, Ontario.

Gower, Richard Hall. 1808. *A Treatise on the Theory and Practice of Seamanship*. Wilkie and Robinson, London.

Gregor, Hugh. 1973. *HMS* Victory. Macmillan Press Ltd., London.

Grimm, Jacob L. 1970. *Archaeological Investigation of Fort Ligonier 1960–1965*. Carnegie Museum, Pittsburgh.

Hall, Jerome Lynn. 2007. The Fig and the Spade: Countering Deceptions of Treasure Hunters. *AIA Archaeology Watch*, August 15, pp. 1–10. Archaeological Institute of America, New York.

Hanson, Lee, and Dick Ping Hsu. 1975. *Casemates and Cannonballs: Archeological Investigations at Fort Stanwix, Rome, New York*. Publications in Archeology No. 14. Department of the Interior, Washington, D.C.

Harris, Jane E. 1979. *Eighteenth-Century French Blue-Green Bottles from the Fortress of Louisbourg, Nova Scotia*. History and Archaeology Series 29. Parks Canada, Ottawa.

Hitchcock, Ann. 2006. FOIA and Protecting Cultural Resources. In *People, Places, and Parks: Proceedings of the 2005 George Wright Society Conference on Parks, Protected Areas, and Cultural Sites*, ed. David Harmon, 471. George Wright Society, Hancock, Mich.

Johnson, Richard E. 1980. Memo to Richard D. Faust, Chief, Southeast Archeological Center, December 12. Biscayne National Park—Research Possibilities regarding Possible British Origin of the Legare Wreck (BISC-UW-20). MS on file, Southeast Archeological Center, Tallahassee, Fla.

———. 1981. The Historical Geography(?) of the HMS *Fowey*. MS on file, Southeast Archeological Center, Tallahassee, Fla.

———. 1988. The Historical Geography of the [*sic*] HMS *Fowey*. In *In Search of Our Maritime Past* (Proceedings of the Fifteenth Conference on Underwater Archaeology, Williamsburg, Va., 1984), ed. J. W. Bream, R. Folse-Elliot, C. V. Jackson, and G. P. Watts, pp. 163–166. Program in Maritime History and Underwater Research, East Carolina University, Greenville, N.C.

Johnson, Richard E., and Russell K. Skowronek. 1983. A Quantitative Analysis of Patterning Potential in Shipwreck Artifact Assemblages. Paper presented at the 1983 meeting of the Society for Historical Archaeology/Conference on Underwater Archaeology—Session 32, Denver, Colo.

Judge Rejects Man's Claim to Salvage English Shipwreck. 1983. *Orlando Sentinel*, July 29, p. B-5.

King, Dean, with John B. Hattendorf and J. Worth Estes, 1995. *A Sea of Words*. Henry Holt and Company, New York.

Laver, James, 1948. *British Military Uniforms*. Penguin Books, London.

Lee, Ronald F. 1970. *Antiquities Act of 1906*. Office of History and Historic Architecture, Eastern Service Center, Department of the Interior, National Park Service, Washington, D.C.

Lenihan, Daniel. 2002. *Submerged: Adventures of America's Most Elite Underwater Archaeology Team*. Newmarket Press, New York.

Logan, Patricia A. 1977. The *San José y Las Animas*: An Analysis of the Ceramic Collection. MS thesis, Department of Anthropology, Florida State University.

Long, George A. 1973a. *Progress Report on Faience Research*. Research Bulletin 12. National Historic Sites Service, Canada.

———. 1973b. *Tin-Glazed Earthenware from the* Machault. Research Bulletin 13. National Historic Sites Service, Canada.

Lyon, Eugene. 1976. The Trouble with Treasure. *National Geographic* 149(6): 787–809.

MacDonald, Peter. 2002. Letter to Major D. B. Trelewicz RE: HMS FOWEY. April 5. Ministry of Defence, Naval Personnel Secretariat, Room 123, Victory Bldg., HM Naval Base, Portsmouth, PO1 3LS (Ref. D/CSAUSNP/NSD16/2/6).

MacIver, Edward. 1733. Deposition to the Governor. *Calendar of State Papers, America and the West Indies, 1733*. Cecil Headlam and Arthur P. Newton, editors. His Majesty's Stationary Office, 1939 #338 ii: 190–191.

MacNeill, Ben Dixon. 1958. *The Hatterasman*. John F. Blair, Publisher, Winston-Salem, N.C.

Mansir, A. Richard. 1981. *A Modeler's Guide to Naval Architecture*. Moonraker Publications, Dana Point, Calif.

Manucy, Albert. 1949. *Artillery through the Ages*. U.S. Government Printing Office, Washington, D.C.

Marcus, Geoffrey J. 1975. *Heart of Oak: A Survey of British Sea Power in the Georgian Era*. Oxford University Press, London.

Marden, Luis. 1957. I Found the Bones of the *Bounty*. *National Geographic Magazine* 112(6): 725–789.

Marsden, Peter. 1974. *The Wreck of the* Amsterdam. Stein and Day, Briarcliff Manor, N.Y.

Marx, Robert F. 1969. *Shipwrecks in Florida Waters*. Scott Publishing Co., Eau Gallie, Fla.

———. 1975. *The Underwater Dig: An Introduction to Marine Archaeology*. Henry Z. Walck, Inc., New York.

———. 1979. *Shipwrecks in the Western Hemisphere, 1492–1825*. World Publishing Co., New York.

———. 1983. *Shipwrecks in the Americas*. Bonanza Books, New York.

Masse, H. J. L. J. 1921 (2004). *The Pewter Collector*. Kessinger Publishing, Whitefish, Mont.

May, W. E. 1958. The Wreck of the HMS *Fowey*. *Mariner's Mirror* 44(1): 320–324.

McNally, Paul. 1977. *Table Glass from the Wreck of the* Machault. Occasional Papers in Archaeology and History, vol. 16. Parks Canada, Ottawa.

———. 1979. *French Table Glass from the Fortress of Louisbourg, Nova Scotia*. History and Archaeology Series, vol. 29. Parks Canada, Ottawa.

———. 1982. *Table Glass in Canada 1700–1850*. History and Archaeology Series, vol. 60. Parks Canada, Ottawa.

Meylach, Martin. 1971. *Diving to a Flash of Gold*. Doubleday, Garden City, N.Y.

Miller, J. Jefferson, and Lyle M. Stone. 1970. *Eighteenth-Century Ceramics from Fort Michilimackinac*. Smithsonian Studies in History and Technology, no. 4. U.S. Government Printing Office, Washington, D.C.

Moore, Warren. 1967. *Weapons of the American Revolution and Accoutrements*. Promontory Press, New York.

Moulton, J. L. 1972. *The Royal Marines*. W. and J. Mackay Ltd., Chatham, Great Britain.

Muckelroy, Keith. 1978. *Maritime Archaeology*. Cambridge University Press, Cambridge.

Murphy, Larry E. 1990. *8SL-17: Natural Site-Formation Processes of a Multiple-Component Underwater Site in Florida*. Southwest Cultural Resources Center Professional Papers, No. 39. U.S. Department of the Interior, National Park Service, Southwest Region, Southwest Cultural Resources Center, Submerged Cultural Resources Unit, Santa Fe, N.Mex.

Naish, G. P. B. 1975. *HMS* Victory. Pitkin Pictorials Ltd., London.

Neumann, George C., and Frank J. Kravic. 1967. *The History of Weapons of the American Revolution*. Bonanza Books, New York.

———. 1973. *Swords and Blades of the American Revolution*. Stackpole Books, Harrisburg, Pa.

———. 1975. *Collector's Illustrated Encyclopedia of the American Revolution*. Stackpole Books, Harrisburg, Pa.

Newman, T. Stell. 1975. Preliminary Historical Studies Plan, Biscayne National Monument, Homestead, Florida. Denver Service Center, U.S. Department of the Interior.

Noël Hume, Ivor. 1968. *Historical Archaeology*. W. W. Norton and Co., Inc., New York.

———. 1969a. *Glass in Colonial Williamsburg Archaeological Collections*. Colonial Williamsburg Foundation, Williamsburg, Va.

———. 1969b. *A Guide to Artifacts of Colonial America*. Alfred A. Knopf, New York.

———. 1969c. *Pottery and Porcelain in Colonial Williamsburg Archaeological Collections*. Colonial Williamsburg Foundation, Williamsburg, Va.

———. 1977. *Early English Delftware from London and Virginia*. Colonial Williamsburg Foundation, Williamsburg, Va.

North, Rene, 1970. *Military Uniforms 1686–1918*. Bantam Books, New York.

Ollivier, Blaise. 1739 (1992). Translated by David H. Roberts. *18th Century Shipbuilding—Remarks on the Navies of the English and the Dutch from Observations Made in Their Dockyards in 1737 by Blaise Ollivier: Master Shipwright of the King of France*. Jean Boudriot Publications, Paris.

Perkins, D. R. J. 1979. *The Isle of Thanet Archaeological Unit*. Graphic Art and Print, London.

Peterson, Harold L. 1969. *Round Shot and Rammers*. Bonanza Books, New York.

Peterson, Mendel L. 1955. The Last Cruise of H.M.S. "Loo." *Smithsonian Miscellaneous Collections* 131(2): 1–55. Smithsonian Institution, Washington, D.C.

———. 1973. *History under the Sea*. Mendel Peterson, Alexandria, Va.

———. 1974a. Diving for New World Wrecks. In *Undersea Treasures*, pp. 131–149. National Geographic Society, Washington, D.C.

———. 1974b. Pioneers in the Search for Gold. In *Undersea Treasures*, pp. 38–59. National Geographic Society, Washington, D.C.

Pope, Dudley, 1987. *Life in Nelson's Navy*. Unwin Hyman Ltd., London.

Rankin, Hugh F. 1960. *The Pirates of Colonial North Carolina*. Division of Archives and History, North Carolina Department of Cultural Resources, Raleigh.

Rodger, N. A. M. 1981. Letter to N. J. Juse, Southeast Regional Office, National Park Service, Atlanta, Ga. NPS ref. #H42-SER-OC; PRO ref. Q 6177.

———. 1986. *The Wooden World: An Anatomy of the Georgian Navy*. Naval Institute Press, Annapolis, Md.

———. 2004. *The Command of the Ocean*. Penguin Books and the National Maritime Museum, London.

Rogers, Jerry L., to Regional Director, Southeast Region. 1986. Review of Draft Report "Archeological Testing and Evaluation of the Legare Anchorage Shipwreck Site, Biscayne National Park, Summer 1983," July 21, H30(418). National Park Service, Washington, D.C.

Romans, Bernard. 1775 (1962). *A Concise Natural History of East and West Florida*. Rembert W. Patrick, editor. University of Florida Press, Gainesville.

———. 1775 (1999). *A Concise Natural History of East and West Florida*. Kathryn E. Holland Braund, editor. University of Alabama Press, Tuscaloosa.

Romans, Bernard, with W. G. De Brahm, Bishop, Hester, Archibald Dalzel, George Gauld, and Lt. Woodriffe. 1799. *A New and Enlarged Book of Sailing Directions for Captain Romans' Gulf and Windward Pilot, Containing Full Instructions for Sailing through the Gulf of Florida; or, the Old and New Channels of Bahama: Together with Directions for the Windward Passage*. Robert Laurie and James Whittle, No. 53 Fleet Street, London. (Original in the John Carter Brown Library, Brown University, Providence, R.I.)

Romans, Bernard, W. Gerrard De Brahm, Capt. Hester, and Capt. Bishop. 1783. *The Compleat Pilot for the Gulf Passage or, Directions for Sailing through the Gulf of Florida, or New Bahama Channel, and the Neighboring Parts*. Robert Sayer and John Bennett, Chart-Sellers, Fleet Street, London. (Original in the John Carter Brown Library, Brown University, Providence, R.I.)

Seidel, John L., and Larry E. Murphy. 1996. Documentation and Stabilization of BISC-20: Lessons in Site Formation Processes and Preservation. Paper presented in Session 33, "From California to the Great Lakes, from Airplanes to Gun Batteries: Current Research in Underwater Archaeology." Society for Historical Archaeology and Conference on Underwater Archaeology Annual Meeting, Cincinnati, Ohio (Saturday, January 6).

Shaw, Simeon. 1829 [1970]. *History of the Staffordshire Potteries*. Reprint, David and Charles Ltd., South Devon House, London.

Skowronek, Russell K. 1979. The Klein Case and the Protection of Cultural Resources on the Outer Continental Shelf (Biscayne National Park). MS on file, National Park Service, Southeast Archeological Center, Tallahassee, Fla.

———. 1981. His Majesty's Ship *Fowey*: Historical Research in Great Britain. MS on file, Southeast Archeological Center, Tallahassee, Fla.

———. 1982. Trade Patterns of Eighteenth Century Frontier New Spain: The 1733 Flota and St. Augustine. MA thesis, Department of Anthropology, Florida State University.

———. 1984a. *Archaeological Testing and Evaluation of the Legare Anchorage Shipwreck*

Site, Biscayne National Park, Summer 1983. National Park Service, Southeast Archeological Center, Tallahassee, Fla.

———. 1984b. *Trade Patterns of Eighteenth Century Frontier New Spain: The 1733 Flota and St. Augustine.* Volumes in Historical Archaeology. Stanley South, editor. South Carolina Institute of Archaeology and Anthropology, University of South Carolina, Columbia.

———. 1985. Sport Divers and Archaeology: The Case of the Legare Anchorage Ship Site. *Archaeology Magazine* 38(3): 22–27.

———. 1988. Testing and Evaluation of the Legare Anchorage Shipwreck. In *In Search of Our Maritime Past* (Proceedings of the Fifteenth Conference on Underwater Archaeology, Williamsburg, Va., 1984), ed. J. W. Bream, R. Folse-Elliot, C. V. Jackson, and G. P. Watts, 149–157. Program in Maritime History and Underwater Research, East Carolina University, Greenville, N.C.

———. 1997. Letters. *Naval History* 11(1): 14.

———. 2002. HMS *Fowey.* In *Encyclopedia of Historical Archaeology*, ed. Charles E. Orser, 231–232. Routledge, London.

Skowronek, Russell K., Richard E. Johnson, Richard H. Vernon, and George R. Fischer. 1987. The Legare Anchorage Shipwreck Site-Grave of HMS *Fowey. International Journal of Nautical Archaeology* 16(4): 313–324.

Smith, E. Ann. 1981. *Glassware from a Reputed 1745 Siege Debris Context at the Fortress of Louisbourg.* History and Archaeology Series 55. Parks Canada, Ottawa.

Smith, George S. (SEAC), Guy Prentice (SEAC), John Cornelison (SEAC), Larry Murphy (SCRU), and David Brewer (SEAC). 1992. Hurricane Andrew Resource Damage Survey, Archeological Damage Assessment, Big Cypress National Preserve, Biscayne National Park, Everglades National Park. September 29 report on file, Southeast Archeological Center, National Park Service, Tallahassee, Fla.

South, Stanley. 1977. *Method and Theory in Historical Archaeology.* Academic Press, New York.

Steffy, J. Richard. 1986. Letter to George R. Fischer dated May 5, 1986. Nautical Archaeology, College Station, Texas A&M University. On file, SEAC, May 20, 1986.

Steffy, J. R., et al. 1981. *The Charon Report: Underwater Archaeology in the Challenge before Us.* Proceedings of the Twelfth Conference on Underwater Archaeology, San Marion, Calif.

Sténuit, Robert. 1974a. Future Challenges, Lost Fortunes. In *Undersea Treasures,* pp. 172–195. National Geographic Society, Washington, D.C.

———. 1974b. Wrecks and Riches: The Lure Below. In *Undersea Treasures*, pp. 8–37. National Geographic Society, Washington, D.C.

Stevens, Robert White. 1867. *On the Stowage of Ships and Their Cargoes.* 4th ed. Longmans, Green, Reader, and Dyer, London.

Stewart, W. Roderick. 1980. *The Guns of the Frigate* Unicorn. Unicorn Preservation Society, Victoria Dock, Dundee.

Stone, Lyle M. 1974. *Fort Michilimackinac, 1715–1781.* Michigan State University, East Lansing.

Swalm, Tod. 1979. South Miami Heights Man Wins Temporary Custody of "Treasures." *South Dade News Leader*, October 29, pp. 2A, 8A.

Throckmorton, Peter. 1974. Archaeology on Old World Wrecks. In *Undersea Treasures*, pp. 104–129. National Geographic Society, Washington, D.C.

Tilmant, James T., Richard Curry, and Richard D. Conant, Jr. 1982. Biological, Hydrological and Sedimentary Characteristics of a Historical Shipwreck in Legare Anchorage, Biscayne National Park, Florida. MS on file, National Park Service, South Florida Research Center, Everglades National Park, Homestead, Fla.

Trelewicz, Denis B. 2001. In Search of Information Pertaining to the Wreck of the H.M.S. FOWEY, a British Frigate. Downloaded 5 September 2006 at http://www.imacdigest. com/hms.html.

Vernon, Richard H. 1984. The Role of Ceramics in Shipwreck Identification: An Example from Biscayne National Park. Paper presented in Symposium 6, Meetings of the Society for Historical Archaeology/Conference on Underwater Archaeology, Williamsburg, Va.

———. 1988. The Role of Ceramics in Shipwreck Identification: An Example from Biscayne National Park. In *In Search of Our Maritime Past* (Proceedings of the Fifteenth Conference on Underwater Archaeology, Williamsburg, Va., 1984), ed. J. W. Bream, R. Folse-Elliot, C. V. Jackson, and G. P. Watts, pp. 160–162. Program in Maritime History and Underwater Research, East Carolina University, Greenville, N.C.

Wagner, Kip. 1965. Drowned Galleons Yield Spanish Gold: Adventurous Divers in Florida Bring Up the 20th Century's Richest Find of Sunken Treasure. *National Geographic* 138(1): 1–37.

——— (as told to L. B. Taylor, Jr.). 1966. *Pieces of Eight: Recovering the Riches of a Lost Spanish Treasure Fleet*. E. P. Dutton and Company, Inc., New York.

Wild, Kenneth S. 1983. Research Design, BISC-UW-20, Legare Anchorage Shipwreck Site. MS on file, Southeast Archeological Center, Tallahassee, Fla.

———. 1988. The Legare Anchorage Shipwreck Project: Data Retrieval and Site Preservation. In *In Search of Our Maritime Past* (Proceedings of the Fifteenth Conference on Underwater Archaeology, Williamsburg, Va., 1984), ed. J. W. Bream, R. Folse-Elliot, C. V. Jackson, and G. P. Watts, pp. 158–159. Program in Maritime History and Underwater Research, East Carolina University, Greenville, N.C.

Zander, Caroline M., and Ole Varmer. 1996. Contested Waters. *Common Ground* 1(3/4): Online Archives.

Index

Page numbers in italics refer to illustrations.

Russell K. Skowronek (*left*) and George R. Fischer (*right*) wearing their City of Fowey coat-of-arms pins at the 41st Annual Conference on Historical and Underwater Archaeology, January 9, 2008, Albuquerque, New Mexico, where Fischer was honored in a symposium titled "The Wrecks We've Gone Down On . . . Papers in Honor of George R. Fischer."

Russell K. Skowronek is associate professor of anthropology and campus archaeologist at Santa Clara University. He founded the SCU Archaeology Research Lab in 1994. Skowronek specializes in the study of the Spanish colonial world. He is the author or editor of several books, including *X Marks the Spot: The Archaeology of Piracy* (with Charles R. Ewen, 2006); *Situating Mission Santa Clara de Asís: 1776–1851: Documentary and Material Evidence of Life on the Alta California Frontier* (2006); and *Telling the Santa Clara Story: Sesquicentennial Voices* (2002). He has published widely in popular and scholarly venues such as *Archaeology Magazine, American Antiquity, Ethnohistory, Historical Archaeology,* the *International Journal of Historical Archaeology,* and the *International Journal of Nautical Archaeology.* He is working on a companion volume to *HMS* Fowey *Lost and Found,* focusing on the ethnohistory and historical geography of HMS *Fowey.*

George R. Fischer was an archaeologist for the National Park Service from 1962 to 1988. In 1967, he established and directed the National Park Service Program in underwater archaeology. In this capacity he directed major underwater surveys at Biscayne National Park, Gulf Islands National Seashore, and Dry Tortugas National Park in Florida and served as principal investigator on more than two dozen underwater archaeology projects in the Southwest and in the eastern United States and Caribbean. In addition to these duties, he served as a courtesy assistant professor and research associate at Florida State University from 1972 to 2002, where he taught underwater archaeology and scientific diving techniques. He makes his home in Tallahassee, Florida, with his lovely wife, Nancy.

New Perspectives on Maritime History and Nautical Archaeology
Edited by James C. Bradford and Gene Allen Smith

Diplomats in Blue: U.S. Naval Officers in China, 1922–1933, by William Reynolds Braisted (2009)

Sir Samuel Hood and the Battle of the Chesapeake, by Colin Pengelly (2009)

Voyages, The Age of Sail: Documents in Maritime History, Volume I, 1492–1865; Volume II: The Age of Engines, 1865–Present, edited by Joshua M. Smith and the National Maritime Historical Society (2009)

Voyages, The Age of Engines: Documents in Maritime History, Volume II, 1865–Present, edited by Joshua M. Smith and the National Maritime Historical Society (2009)

HMS Fowey *Lost and Found: Being the Discovery, Excavation, and Identification of a British Man-of-War Lost off the Cape of Florida in 1748*, by Russell K. Skowronek and George R. Fischer (2009)